QUESTION EVERYTHING

THE RISE OF AVID
AS AMERICA'S LARGEST
COLLEGE READINESS PROGRAM

JAY MATHEWS

JB JOSSEY-BASS™
A Wiley Brand

Cover image: © Shutterstock/Digital Storm
Cover design: Wiley

Published by Jossey-Bass
A Wiley Brand
One Montgomery Street, Suite 1000, San Francisco, CA 94104-4594—www.josseybass.com

Jossey-Bass books and products are available through most bookstores. To contact Jossey-Bass directly call our Customer Care Department within the U.S. at 800-956-7739, outside the U.S. at 317-572-3986, or fax 317-572-4002.

Wiley publishes in a variety of print and electronic formats and by print-on-demand. Some material included with standard print versions of this book may not be included in e-books or in print-on-demand. If this book refers to media such as a CD or DVD that is not included in the version you purchased, you may download this material at http://booksupport.wiley.com. For more information about Wiley products, visit www.wiley.com.

Library of Congress Cataloging-in-Publication Data is on file.

ISBN 978-1-118-43819-0 (cloth)
ISBN 978-1-119-03944-0 (ebk.)
ISBN 978-1-119-03945-7 (ebk.)

Printed in the United States of America
FIRST EDITION
HB Printing 10 9 8 7 6 5 4 3 2 1

CONTENTS

To Linda

FREE Premium Content

This book includes bonus videos that can be viewed on our Web site when you register at **www.wiley.com/go/avid** using the password *38190.*

INTRODUCTION

What works in schools, and what doesn't? For the last three decades, in articles and columns for the *Washington Post* and in five books, I have focused on that question. Never in my quest for answers have I had as many surprises as in my investigation of the Advancement Via Individual Determination (AVID) program.

I knew a little about AVID before I started this book. I had been invited to speak at one of its conferences in 1999. It seemed to be a thoughtful program based on the work of a terrific teacher, Mary Catherine Swanson. But I had much to learn.

AVID has become the nation's largest college preparatory program by far, with about four hundred thousand students in five thousand schools, in forty-four states and several countries. There are several aspects to this success that I did not initially understand. The excitement and commitment it inspires in teachers are extraordinary, even though AVID is rarely mentioned in our heated national debates over education reform. Once a school adopts AVID, even in a small way with a few classes, teaching practices and standards begin to improve throughout the campus. Students and their parents swear by it, although newspapers and magazines like the ones I write for usually ignore it.

What's going on?

This book was written to answer that question. Before I explain how Swanson created this extraordinary challenge to the usual ways of educating average students, let me outline the central tenets of the AVID program:

1. Teaching and enforcing orderly learning—keeping well-organized binders, making time for homework, cooperating with other students—can reap enormous benefits.
2. Students can and should be taught how to take notes, one of the most neglected skills in education.

1

3. Learning standards should eventually take all students, including average ones, to the most challenging courses in high school, such as Advanced Placement and International Baccalaureate. Every child deserves a taste of what college demands.

4. In order to push learning beyond memorization and repetition, students must see each concept as a response to an important question. They should practice inquiry-based learning, using it with each other so that it will be second nature once they get to college.

5. Regular access to well-trained tutors is essential. This is the only practical way to bring average students to the point where they can handle the demands of college and the workplace. Tutors should focus not on answering questions but on showing students how to arrive at the answers themselves.

6. The demanding college-level courses and tests that have become the measure of high school quality won't raise standards unless students have support in dealing with them. Educators must be there daily to make sure that students are managing their time, taking notes, benefiting from tutors, and asking the right questions.

7. Applying for college or other training after high school, particularly for average students, cannot be left to overloaded counselors. Writing essays, preparing forms, seeking financial aid, visiting colleges, and choosing extracurricular activities should be a part of a regular class.

8. Programs work best when both teachers and students feel that they are part of a free-thinking family. AVID students bond with each other and their teachers. The teachers are free to be creative in their lessons and to advocate for their students outside the classroom. That motivates and excites them as they head for school each morning.

It took me some time to comprehend what AVID does. I knew that requiring students to take notes, keep their papers in order, be tutored regularly, and apply for college were best practices proven to boost achievement. I thought that was the essence of AVID: because the AVID program did those things, it was good.

I am still embarrassed by my simplemindedness. I was startled to discover that those approaches had a depth unlike anything I had seen in other school programs. AVID teaching was inquiry based. The Cornell notes invented by Walter Pauk and required by AVID, and the intricate tutoring procedures AVID founder Swanson developed, forced students not only to absorb new information but also to ask questions that got to the conceptual root of their lessons.

AVID students learn not just by remembering what is taught but by conceiving what vital questions are at the heart of their lessons. This is something I rarely had to do as a California public school student, or even as a Harvard College undergraduate. I memorized as much as I could and almost never tried to turn the content into conceptual questions until I was asked to do so on an exam.

I missed out on a better way of learning, and I am not alone. It is difficult to find anyone in this country who has ever been taught how to take good notes. AVID students write down the important points and facts, but they also jot down what appear to be the questions the lecture or book is answering. They learn to discuss the subject with others and link the lesson to other reading. That helps them remember the material and use it intelligently on exams and in life.

The question-making demanded by the AVID tutoring process goes even further. I was skeptical that average high school students could do it. But as I watched carefully, interviewing many teachers and students, it became clear that AVID kids were getting the idea. As a former tutor in Washington DC–area schools, I felt sorry that my tutees had received such inadequate assistance from me. Some top-rate private tutors do what AVID does, but they are rare.

Tutoring sessions, usually every Tuesday and Thursday, are the core of AVID. Most of the money spent for the program goes to pay the tutors. The process is unlike anything I have ever seen in thirty years of education reporting. Each tutor works with no more than seven students. They are trained to stifle their instinct to help struggling students by giving them the answer. In an AVID tutorial, that is the worst thing you can do. Instead, the tutor nudges students toward the questions that will suggest the answer. The students themselves employ that question-making more often than the tutor does.

Inquiry-based tutorials are difficult to do. It takes months for students to get the hang of it. Some AVID tutorials are ragged and disorganized, but even the weaker ones I saw appeared to be more enlightening than the non-AVID tutorials I have observed and participated in over the years.

Emory University English professor Mark Bauerlein has pointed out the fallacy of our popular notion that the best way to improve high schools is to make the teaching livelier and more relevant to students' lives. There is nothing wrong with doing that, but it isn't enough. As Bauerlein, who teaches college freshman composition, points out, college courses like his are inevitably going to be boring and off-putting to a large number of students. He has to teach rules of grammar, organization, and usage, not fun for many students. High school students must learn to deal with courses they don't find engaging if they are going to succeed in college. AVID's frequent lessons on time management and its tutorial emphasis on what to do when stuck on a problem prepare students for such challenges.

In a way, this book is my attempt at question-making. How did AVID evolve into a national movement? Why hasn't it received more public notice? Why are the teachers, principals, and counselors in AVID so passionate about it? How much further will it go? Does research on its results back up the enthusiasm of its participants?

Those of us immersed in the raging national debate over how to improve our schools should note that AVID has little to do with the issues on which we so often disagree. The program doesn't tell us if it is OK to assess and pay teachers based on student test scores. It doesn't care if the students it serves are in traditional public schools, charters, or private schools. It is unrelated to school vouchers or teacher tenure or corporate motivational techniques or test security or competing curriculums. The fact that such hotly debated issues are largely irrelevant to this powerful program explains in part why it has become so influential while remaining little known. It also makes me wonder if our big arguments are as important as we think they are.

AVID is trying to grow and improve. It now reaches elementary schools as well as colleges. Its teachers want to involve many more students than they do now, and to move beyond AVID's emphasis on average students to a schoolwide approach. That requires more experience with students who don't fit the AVID profile and with the many school district administrators who have trouble, as I did, understanding what AVID does. The program also wants to bring its methods into more large urban districts. The collapse of an ambitious AVID program in Chicago shows that such growth will take time, hard work, and some luck.

AVID's great strength is its popularity with teachers, who see it as an exceptional way to engage students and deepen their learning. They and their students sense from the beginning the unusual nature of the enterprise. Teachers can be creative in the classroom and advocate for their students outside the classroom when old rules and procedures are denying students the challenges they need. AVID teachers like the focus on preparing students for college rather than just raising state test scores, a numbers game they distrust.

The power of what Mary Catherine Swanson created in a San Diego ninth-grade classroom in 1980 is best understood through the stories I tell here of those teachers, and their students. They still have lots of questions. That is the best you can say about anyone in AVID or any other effort to improve our schools.

 WATCH CLIP 1: "PEOPLE LIKE ME DON'T GO TO COLLEGE"
AVID students turning self-doubt into positive self-talk.

www.wiley.com/go/avid1

TAKING AVID HOME

It wasn't until Kande McKay moved two thousand miles from Madison, Indiana, for her third year of teaching that she realized how little her students were accomplishing back home and how much more they could do if she asked them to.

She had grown up in Madison. The town of fifteen thousand was a twenty-five-minute drive up the Ohio River from Louisville, Kentucky. Her mother owned a children's clothing store. Her stepfather ran a construction firm. At Madison High School, she was a good English student, with a budding interest in journalism. She was a cheerleader, popular with teachers and students. She loved the place, so she came back after graduation from Ball State University to teach at the school.

Then her life changed. She met a visitor from California, married him and moved to the San Francisco Peninsula where he had grown up. While he joined a construction firm in Mountain View, she got a job as an English teacher at Los Altos High School. There she encountered AVID, a way of teaching that made what she had been doing in semirural Indiana seem weak and wasteful.

RAISING THE BAR: HIGHER EXPECTATIONS ACROSS THE BOARD

At Los Altos High, "They expected kids to perform; there were no excuses," she recalled years later. "You could do rigor, essentially, and that was something I always wanted to have in my classrooms, but wasn't sure how." At Madison she had tried to make her English and yearbook classes rigorous, but students resisted. Like most teachers in America, she went with the flow. She developed warm relationships with her students. She tried to coax them along. That was her great strength as a teacher. But she did not ask them to extend themselves very far.

"I taught at Madison for two years, and I taught the same way my teachers had taught me, which was read the book, take the quiz, that kind of thing," she said. "Even at Ball State, even though they were very good at teacher preparation, I don't think they taught us to work backwards, as AVID did. They didn't talk about figuring out what I wanted my students to be able to do and work backward from there.

"The first two years I taught, it was, well, they either get it or they don't. Either they get it and they pass, or they don't and they fail. Teachers were there to dispense the information and record the results." That summarized the way teachers felt about their work all over the country, particularly when they were dealing with average kids with average parents who had not graduated from college. The teachers, and in many cases the parents, doubted their children could handle difficult courses, like the math McKay herself had struggled with as a student. They were similarly pessimistic about demanding homework.

AVID had been invented by an English teacher, Mary Catherine Swanson of Clairemont High School in north San Diego. Swanson was similar to McKay in many ways. Both were conscientious and energetic, with leadership skills. But Swanson had more than ten years in the classroom and was a department chair when the idea for AVID occurred to her. She knew much more than beginning teacher McKay did about how to motivate students to do things they did not want to do and that other educators thought they were incapable of doing.

Swanson had started AVID in 1980 to handle a crisis at her school, a sudden influx of low-income students being bused in from south San Diego. Many teachers at her school thought such kids would need a watered-down curriculum, just enough to get them to graduation. It was assumed they lacked the parental support, motivation, and study habits to qualify for college. Swanson thought differently. She found thirty-two of the newcomer students, most of them Hispanic or black, who were willing to work harder to learn how to handle the honors and Advanced Placement classes they would need to be admitted to four-year universities.

The idea worked. By 1998, when McKay arrived at Los Altos High, AVID had spread throughout California and was popping up in other parts of the country. By 2015, it would be by far the largest college preparation program in the country. The positive reaction McKay had to AVID's higher expectations was by then common. The program would be important not only in schools with many low-income minorities but throughout the US education system, because it responded to educators' widespread frustration with inadequate time for and interest in learning at a deep and engaging level.

In the 1990s, as McKay was learning about AVID, US schools in general were stalled. Since the mid-1970s, seventeen-year-olds had shown no significant increases in math or reading achievement. The gains for thirteen- and nine-year-olds were not much better. Many states were attacking the problem with more tests. Students would be given annual exams in math and reading, and sometimes other subjects, to see if they had reached a level considered proficient for their age group. In 2002, President George W. Bush had signed the No Child Left Behind law. It required such tests in all states. Schools that did poorly were labeled "needs improvement" and forced to do more to get their scores up.

Teachers complained that the law did not measure everything they were trying to do. It ignored teachers handling subjects other than math and reading. It overlooked the ravages of poverty that left many urban and rural schools near the bottom of the proficiency rate lists.

There was also a discomforting fact that the debate over No Child Left Behind usually ignored: the proficiency standards established by the states were low. In many cases a student could miss half the questions on a state exam and still pass. Politicians and educators rarely acknowledged that the vast majority of students did not devote much time to their studies.

Time-use studies by the University of Michigan Survey Research Center showed that the average fifteen- to seventeen-year-old did less than an hour of homework a day, while spending more than two hours a day watching television or playing video games. The annual UCLA survey of college freshmen nationwide indicated that they averaged no more than an hour a day of homework when they were in high school, even though they were the top students, the ones headed to college. Those not going to college did far less.

Low expectations for teenagers were an embarrassing fact of American life, woven into the national culture. A frontal assault on habits so engrained was unlikely to succeed. AVID did not attack the problem directly. Instead it undermined the resistance to hard work by offering students willing to seek a higher standard the kind of support they needed. This approach appealed to many ninth graders, and also to sixth and seventh graders when AVID moved into junior highs and middle schools. They and their parents were already worried about dealing with schools that were bigger and more frightening than elementary school. They would have meaningful contact with caring educators and perhaps more personal safety and protection from harassment than students who did not sign up for AVID.

In the largely suburban schools where AVID first blossomed, the students most likely to be recruited were those whose parents had not attended college and did not understand how to prepare for college. But those parents had moved to these neighborhoods in part because they thought their children would have a better education and have a better chance for college and better jobs than the parents had had. For them, AVID was a response to those hopes.

BEYOND ROTE MEMORIZATION: LEARNING TO ASK THE RIGHT QUESTIONS

Once students at Los Altos were in AVID, McKay was amazed to see, they were given something rare in even the best high schools—a style of teaching that was geared to conceptual understanding, not just memorization of facts and formulas.

AVID students were required to keep binders that were inspected each week for completeness and neatness. The binders carried all of the students' class materials and notes. In class, students were required to take Cornell notes, which led to the big questions their lessons were designed to answer, rather than just the names and dates they were supposed to remember.

The most important part of AVID, McKay thought, was the inquiry-based tutoring. Students attended their AVID elective class five days a week. On Monday, Wednesday, and Friday, they learned how to take notes, question teachers, manage their time, plan for college, plan for life, make effective presentations, write persuasively, and develop other skills that the regular classes did not have time for. On Tuesday and

Thursdays, the tutors arrived. They were usually local college students trained in AVID methods. They helped students work on problems they were having in their other classes.

WATCH CLIP 2: INTRODUCTION HANDSHAKE
Introducing oneself to others is one of the many life skills that students learn in AVID classrooms. In this clip, AVID teacher Vanessa Aleman discusses how she uses the Introduction Handshake activity to help her seventh-grade students prepare for life outside the classroom.

www.wiley.com/go/avid2

The AVID rule was that you had to be in advanced classes in your regular subjects, such as honors Geography in sophomore year or Advanced Placement English in senior year. The AVID students would be getting the best and most challenging teachers the school had. That meant they were more likely to run into concepts they had trouble understanding. In most schools, students struggling with difficult subjects sought help from their parents or friends or their teacher, none of whom had much experience in tutoring for understanding.

AVID tutors had such training. Watching what they did was eye opening to McKay. The average tutor in American schools would sit down with the child, ask her to open up her homework, and ask if she had any questions. If there were none, the tutor would check the work, look for mistakes, and explain how to get the right answer.

That was not what AVID tutors and students did. At the beginning of each tutoring period, the students would turn in forms on which they described a point, or points, of confusion they had reached in their studies. The teacher would check the forms and organize a tutoring group of no more than seven students, for each of the subjects in which students sought help. In most AVID classes, there would often be two or three math groups—the most difficult subject for most students—and an English group, a history group, and so on.

Tutors were trained to avoid at all costs giving a student the answer. The students got the same training. They were shown how to help classmates figure out the answer by asking questions that pointed in the right direction. If the student did not understand why the United States got involved in Vietnam, the tutor would not say that Washington was worried that Communist influence would spread throughout Indochina. The tutor would instead have the student stand up and go to a blackboard or whiteboard in front of the tutoring group. The tutor would sit in the student's seat while the student wrote on the board his point of confusion and how far he had gotten in figuring it out.

The tutor was not supposed to ask questions. The students were. If they hesitated, the tutor would call on them to get the discussion going. For this example, good leading questions might be "What was changing in Indochina after World War II?" "Did you read the previous chapter on the international foreign policy of the Soviet Union and China?" "Did you review the chapter on the Korean War?" or "Why did the United States resist the Soviet effort to choke off West Berlin?"

Usually the confused student would make progress, sometimes finding the answer quickly. If not, he would be prepared to go back to his teacher with better questions. After he sat back down, another confused student would take his place.

McKay wanted to be part of that. She began to use AVID techniques in her sophomore and senior English classes. She attended the required week of training at an AVID Summer Institute in Asilomar, California. In her second year at Los Altos High, her skills improved. She told her friends back at Madison High in Indiana, particularly English department chair Carol Martin, about AVID. McKay's first child was born in July after her second year at Los Altos. Two months later, as she prepared for a new school year, thinking about taking over one of the AVID classes, her life changed again, this time much for the worse.

Her husband, at age thirty-two, had a stroke. There was no warning, no clue that it could happen to such a vigorous man. He lost control of the left side of his body. His brain swelled so much he needed a craniotomy to relieve the pressure. McKay now had a disabled husband and a two-and-a-half-month-old baby. She did not work the fall semester. "It was just kind of crazy for a long time," she said.

She and her husband had to give up the house they were renting in Los Altos and live with his parents in nearby Redwood City. It occurred to her that they might be better off, as he recovered, if they moved back to Madison. (They had been renting an eight-hundred-square-foot house for $2,000 a month, when they could buy a sixteen-hundred-square-foot house in Madison with a mortgage of just $600 a month.)

Somebody had to work, so McKay went back that spring semester at Los Altos High. But during spring break, they visited her family in Madison. McKay's husband got better, but she felt they needed to be in Madison. Her husband's parents were supportive, but they were older and found the situation a huge strain. Madison High took McKay back. The journalism teacher whose class she had loved had decided to retire, and she replaced him. Within a year, she was the AVID coordinator for a new program, working to persuade American teenagers of the importance of setting goals higher than they had ever considered possible.

TORTUOUS JOURNEY OF A TEACHER'S IDEA

T he standard hero-teacher movie plot requires a beleaguered educator with fire in his eyes, yelling at interfering administrators and rallying kids as the background music rises. Mary Catherine Swanson, the creator of AVID, had plenty of enemies and crises, but she rarely raised her voice. In the classroom and at faculty meetings, she was always crisp and professional. She came to school immaculately dressed, with a friendly smile and her blonde hair piled high.

She eventually proved to be one of the country's most creative and productive educators. With the help of a few friends, she invented one of the most effective means ever for raising the achievement of average students. But she always looked and sounded like a docent at an upscale art museum, which may be why she was so often underestimated.

Swanson was born September 3, 1944. She grew up in Kingsburg, California, fifteen miles southeast of Fresno. Her father, Ed Jacobs, a graduate of the Columbia Graduate School of Journalism, was publisher and editor of the *Kingsburg Recorder*, the local paper. She wrote columns for the student newspaper at San Francisco State and had won a fellowship to the Columbia Journalism School herself, but instead married Tom Swanson, an economics major at UC Davis. They moved to San Diego, where she became a high school English teacher.

They had a son, Tom, in 1972. Swanson's reputation at Clairemont High School in northern San Diego was growing as her husband made progress in the banking business. By 1980, she was chairman of the English department. She had many ideas for improving instruction. Meanwhile, a recently constructed high school in the area had drained away many of Clairemont's affluent white students. She was offered a chance to create the English department at the new school, but chose instead to stay at Clairemont and help the large numbers of low-income Hispanic and black students being bused into the school to take the place of the departed afflu-ent kids.

The plan seemed to be to shove the newcomers from south San Diego into remedial classes. Swanson thought that was a terrible idea. With good teaching, she told the principal and her colleagues, the new kids could be made ready for the same advanced courses the school had offered for years to the children of doctors, lawyers, and business executives. She had gotten great satisfaction from finding ways to build the skills and under-standing of struggling students. Now she had much more of them to work with. Her friend and mentor Jim Grove, a legendary English teacher at the school, supported her decision and helped her set up in the summer of 1980 what would be called AVID.

AVID to Learn: Advancement Via Individual Determination

Swanson and Grove envisioned one elective class for students from poor families who dreamed of going to college. Making the program part of the school day, rather than an after-school attachment as such efforts usu-ally were, was key to its success. With the help of student tutors recruited from Grove's seminar class for gifted students and from the University of California, San Diego (UCSD), Swanson planned to teach time manage-ment and study skills that would ready the new students to take AP classes and get into good colleges. As department chair, she would also create an English course, taught by her, for the same students to strengthen their reading and writing abilities.

Grove had an unusual feel for such students. He and his brothers had been placed in an El Paso, Texas, orphanage because their parents were too stressed and inebriated to raise them. An insatiable desire to read saved him. He saw Swanson's class as a refuge for children like himself, avid to learn. Swanson said she thought AVID might be a good acronym for her class, but what words would it stand for? They tried out Achievement Via Individual Determination. That didn't sound big enough to Swanson. She wanted to provide not only academic success but also a way forward in life. They changed the name to Advancement Via Individual Determination.

She still needed an administrative endorsement to go ahead. Swanson's vice principal didn't think AVID fit the rules for new courses or the school's budget. Because he was retiring, her principal told her to go ahead anyway. Swanson told him that if the idea failed, it would be her problem, not his. She got recommendations from friendly middle school teachers of eighty students who fit her profile of average kids whose parents hadn't gone to college. Fifty of them signed up. She chose forty. Only thirty-two appeared in her classroom the first day of school, but that was enough.

The Community Outreach Program at UCSD supported the AVID idea. They agreed to recruit college students as tutors. The program's outreach director helped Swanson write grants to fund the program. (She discovered later that the director absconded with money meant for her and others and moved to South Africa.) Luckily, the Bank of America came up with $7,000, a good start.

One of the signs of Swanson's genius was that she realized from the beginning that she had to create not just a class but a family. Her students needed not only good teaching but a place to feel secure and comfortable. This would eventually be recognized as one of AVID's great strengths, but at the time it seemed to many at Clairemont High like one more weird Swanson idea. She got rid of the narrow desks in her classroom and replaced them with wide tables and chairs from the cafeteria. Her students could look at each other and learn in groups. She begged carpet samples from a rug store and taped them together for a cozy reading nook. She created another corner full of catalogues for college searches, with an old typewriter to prepare applications. The year-old encyclopedias that were dumped each year by the library went to her room. The huge letters *AVID* in garish Clairemont High orange and blue decorated the door of room 206.

When she was told there were no vacancies in the honors courses in algebra and history she wanted for the AVID students, she conceived an after-dark caper to make room for them. A friendly counselor gave Swanson a key to the office that had the class lists. The night before school opened, she reprogrammed the students by hand, putting all the AVID kids in the top spots. When several gifted students found themselves bumped off the list, their parents protested and more classes were created, which in Swanson's mind was what should have been done for the AVID kids in the first place.

On the first day of school, the students filed into Swanson's warmly decorated room, happy to have a teacher who seemed so encouraging. But their mood quickly changed. They were each issued a three-ring binder and told that they must keep all of their notes and papers from all of their classes in it. They had heard first-day-of-school neatness lectures before. The problem was that Swanson meant it. There would be regular binder checks, a phrase that would trouble future generations of AVID students.

They would lose five points for failing to have two pens and two pencils in a plastic pouch; papers in order from newest to oldest; no loose paper; name, date, and subject on all papers; and blank paper in the back of each section. They would lose twenty points if they failed to have a parent signature on every homework assignment. Twenty-five points, at the rate of five points a class, would be lost if their grades and homework assignments were not recorded for English, science, math, history, and AVID. They would lose a total of fifty points, at a rate of ten points per class, if their notes or logs for each subject each day were missing.

The adolescent resistance was fierce, but Swanson stuck to her system. She was both supportive and demanding. She told her students that hard work would make them smart. If they made an effort, she would always be at their side. Her first class of students kept their binders clean and took Cornell notes each day. The tutors helped them strengthen their weaknesses and engage in intense discussion of the key points, which made them easier to remember. Their reward was a surge of accusations from other teachers that they were cheating.

Jonathan Freedman, author of the 2000 book about AVID's beginnings, *Wall of Fame: One Teacher, One Class and the Power to Save Schools and Transform Lives*, gave a detailed account of the most serious incident. A biology teacher told Swanson that her students could not have done so well on his most recent exam without some unethical assistance. Swanson was enraged. But true to her commitment to proper form, she held it in and invited the teacher to come to her room and give her students an oral quiz on anything he liked. That would show, she said, that what he taught was in their heads, not on a cheat sheet.

The biology teacher got some intriguing answers during an hour-long examination. To one student he said, "You wrote 'ontology recapitulates phylogeny.' What does that mean?"

"It says story of one creature repeat history of evolution of species," the student replied, according to Freedman. "But this old theory just gross generalize. Young people not have to repeat same old story of ancestors. Mrs. Swanson teach we can 'advance via individual determination.' That spell AVID."

"Trace the circulation system of the fetal pig," he asked a girl.

"Your heart pumps blood from aorta to the lungs, where it picks up oxygen, and heads out to the organs and tissues," she said. "Then the veins carry back the carbon dioxide to the lungs, where it's exhaled." She traced the blood back to the heart. "You know where Interstate 8 crosses the 5? That's the aorta of San Diego."

They passed the impromptu exam, but doubts about the program persisted. Swanson saw bias in those negative feelings from her colleagues. She recommended that her students do something about it, a lesson in how a professional handles such unpleasantness.

OVERCOMING OBSTACLES AND TAKING THE HIGH ROAD

"Dear Teachers," said the letter the AVID students sent to the Clairemont faculty. "We are enrolled in your college preparation classes without the prerequisites. Sometimes we are going to struggle in your classes. The reason why we are there is that we want to go to college. We are also enrolled in an elective class called AVID where we receive tutorial help with our work. If we are not doing well in our classes, will you please tell our AVID teacher, Mrs. Swanson, so we can work more effectively? Also would you please stop by our AVID classroom, room 206, during fourth period any day to see the kind of work we do in our study groups from the binders that we keep? Sincerely, The AVID Students."

They began to take AP courses and do well on the exams. Every member of the first AVID graduating class went to college. Statisticians at the San Diego school district headquarters found a surprising anomaly in data from Clairemont High. Unlike other high schools with large minority populations, achievement scores in reading and math at the school were above the district average. Even more confusing to school district officials was the fact that AVID students were testing higher than low-income minority students enrolled in the Achievement Goals Program (AGP), a much larger effort sanctioned by the school district. Over the years, the AVID program developed a 93 percent college-going rate, much higher than that attained by AGP kids. This led to a bizarre effort by the director of the district's seminar program for gifted children to recruit Swanson and shut down her project.

According to Swanson, it was the seminar director's theory that the AVID students were scoring so well because they were gifted, not because Swanson had found a viable formula for engaging average kids. Swanson held her tongue and invited him to administer IQ tests to see if her students were, as he thought, unidentified anomalies. The tests showed otherwise. The average AVID student's IQ was 101, with 90 the lowest and 115 the highest. The district defined giftedness as 145 or above.

The seminar director did not give up. His program was in trouble because almost all of his students were white. The school system was under a court order to integrate. The director decided that, whatever their IQs, the AVID students were doing well with enriched instruction and would thrive in the seminars. If they were admitted, the seminar program would become more racially diverse and Swanson's AVID idea, an embarrassment to status quo defenders like himself, would go away.

In the summer of 1985, the seminar program director called Swanson at home. "Mrs. Swanson, you're coming to work for me," he said. It was obvious to her that he had not cleared his plan with anyone. She told him she wouldn't do it. "Mary Catherine, you will not be able to get along in your life on good looks alone," he said. "At some point you are going to have to produce something."

Swanson was not in the habit of letting such remarks go unchallenged. She complained to her principal and to one of the deputy superintendents. The seminar program director called her again. "I understand you are not going to work for me," he said. "Let me tell you one thing. I will see to it that your career is ruined in the San Diego city schools." Swanson's friend Mary Barr, head of the district's language arts department, helped her make another complaint to another deputy superintendent, but nothing came of it. Instead, Swanson had to deal with an even more unpleasant surprise: a new Clairemont principal who could not stand having such a successful teacher on his staff.

At the beginning of AVID's sixth year, with four AVID elective classes running, Swanson's principal introduced her to his replacement. "I want you to know what a privilege it has been to work with Mary Catherine," he said to the new man as she stood there. He described her work creating and running AVID, heading up the English department, and instigating many schoolwide reforms. The new principal never smiled or showed the least bit of interest in what he was hearing, Swanson recalled. The only comment he made to her—Swanson insists this actually happened—was that she had snot in her nose. It became clear that he considered both her and AVID a problem, not an asset.

AVID was getting favorable newspaper and television coverage. The district superintendent, Thomas Payzant, had praised the program during a television interview. But Swanson's request to the district for funds to pay her tutors had gone unanswered. The $7,000 grant from Bank of America had been spent. Without more support, the program would die.

Since 1980, 170 AVID students had graduated and gone to college. Another thirty were on their way to doing so in the spring of 1986. The new principal said little about this. He treated the program as a trivial annoyance. He began to complain about Swanson's work. He didn't like her teaching methods. The final insult was a last-minute work project he knew would get in the way of her helping her 120 AVID students complete the year successfully.

The principal had failed to organize the preparation of a six-year report to the Western Association of Schools and Colleges. The association would decide if Clairemont's accreditation was renewed. With the deadline a month away, he dumped the project on Swanson's desk. When she protested that she had several classes to teach, he told her that her tutors could run them while she monitored the work from the library. (Swanson was paying the tutors with $1,000 of her own money because she could find no other source of support.) The principal said she was to collect all the information and type the report herself—no secretaries could be spared.

She got it done, but decided it would be the last chore she ever did for the man. She arranged for Don Thorpe, a thirty-eight-year-old English teacher she trusted, to take over the AVID program. In class, Thorpe appeared to be looser and softer in comparison to Swanson's strict adherence to form, but he kept the classes humming and maintained the standards. "I had learned to adjust my teaching style to accommodate lackadaisical students, busy parents, and, more often than not, neutral school administrators who were too preoccupied with issues other than what was going on in the classroom. Teaching AVID changed all that," he said later in an essay.

Swanson submitted her letter of resignation. She looked for a way to relocate and expand AVID. The obvious choice was the San Diego County Department of Education, which was separate from the San Diego Unified School District of which Clairemont High was a part. But when she asked her friend Barr, who had moved to the county department, she said there were no openings.

Then another county education department official, Jack Tierney, found a need for AVID. The *Los Angeles Times*'s Scott Harris had written an article about AVID and its lack of funds. "Minority Students Avid Fans of College Readiness Program," the headline said. On a trip to Sacramento, Tierney found that Assemblywoman Sally Tanner had passed a bill to improve minority performance on college entrance examinations. The state was putting out a request for proposals to spend the money.

Tierney knew that Barr had worked in the San Diego district. He asked her about AVID and Swanson, and Barr told him it was the real thing. Tierney called Swanson. Soon Jerry Rosander, the county superintendent of education, was in room 206, talking to her students. Swanson did not know Rosander. He seemed chilly and uninterested; she didn't detect much warmth even when her students told their stories.

He began to tell the students about his own childhood. He was one of nine children of a rural immigrant family. His father died when he was in the eighth grade. He got a job sweeping out the local newspaper office. The editor took an interest in him and had him writing bylined stories before long. Rosander was still an awkward high school student, but he became more confident of his abilities. He dared to apply to UC Berkeley and got in. Now he was a county school superintendent, more successful than he had ever expected. "It was that newspaper editor who taught me carefully and gave me the courage to go on to college," he said, looking at Swanson. "Today, I have met his daughter, who is doing the same for you."

It was one of the most touching moments of Swanson's life, giving her goose bumps when she thought of it. It looked like she had a chance. In the third week of June, as she packed up her classroom, Tierney called. The grant came through. The county wanted her. It would pay half of her salary, and the grant would pay the rest. Rosander was pleased to have Ed Jacobs's daughter on his staff, but what he and the county hierarchy really wanted was to expand AVID. "You've got to replicate this thing," Tierney said.

WRITING, INQUIRY, AND COLLABORATION: BUILDING FROM THE GROUND UP

In July, Swanson moved her files into a trailer in the middle of the county Office of Education parking lot. Her one-sentence assignment read: "Disseminate AVID throughout the San Diego County Schools." Wearing high heels as usual, she lugged twenty-six file boxes up the steps and stacked them in the cramped quarters. The trailer had three desks and three chairs but no file cabinets. There was no phone, no restroom, no insulation, and no fan or air conditioner. But she had a task that would challenge and engage her, like the work she gave her students, so she plowed ahead.

The forty-two school districts in the county had no clue what she was doing. AVID was complex, and could not be communicated by just visiting their offices. So she wrote a user's manual. For that, she needed to buttress her classroom experiences with research. She used the county's large, air-conditioned professional library, where she found that AVID was in tune with much expert opinion. For example, mathematics professor Uri Treisman at UC Berkeley and psychiatrist William Glasser, who had an institute in Arizona, said students gained a deeper understanding of their lessons when they worked together.

She persuaded one of her former AVID tutors to live in her guest room that summer and help her put the manual together. By September, the *AVID Handbook and Curriculum Guide* was done. It was over five hundred pages, organized like any good AVID study guide into a three-ring binder with sections and thumbnail indexes. It was easy to revise. Just unsnap the binder, pull out the old pages, put in the new, and snap closed.

Tierney let Swanson roam through the county's test score database. The numbers were helpful when she began visiting districts. She walked into the office of the superintendent or deputy superintendent loaded with information. She asked, Was this district committed to equal education for all students? Of course, she was told. She would show data comparing their results to other districts in the county. San Diego County had many affluent areas. Those schools did well. Then she would show the data for their minority students. That was not so good, but there was hope, she said. She pulled out the numbers on Clairemont High. She showed how it compared to other schools in the San Diego district. Despite the fact that it was no longer majority white, its test scores were at the top.

The superintendents were curious. Why was that? She plopped the three-inch-thick AVID guide binder on their desks. "It is the result of a focused process of learning based on writing, inquiry, and collaboration," she said. The three words were to her the distillation of AVID. Writing, inquiry, and collaboration were an AVID acronym, WIC, later expanded to WICOR, for **w**riting, **i**nquiry, **c**ollaboration, **o**rganization, and **r**eading to learn. "The AVID curriculum was developed in my classroom by dozens of students, tutors, and teachers," she told the superintendents. "The program begins with recruitment and ends with college admission." The guide showed how to implement the program, step-by-step, week by week. Ninety-three percent of AVID graduates went to college, a fact often emphasized in the newspaper clippings she gave them. Most of those students were still enrolled in college, she said.

She knew that the superintendents' most important concern would be cost. She saved that for last. The program would not be expensive. State funds would pay to train teachers, so the only money needed from the district was for tutors to be paid minimum wage. She had managed to do that for five years at Clairemont for only $7,000.

If a superintendent showed interest, she drove to the local high schools and talked to the principals. Some appreciated what Swanson had done. Some had seen the news stories about her. She invited them and their teachers to visit the AVID classes at Clairemont, still going strong under Thorpe. Bill Honig, the state superintendent of public instruction, also visited.

She tried to interest the San Diego city district in having the program in some of its schools other than Clairemont. This seemed insane to many of her friends. Powerful San Diego administrators considered her a self-important, ungrateful traitor, a media celebrity who had made them look bad after the city district had done so much for her career. They thought she was pumping up her program as better than theirs. She had gotten the state grant they had also applied for. But Swanson had read her assignment in the grant. It said to disseminate AVID through San Diego County schools. The city was part of the county.

At Barr's recommendation, she met with the city's four area assistant superintendents, three women and one man. She gave them a fifteen-minute pitch and paused for questions. There were none. She presented copies of the handbook, but they showed no interest. "We do not need your help in our schools, thank you," one of them said as they left.

That turned out not to be a unanimous opinion. San Diego city school board president Dorothy Smith asked Swanson for a meeting after work hours. She told Swanson she wanted to get AVID in all the city high schools despite the district's resistance. Swanson thanked her, grateful for an unexpected ally. In December 1986, the board voted to put AVID in all seventeen comprehensive high schools in the city.

Swanson learned some useful lessons about money in schools. When funding ran out for tutors, Swanson's friend, the Clairemont High financial secretary, helped her search for leftover categorical monies. If the regulations for using those funds included activities AVID was doing, they used the money, usually for tutors. Getting money for new programs was trickier, but if a budget allocation seemed to fit the program's purposes, it could be done. For AVID supporters in school districts, the favorite budget lines were training and curriculum, as AVID supplied both.

By 1988, there were thirty-six schools with AVID classes, all in San Diego County. Then Riverside County asked if it could use the program in its lowest-performing school, Ramona High. The San Diego County education office gave its permission, beginning the spread of AVID throughout California, with the San Diego county office remaining its headquarters.

Growing Pains: Expanding AVID without Going Broke

In 1989, Swanson inaugurated what would become a major part of the AVID experience, the Summer Institute. The first Summer Institute in 1989 had only 450 participants, but that was many more than Swanson expected. She had been training teachers in makeshift weekend and summer sessions, but the process was not detailed or intense enough to meet her standards. The first Summer Institute started on a Monday morning and went until Saturday lunch. Swanson could not afford a hotel, but an auditorium rented from the University of San Diego across the road from county education office headquarters suited her needs.

AVID educators signed up for one of eight strands, each focused on an area important to the program. New teachers enrolled in Implementation. Those with AVID experience could do strands on administration, counseling, English, history, science, math, or foreign languages. The opening keynote speaker was Henry Gradillas, the principal at Garfield High School in East Los Angeles. He had been the prime supporter of Jaime Escalante, the AP Calculus teacher made famous by the film *Stand and Deliver*.

Swanson had been struck by the similarities between her students and Escalante's. Both groups were low-income kids who had risen to the challenge of more rigorous teaching. Both groups of students had been accused of cheating and had to retake exams to prove their worth. Swanson was aghast at some of Escalante's methods. He would threaten parents with investigations of their immigrant status if their children missed school. She preferred her polite ways, which she thought had more influence over time. She was fourteen years younger than Escalante and, unlike him, had grown up in the United States. She had a much better sense of how to organize a large program and had more time before retirement to get it done. Escalante didn't want to administer anything.

He just wanted to teach his kids. Swanson understood that joy, but was willing to give it up to have more impact.

Swanson continued to receive more recognition. In 1991, she won the Dana Medal, an education award usually reserved for university presidents or renowned professors. That same year, the Department of Defense Dependents Schools, with campuses all over the world, asked for AVID. Kentucky called, which forced Swanson to consider the consequences of national growth. Harry Weinberg, who succeeded Jerry Rosander as San Diego County school superintendent, gave her permission to add a state on the other side of the country. He also suggested she think about creating a nonprofit corporation to handle future requests.

A young education reformer named Ron Ottinger, son of a former New York congressman, had been elected to the city school board and had to resign his job in the superintendent's office. Swanson hired him to set up the nonprofit, created in 1992 and named AVID Center. The next year, Eric J. Smith, one of the nation's strongest supporters of AP and IB courses for inner-city students, asked to introduce AVID to the Newport News, Virginia, school district, where he was superintendent.

The issue was how to bring AVID to more schools and not go broke. The program could charge districts for training and curriculum, as AVID was doing in San Diego County, but that was not enough. Swanson argued that they needed to charge districts an annual fee for networking and consultations. Ottinger said that was not something programs usually did, and that as a school board member he would not vote for it. Often educational organizations charged only a one-time fee for the start-up concept, materials, implementation, and training. That appealed to budget-conscious superintendents and school board members, but it also meant that if they had trouble making a program work, they were not going to get much help. Swanson saw AVID as a fluid, creative program that good teachers could adjust to their local conditions, and add flourishes that AVID might adopt. That required close and regular contact. The Summer Institutes would let educators to catch up on changes and get new training, but during the year they would still need advice. AVID coordinators always had questions about unforeseen crises.

The new AVID board comprised Swanson; Ottinger; math professor Uri Treisman; Clarence Fields, a member of the first AVID class who worked for Xerox; and some local businessmen. They eventually approved Swanson's annual fee idea. It took time to calculate what it would be, but a schedule was arranged that school boards found affordable. That money plus the curriculum and professional development fees paid AVID Center's staff, except for the executive director. For the first ten years from 1994 to 2004, Swanson took no salary. Her husband was doing well in the banking business. They had just one child. She did not want anything to get in the way of attracting the best people she could find.

A typical school in the late 1980s would purchase the AVID curriculum and send about eight teachers to a Summer Institute for a first-year cost of about $7,000. Annual costs settled down to about $1,000 a year, mostly for tutors. AVID Center's first headquarters was a recently relocated Victorian house near San Diego's Old Town where Swanson leased space. The first staffer was Ottinger. An inch-thick business plan was adopted in 1996.

Nationally, most states were adopting programs to create annual tests that would rate schools and inspire more funding for those that were not meeting learning standards. By 2002, this system would be nationalized by the passing of No Child Left Behind. That would create more demand for AVID.

AVID in its early years had proven to be effective and appealing, mostly because of Swanson's insistence on keeping up its standards and hiring people who shared her values. Regular state funding for the AVID nonprofit organization began in 1996. Swanson had a stroke of good fortune when a former teacher and former state senator named Gary K. Hart, who had been the most pro-AVID member of the California legislature, was named state secretary of education in 1999. The chairs of the education committees of both the senate and the state assembly were also AVID supporters.

The state backing put AVID's California growth on a solid footing. But outside California, it continued to depend on activists like Eric J. Smith who had both power and strong views on challenging minority kids, as well as on chance meetings that changed educators' lives and brought word of AVID to new places.

BOISE SCHOOLS CHANGED BY LOVE

In 1997, Stacey Curry, a principal at a middle school near Fresno, California, attended a middle schools conference in San Diego and learned about AVID. This otherwise ordinary moment would lead to an explosion of AVID schools in Idaho, of all places, and the greatest expansion of Advanced Placement (AP) testing ever in the mountain states. The reason takes some explaining. It is a telling example of how AVID grew by happenstance and accident because that was the way Swanson wanted it.

NEW BEGINNINGS

Eighty-eight percent of Curry's students in Fresno were Hispanic. Ninety percent were from low-income families. She was struggling to find a way to raise them above the low level of learning typical of poor children. AVID offered a chance to do that in ways she had not seen before. "Oh my gosh, this makes sense," she recalled thinking. "We can do this. I loved the fact that it opened up the possibility of acceleration for kids who would never be doing that otherwise, whose parents would never dream of them doing that."

She attended the AVID Summer Institute in San Diego in 1998 with several of her teachers. She built the program at her school. In 2001, when she was hired to be an assistant superintendent for the small district of Riverdale, also near Fresno, she implanted AVID there, too.

Then she fell in love. Her mother, sister, and brother had moved to Boise, Idaho. While Curry was visiting them one summer, her mother introduced her to a man who worked for the Idaho Department of Commerce. They clicked. They tried a long-distance romance, but she was building a middle school program and working on her doctoral dissertation. It was too much. They broke up.

Then they got back together, and Curry moved to Idaho. "I decided as much as I loved my career, I preferred to marry the man who would become my husband," she said. "I knew I could get a job in the classroom wherever I went."

She started teaching seventh-grade reading in the Meridian school district, near Boise. Her administrative experience and wealth of ideas were obvious, so a year later the Boise school district hired her to be principal of Fairmount Junior High School. Morale at the school was low. There had been a significant shift in the demographics of its neighborhoods. It had become a majority low-income school, and average achievement rates were declining. Her supervisors wanted her to fix that, but only after she had boosted morale. "Let's get them happy first before we try anything else," one headquarters supervisor told her.

"It was not my nature to do that," she said. "We didn't get them happy, but we started them with AVID."

Her staff was complaining, as were educators everywhere, about the No Child Left Behind law that required all schools to give annual tests and be judged by the result. The law required that they make "adequate yearly progress" or be forced to make reforms. Curry told her new colleagues that the complaining had to stop. "The kids are here," she said. "They walk through our door every day no matter what color they are or how poor or how rich they are, and it is our job to give them opportunities to go to college."

About eight months into her new job, she called Boise schools superintendent Don Coberly and his chief deputy to discuss a plan she had drawn up for her school. "They thought I was this crazy lady from California," she recalled. But they came to her office and listened.

Coberly, Curry knew, was devoted to expanding opportunity for high school students to take AP courses and tests. Curry told him that if he let her pilot the AVID program, "it will fit nicely with my demographic and also with the greater goal of Advanced Placement." She gave them a four-page summary of what she had in mind. She had put it together for staffers at her junior high. Before she sent the staffers to San Diego for a summer institute, she wanted them to know what AVID was.

She emphasized the support the AVID elective classes would give to nontraditional students never before welcomed to AP. Those junior high school students of hers would be going to Capital High School. With AVID they would be better prepared for that school's growing AP program. It would give her school and the high school more rigor, with support.

AVID was just another acronym to Coberly. He needed something to get more low-income students ready for challenging work. He listened carefully. After twenty minutes he said, "Wow—this is what we have been waiting for." Coberly got a grant from the district's education foundation, funded by donations from local businesses and parents, for half of the cost of the AVID start-up at Fairmount. Curry would have two AVID elective classes in eighth grade and one in seventh grade. The money Coberly secured allowed her to add Capital High School teachers to the group who would get training at a summer institute.

There was resistance. An English teacher who had been at Fairmount many years said she would not permit AVID kids in her accelerated class. It was just for elite kids, she said. Curry heard an unspoken message: "These are the kids I normally teach, which means I don't have to do much. They do their homework. I don't want those lower-level Hispanic kids in my class. They would water down our accelerated program. It would ruin it. We are not going to do it."

Curry showed the teacher the data indicating that once they were challenged by AVID, children did much better. "I tried to bring her on to the AVID site team," Curry recalled, "along with five other teachers who seemed to agree with her."

But if they could not be persuaded, they were going to have to cooperate or go. "At some point as an administrator, after you have spent two years making dissenting teachers comfortable with the change, you then say we are doing this, and we are going to move forward. And you just go." Curry's impression, shared by other AVID coordinators around the country, was that such teachers ended up with AVID students in their classes, who with all that support did better than expected.

The English teacher who had made a fuss retired, so Curry did not have to deal with her anymore. Coberly said that the teacher had been his close friend, someone whose professional capabilities deserved respect. "She had reached retirement age," he said. "Frankly, I think if she had had a little more time, she would have come over to our way of thinking about AVID."

"COME TO JESUS": CHANGING ATTITUDES
AND INCREASING CLASSROOM RIGOR

Two of the naysayers in the English teacher's group did take AVID kids into their accelerated classes. Curry calculated that they were "probably 60 to 70 percent committed to the program." They remained at the school and were better at accepting AVID principles than they were before, "but they were still not totally sold," Curry said.

At Fairmount, some parents initially resisted the change, or were uncomfortable with it. Fairmount had about thirty students in an accelerated seventh-grade English class. Instead of mixing AVID students into that group—the usual procedure when the program began at a school—Curry created a separate English class for AVID seventh graders. It was a way for the AVID and English teachers to focus on raising the standard for those kids. The second year, more accelerated English sections were created for seventh and eighth grades so that AVID students could be mixed with the traditional accelerated students, producing more bad feeling.

In the long history of attempts to bring capable low-income and minority children into advanced classes, misinformation has often been a problem. When accelerated students see kids not in their peer group suddenly assigned to their classes, they tend to assume that the class has lost its honors status and is being dumbed down.

When that happened at Fairmount, Curry convened what she referred to as "a little come-to-Jesus meeting" for parents. She met first with the parents of the traditional advanced students, then with the AVID parents. She told the parents at the first meeting that their children were getting the accelerated curriculum as before, but this time the AVID children were getting it, too. She explained that the AVID students were taking a special elective class that prepared them for advanced work in ways supported by research. Their children would get the same benefit of the AVID emphasis on organization, note-taking, and critical thinking.

"I haven't done a good job over the last year meeting with you," she said to them, "so let me refresh you and go back through what we are doing. What you may be hearing from your kids is that it is different, but it's not. . . . If you want our school to be a great school for your kids, we need to give every kid the opportunity for more rigor. We need to support that."

The parents came around. The program at Fairmount continued to grow, in time introducing AVID techniques to every classroom for all children, whether designated for AVID or not. It became an AVID National Demonstration School, a place to send visitors who wanted to see how the program worked at its best.

Fairmount's school population in 2012 was about 70 percent low income, but the level of its classes had gotten much better. When Curry arrived in 2003, the school had twenty-three remedial courses in several subjects. By 2012, there were only two. When Curry arrived, there was just one section of Algebra I for eighth graders. By 2012, there were five.

That growth at Fairmount fit Coberly's plans to increase the number of students in AP. In 1981, the Boise school district gave only ninety-five AP exams. In 2000, that number had reached 950. In 2012, the district gave a total of 3,436 AP exams, one of the heaviest concentrations of college-level participation in the country. All four high schools were on the *Washington Post*'s Most Challenging High Schools list, putting them among the top 10 percent of schools in the country measured by AP, IB, or Advanced International Certificate of Education test participation. Passing rates on the AP exams in Boise schools ranged from 65 to 83 percent, all above the national passing rate for AP.

By 2012, there were 850 students in AVID classes in Boise. Coberly said he did not think AVID would have experienced nearly as much growth if the district had not already been in the midst of a major expansion of AP. Some principals and counselors resisted. "They were just worried that what we were doing was going to cause a number of students to fail," he said. "They feared that if some students got into accelerated algebra they would fail and then that would change their attitude and they would feel like they were failures all around."

"Our response was, 'How will we know if that will happen if we don't give them a chance?'"

When one of the junior high principals dragged his feet on instituting AVID, Coberly found that persistent persuasion solved the problem. "We didn't make any changes in the administration or the counselors or the teachers," Coberly said. "We just worked on changing the attitude."

When the recession hit in 2008, Coberly and his school board had to cut $22 million from its $200 million annual budget. Voters approved a tax increase that raised about $14 million. AVID spending was not affected. The district cut more than a dozen administrative posts and put off new textbook adoptions for three years, but AVID was given the highest priority by the Boise school board, thanks to a California principal who decided to follow her heart to the Gem State. Students also wandered into AVID in the same unpredictable way.

"Prove to Me You Got an A in Everything"

Students qualified for AVID in many ways, although Jesus Medrano's route to the program was different from most. He was smart, but didn't like school. As a ninth grader at Southwest High School in San Ysidro, south of San Diego, he did not see the point.

Take math, for instance. He was good in that subject. At San Ysidro Middle School, he had been advanced to the Algebra I class in seventh grade. It was easy, but he was not motivated. He was a troublemaker in class, often loud. His grade was not good. He was put in Algebra I again in eighth grade. To him that just made it worse. What sense did it make to enroll him in a class he had already mastered? His behavior was again bad. That led inexorably to his being assigned to Algebra I a third time when he reached ninth grade in 1998 at Southwest High.

This did not surprise Medrano. San Ysidro Middle School had the reputation for being the worst of the three middle schools that fed into Southwest. "They liked to place us in classes where we didn't belong," he recalled years later. Just knowing he was from that middle school was enough for schedulers to assume he wasn't worth much, Medrano thought. He told his counselor he didn't belong in Algebra I, but he was ignored. His parents weren't involved in his schooling. They had stopped checking his homework when he was in the third grade. By high school, his education choices, what few he was allowed, were his.

His teacher for his third year of Algebra I was "not one of the better teachers," Medrano recalled. The man handed out worksheets. He handed out quizzes and tests. That was about it. Medrano got A's in all of his assignments, but a D in the course.

"Why did I get a D?" he asked the teacher. "I got an A in everything."

"Prove to me you got an A in everything," the teacher said.

Medrano was accustomed to indifferent teaching, but this was unbelievable. "Aren't you supposed to keep the records?" he asked.

HIGH EXPECTATIONS BEGET HIGH PERFORMANCE

At about the same time, someone at Southwest High finally noticed that ninth grader Jesus Medrano, despite coming from San Ysidro Middle School, had had good grades on his transcript. The new take on Medrano was that he could be difficult but had great potential. That meant he was enrolled in AVID. He didn't object. His friend Angel was also in the ninth-grade AVID elective class. They enjoyed going together in their favorite T-shirts and baggy pants and disrupting the proceedings.

The ninth-grade AVID teacher, Ms. Matthews, called them on their behavior. They were slow to respond. Medrano detested keeping his papers in a binder. He only made a pretense of complying with Cornell notes. His pages might be marked off properly, but the notes were sparse and the key questions slapdash.

Then he was suspended for three days for using a vulgarity in his English class. This surprised him. He used the word often, but usually in a whisper or in his head. He had not realized that language was such a sensitive point. On the surface, he did not seem to take it seriously. He was not contrite. He spent the three days of his suspension at home watching TV. But, he acknowledged years later, he was embarrassed that his mother and grandmother had to come and pick him up at school. They told him he had dishonored his family. That stuck with him.

He was doing things outside of school with great future benefit, even though he thought of them as aimless amusement. He loved video games. His father had never gotten further than third grade in school, but he had skilled hands and a curious mind. He bought an old computer at a swap meet. With his son, he took it apart and put it back together again. "We couldn't afford it," Medrano recalled, "but he bought a better computer, a modern one. We took that apart and saw how everything worked. It was a challenge. It was fun."

Medrano didn't like sports. Then five foot four, he thought he was too short to be much good. He preferred to hang with his friends and see how well he could do in school while doing the least amount of work. At the end of his freshman year, Matthews told him: "You have a big chip on your shoulder, and I expect you to do much better next year."

Somewhat to his surprise, he did. Binder checks and Cornell notes became less annoying. As an AVID student, he was put in honors courses where there were better teachers. His geometry teacher, Mr. Powers, was the opposite of the ninth-grade Algebra I teacher who didn't bother to keep a grade book. Powers was energetic, challenging, and encouraging. He gave a test every Friday. Medrano loved taking exams, particularly when the teacher was recording the results. Powers was not effusive. He didn't make a point of telling Medrano he was doing well. The way he recognized good work was to suggest that the student do some extra problems. "He would say, 'Let's have some fun,' and he would have a math competition I qualified for. If that went well, he would say, 'Why don't you do this puzzle?'" Medrano recalled.

The three years of first-year algebra had put him behind, but Powers thought he could catch up. He arranged for Medrano to take trigonometry the summer after his sophomore year so that he would be ready for precalculus junior year and calculus senior year.

His happiness with his math teacher contrasted with what he encountered in other classes. The rule that AVID students had to be placed in advanced classes did not apply to all subjects, as in some cases advanced classes were not available. He didn't recall doing anything in ninth-grade English. "We were supposed to do *Wuthering Heights*, but I don't remember reading it at all. The teacher was not imaginative and was not demanding. She gave us papers to do and they were due a month later," he said.

He had a similar experience in tenth-grade biology. "He would talk for about five minutes," Medrano recalled, "and then we would watch a video about whales, or something. Every day there was a video. The teacher said, 'Write a page about what you learned and then give it to me.' Everything was based on the videos. He would give us a test every month or so. I got an A."

But by eleventh grade, he found both his courses and his attitude improving. Because of AVID, he had more of a feeling of responsibility. Powers continued to nudge him into challenging territory. Medrano was in precalculus his junior year, doing so well he asked if he might take AP Calculus AB at the same time. Powers and his counselor gave him a calculus placement test. Out of fifty questions he missed only a couple, so he enrolled in calculus at the same time that he was taking precalculus. He scored a 5, the highest possible score, on the AP exam and enrolled in AP Calculus BC his senior year.

His math skills were so advanced that Matthews had him act as an AVID math tutor on days that she was shorthanded. He bonded with his World Cultures teacher, Mr. Volton, by joining the school's Academic League team. "He would treat us like we were in college," Medrano remembered. "He wouldn't put up with any nonsense. People were afraid of him because he was loud." Medrano thought the tough-guy routine was amusing, and sometimes laughed. Volton did not like that but humored him.

COMPETING FOR HONORS AND BREAKING NEW GROUND

The thrill of the competition with other students led Medrano to show up for Academic League practice every day after school, sometimes staying as late as 6 p.m. By junior year, he was loaded up with demanding courses. He had AP English Language and AP US History, as well as honors Chemistry and AP Spanish. He had no time for an AVID elective course that year, but kept in touch with Matthews as he began to apply to college.

The honors Chemistry course had a very tough teacher. Medrano liked that. Students said that this was the course that determined who would be valedictorian because every year many of the straight-A contenders for that honor would get mediocre grades in chemistry. The teacher started the course with a test in what she called basic math. "If you can't pass this, you can't be in my class," she said. The next day, as she passed out the graded exams, she said, "In all my years of teaching this course, only one person ever got a perfect score, and that person went to MIT, the only person in the history of the school who did that. This year we have another person who got a perfect score."

Medrano recalled hearing several students from Filipino families, smart kids who sat at the front of the room, speculating that a girl in their group must have had the perfect score. She was a straight-A student. She was sure to be the valedictorian. At Southwest High, the students of Filipino descent were thought to be at a higher academic level than those of Mexican descent. Filipino parents were likely to be high school or even college graduates. But it was Medrano, born of Mexican parents, who got the perfect score.

He rarely did much homework. His free time was spent reading for pleasure, including some math and chemistry books he was never assigned in school. At home he would play video games and watch TV with his family. He had enough time at school to keep up in class work. He didn't want to be bored. Both his English and history teachers saw that.

AP English Language class was his favorite. There was lots of reading and writing. The teacher was entertaining and lively, once enthralling the class with his story of changing a flat tire. That teacher did not, however, prepare his students well for the multiple-choice section of the AP test. Medrano scored only a 2, which bothered him.

The AP US History teacher, Mr. Winters, was more effective. He emphasized at the beginning of the year that AP US History at Southwest had a very low passing rate on the AP exam, only about 10 percent. His mission was to pull up that percentage. Every minute had to be put to use. They wrote a great deal. Medrano got a 4 on the AP exam, but thought he should have done better.

By the end of Medrano's junior year, he was immersed in college planning, with the help of his counselor and Matthews. Medrano had a college-educated uncle who took him on a business trip that included a visit to UC Berkeley. His counselor and AVID teachers had high hopes that a student with such a keen intellect, who read for pleasure in his free time and whose parents had never gotten to high school, would be selected by one of the nation's top-ranked colleges. He enrolled in a special AVID college prep class for seniors that met after school. On many days he would be at the high school from 6:30 a.m. to 6:00 p.m.

In his senior year, he wanted to take at least five AP classes, an unheard of number for his school. He asked Matthews how many she thought he should take. "Why don't you take them all?" she said. He took eight. He scored a 5, the highest possible score, on Calculus AB his junior year and a 4 on Calculus BC his senior year. The Chemistry test was to him the easiest AP. He earned a 5. He got a 4 in Physics B, the first person at Southwest ever to pass that test. He scored a 3 in European History, a 4 in Government, and a 4 in Art History. There was no Art History course at Southwest, but Medrano and two friends shared that interest and studied on their own. One friend got a 4 and the other, a 5.

His counselor suggested that he try Harvard, but Medrano said it was too pretentious. He applied to MIT, Princeton, Caltech, and four UC campuses—Berkeley, Los Angeles, San Diego, and Irvine. He got into all of the UCs and MIT, was waitlisted at Princeton, and rejected by Caltech. Unlike many Hispanic students from low-income neighborhoods in California, he had no qualms about attending school far away. He was not very interested in Princeton, but got excited when an official in the MIT admissions office called to invite him to visit the campus.

"That would be great," he said, "but I can't afford it."

"No, no, no," said the MIT official, accustomed to that response from the children of parents who never went to college. "We cover all costs, including the airfare."

Medrano liked the way the city of Cambridge surrounded the MIT campus. "The people were a little more normal than I expected," he recalled. "They were very bright people and very cool to hang with." He chose MIT, not bothering to wait to see whether Princeton took him off the waitlist.

KEEPING ORDER AND KEEPING AFLOAT: LEVERAGING AVID IN COLLEGE AND BEYOND

When he arrived at MIT, Medrano decided that the healthiest way to adjust was not to expect too much of himself. If I get a C, he thought, I am OK. I'll graduate. I'll be fine. "That was a big advantage, because when I failed, I could take the challenge and do better next time," he said. He got all B's his first semester.

He got up before 4 a.m. to study. He planned his days and weeks as he had done with his AVID calendar. He remained a math major and finished in four years, but took so many other courses that, he realized, he could also have majored in economics or computer science. His grade-point average at graduation was a 3.7 on a 5.0 scale.

He managed this despite a series of family crises during his senior year in 2006. His grandmother died. His father was arrested for drug trafficking and sent to prison for two years. His mother, never before separated from her husband, was profoundly depressed. Medrano had to miss the deadline on some midterm papers and drop two classes. When he emailed his counselors as he left for California, they suggested he delay graduation for a year. He said, "No, I'm a senior. I'm going to graduate now." He got an A in the one last class he needed. He felt a brief moment of satisfaction, then jumped into one of the most miserable times in his life.

He had a degree from MIT, but that wasn't much good for helping his mother and the rest of his family cope with their losses. There was no money. Bills were due. He had a younger brother and sister to take care of. He looked for a job he could do from home. He got some paid speaking engagements, telling his story to AVID audiences. Finally, after the home situation stabilized, he got a job at Grumman Aircraft in Rancho Bernardo, working on drones as a guidance control engineer.

His mother found a part-time job as a lunch attendant at an elementary school, something Medrano was hoping would take her mind off of his father. She drove him to his job each day, a forty-five-minute trip, and picked him up at night. The family had only one car. His salary helped catch up with six months of unpaid bills, but the situation was exhausting. When they caught up financially, Medrano persuaded his mother to let him rent an apartment with a friend near his job so he would not have to do the long commute. His father got out of prison, but died in 2012.

Medrano had learned in AVID how to have an orderly life. It had gotten him through college and through a bewildering series of family tragedies. He was able to move forward to the life of his dreams, just as the AVID people he once distrusted had said he would. He met a young woman joining the human relations staff at Grumman's the same week he got his job there. She had a daughter. They married in August 2011, and in February 2013, they had a baby, Adrian Ismael Medrano. Two months later, he accepted an offer to be a software developer at Yahoo! in Sunnyvale, and moved with his family to their new home in San Jose, at the heart of Silicon Valley.

He no longer had to deal with people who thought he was a loser because he had gone to San Ysidro Middle School. Work and life could still be hard, but he knew how to deal with them, his papers in order, budgeting his time and taking notes that focused on the big questions.

SHOWING AMERICA HOW TO
TAKE NOTES

Few Americans learn to take lecture notes. They have notebooks in high school, and often scribble in them when the teacher is speaking. But they really don't know what they are doing. Rarely does anyone show them how best to break down a lecture or book. Most high school and college students write what seems important, but get no lessons in the best ways to record what they are learning.

One of the biggest surprises for people coming in contact with AVID is to learn that there is a proven way of taking notes effectively, and that AVID requires it of its middle and high school students. Eric Welch, a social studies teacher in Fairfax County, Virginia, first tasted the power of thoughtful summarizing at a 2005 summer institute session on Cornell notes, the system Mary Catherine Swanson adopted three decades ago. "I saw this fed into so many different aspects of learning," he said. Soon he was the AVID coordinator for J.E.B. Stuart High School, one of the highest-achieving schools in the country with a majority of students from low-income families.

CORNELL NOTES: DEEPER LEARNING THROUGH EFFECTIVE NOTE-TAKING

The AVID note-taking system was developed by Cornell University education professor Walter Pauk in 1949. The student divides a sheet of note paper into two columns, the one on the right twice as wide as the one on the left. The student adds a horizontal line about two inches from the bottom of the page. He takes notes in the right column, using a number of symbols and abbreviations. Questions and key words go in the left column. Afterward, the student reviews the notes, revises anything that needs changing, adds questions to the bottom of the left column that have not occurred to him before, and writes a brief summary at the bottom of each page.

The process deepens learning and augments review, its advocates say, but it takes patience and perseverance, qualities not common in adolescents. From the beginning, AVID teachers recognized that Cornell notes would not do the job for which they were intended if students only used them in their AVID elective class. Swanson began to teach Cornell notes because without the notes, she would have had no idea what her AVID students were being taught in their other classes. The tutors she had hired would have been unable to help her students cope with those classes, which was the purpose of AVID.

"I didn't know a good system of note-taking," Swanson said. "I myself in college had taken notes and not in the most advantageous way." By October of the first year of AVID in 1980, Swanson saw that the haphazard way her students were taking notes would not work. It made them too dependent on their tutors. When her college student tutors had to take a week off to take their midterm exams at the University of California, San Diego, she tried to fill in for them. Her students told her to give up. Only their tutors knew enough to provide them the answers they needed to prepare for exams or complete homework.

Swanson moved, haltingly and with many setbacks, toward an inquiry-based system of both tutoring and note-taking. Her students had to be thinking about the key questions being addressed as they took notes on lectures and reading assignments. They had to be asking themselves the essential questions raised by the material and see for themselves where they needed to go to get the answers.

That kind of note-taking was familiar to one of Swanson's tutors, Nina Manzi. She had learned the Cornell system. It sounded good to Swanson, so she and Manzi trained all of the AVID students and AVID tutors in the method. "I would lecture to the class like the classroom teachers would lecture, using some AVID topic such as how best to manage their time," Swanson said. "Nina would have the overhead projector, which is what we used in those days, and would take Cornell notes on what I was saying and show the kids how to do that."

"Out-Loudness": Active Question-Making for Independent Thinking

In a hand-typed personal letter to a student, now a treasured AVID document, Pauk emphasized the importance of inquiry in the note-taking process:

> Question-making is not easy! Question-making was very hard
> for me; but, as I battled to come forth with a question, I became
> better and better at the thinking process. You see, Pamela, I
> had to keep asking myself, "What is the lecturer trying to say?"
> It seems that you have to talk out-loud to the words on that
> page . . . "What are you getting at?" You see, too, that this
> "out-loudness" puts you in almost a person to person mode.
> You're no longer a passive reader of the notes. This goes for text-
> book reading, too.
>
> One does not learn through the eyes alone. One learns
> through the processing of information by the brain. Words very,
> very seldom imprint themselves on the brain; but one's think-
> ing does.

As AVID developed, the acceptance and encouragement of AVID methods by non-AVID teachers became critical. Some teachers discouraged note-taking, having found that students did it poorly, if at all. Some teachers would hand out notes they wrote themselves, or worksheets that were the equivalent of notes, with all of the relevant information included.

Students told their AVID teachers that there was no point taking notes in those classes. So AVID teachers from the beginning, including Swanson, had to persuade their colleagues to change their ways. In the meantime, they would tell AVID students to take Cornell notes on the worksheets, as the sheets would rarely be organized to encourage the question-making that Pauk, Swanson, and many other educators considered so important to learning.

Swanson didn't go to other teachers and point out their flaws. That would have violated a sacred rule of teacher culture: never act as if you know more than your colleagues. Instead, Swanson said, "I went into teachers' classrooms and watched how they questioned kids." She got permission to be in their classes with a white lie. She told them her kids were just not getting what they were teaching, and she and her tutors would only be able to transmit the teachers' good lessons if they heard them personally.

It was a distressing experience for Swanson. "They would ask the class a question," she recalled. "They knew the answers they wanted. Kids would raise their hands. Always the same kids, of course. They would say to the first student, 'Yes?' and that student wouldn't give them the answer they wanted. They would call on one more student, and that student wouldn't give them the answer they wanted, so the teacher would give the answer that she wanted, and move on with more content. The kids never understood why that was the answer." Their teachers didn't think it was their job to tell them.

"What she should have done was ask them a question that might lead in the right direction to the answer," Swanson said. "Our teachers weren't doing it, and I don't think Clairemont was much different from any other schools."

AVID teachers across the country are trained to embrace the question-making emphasis. At Stuart High in Fairfax County, Welch said he had success in his government classes giving weekly quizzes at which students are allowed to use their Cornell notes. "When they come back from college," he said, "they say they learned how much note-taking helps." They could not survive if they did not know how to pursue their own studying and thinking in that way.

Teachers Afraid of Tough Courses

Rob Gira (pronounced ji-RAH) was teaching English at Vista High School in northern San Diego when he realized that his fear of putting ordinary students in Advanced Placement (AP) courses was stupid and wrong. It was part of his gradual awakening to the untapped potential of American teenagers. Years later, that insight would make him one of AVID's most influential executives, a master at designing programs for average kids.

He began working at Vista in 1976 at age twenty-six. The school's demographics were changing, as they were elsewhere in the state. The Hispanic population was growing rapidly. Many more low-income kids were enrolling in suburban schools that previously had been mostly middle class.

The Vista staff saw that Gira was tall and friendly. Gradually they learned he was also smart, imaginative, and resourceful. He had found a way to get through college even after his basketball scholarship at Chapman University had evaporated because of an injury. At Vista, he realized that what he had learned in teacher training at San Francisco State would be greatly enhanced if he asked his students what was working for them and what wasn't. He benefited from an after-hours program called the California Literature Project, sponsored by the same San Diego County Office of Education that supported AVID and the entrepreneurial English teacher who would change Gira's life.

Accelerating Students through Engagement

The Literature Project encouraged good writing and writing instruction, taught seminar style. "It helped me understand collaborative grouping and really differentiating instruction so you are not doing the cookie-cutter thing," Gira said years later. That served him well when he began to see that more Vista students were ready for a challenge than were being offered it.

An English teacher named Pat Prather, later to be the California director for AP's counterpart, International Baccalaureate (IB), asked the Vista principal to offer AP English Literature to the school's best seniors. AP Calculus and Physics were added, but not for very many students. Gira was intrigued when a friend who was teaching AP English Literature to seniors mentioned that the school had an English class for gifted juniors who were not getting a comparable challenge. Gira thought another AP course, English Composition, might work for the gifted class. He set it up cautiously. He was a good writing teacher, but the AP reputation was intimidating. He was so afraid of failure that he picked only eight of those bright juniors to take the AP final exam, a three-hour ordeal written and graded by outside experts.

Years later, Gira was critical of himself and the other Vista teachers for being slow in seeing the potential of AP and other challenging courses to turn young lives around. "We were classic gatekeepers," he said. "We also got the IB program, and we figured we had brought in this rarified air; only a few can sniff it. We kept it pretty limited."

He shared the view of many teachers that kids would suffer blows to their self-esteem if brought into AP or IB too soon, leading them to flunk the exam. But that was not his main fear. "I myself was intimidated by the fact that I was now an AP teacher. I was frightened by how bad I was going to look, how bad I was going to gum this up if I didn't do it right, and I needed to prove to my colleagues that our kids could do it. So I started with a small group of kids. It was more about me, more about how I would look."

Gradually he saw what he was missing. Like other teachers, he had classes at every level, from AP down to remedial. "When I did research on the backgrounds of the noncollege kids in my remedial classes, lo and behold I found more than a few had been identified as gifted at one time. The reason they were in remedial was they had not been engaged. They had problems. So they were stuck into the remedial classes, and I realized we were pretty arbitrary about student opportunity, about whom we offered a chance to grow."

AVID arrived at Vista High in 1987. It was one of the first San Diego county schools to participate in the program Swanson was running from the county Office of Education. The superintendent of the Vista school district, Rene Townsend, liked Swanson and liked AVID. She adopted it for both Vista and Rancho Buena Vista High, which opened that year.

"My first impression was that it made sense," Gira recalled. "It was an opportunity to accelerate students. That fit my thinking that we were holding too many kids back." He thought of two girls who had been in his junior gifted English class, the one he had turned into an AP English Composition class and also part of the IB program. "They would have been perfect for AVID," he recalled. "They were Hispanic girls. Their families were very poor. The barrio was just adjacent to the high school. Nobody there had gone to college. They got enough support from us through IB to both get full IB diplomas, and both went to Harvard."

"That was kind of a wake-up call for me," he said. "Like a lot of people, I hadn't really seen the potential; I didn't have that vision. But seeing those young ladies that I had an opportunity to work with and really asking them a lot of questions while I had them in my English class, I realized—hmmm—there are probably more kids like this."

He was also impressed by the quality and energy of the teachers who were joining the AVID program. They were his friends. As he moved into administration, he became more committed to making AVID a priority. He transferred to the new Rancho Buena Vista High School campus as an assistant principal, then came back to Vista in 1991 as principal.

AVID was doing so well at Vista that the AVID coordinator, Cindy Bishop, and the rest of her team suggested they apply for something Swanson had invented called a validation. It was similar to the school assessments done by International Baccalaureate. An AVID team visited a school's AVID elective and other classes with AVID students. The team interviewed staff and students and looked at data. How vigorous had the faculty been in applying AVID methods? What impact did AVID have on schoolwide performance, as measured by such factors as the number of students passing all of the course requirements for the state university systems and participating in AP?

Vista received a high validation, one reason why Swanson took notice when she heard in 1994 that Gira, then forty-four, wanted a change. She matched his salary and persuaded him to join AVID Center, her new nonprofit located in a Victorian house in San Diego. She insisted on collegiality. Big decisions were made by consensus after long meetings in which everyone had a say. After a few months of this, Gira observed that AVID staffers had the strongest bladders he had ever encountered. This phenomenon was henceforth referred to as "the Cult of the Iron Bladder."

Gira was hired in June and told that he had less than two months to prepare a weeklong strand training for administrators at the upcoming summer institute. "I had to develop a syllabus for those four-and-a-half days because AVID did not have a syllabus for that strand," he recalled. "I had never written a syllabus before."

CONTINUALLY IMPROVING

He quickly saw why Swanson had been able to turn her one-classroom program for thirty-two kids into one of the hottest educational ideas in the state. "I don't think I have ever met anyone as focused as Mary Catherine," he said. "She has the ability to concentrate and really turn her attention to a problem. She has this weird combination of creativity and organizational skill that is just phenomenal. She always follows up. She never forgot anything. She always had twenty things going."

"She was very developmental in her approach to AVID," he said. "She understood that AVID was not fully formed. She had been implementing it for six years at Clairemont and then went to the county office and had to write the curriculum, and she was continually improving. That was her mantra."

Swanson said she hired Gira because he had done such a good job supporting AVID at Vista High. He had not taught an AVID class, but he knew the program well. "I found out he could do a whole plethora of things," Swanson said. "Other than budgeting—he is no good at budgeting at all—but when it comes to programmatic things, he is extremely good, very creative. He has great follow-through. He knows how to test things out with teachers to see if they work. He is a good staff developer. He is an excellent writer."

The growth of AVID was episodic and unpredictable. Swanson kept trying to improve the model. Excited teachers who had seen it work passed the word, but Swanson and Gira made little effort to promote it. "It didn't hurt to have a charismatic figure at the top who was also very real," Gira said. "Mary Catherine was a teacher. It was a teacher-based program. Because of that, it had authenticity with good teachers."

The California state government began to provide regular funding for AVID in 1996. AVID got a further boost in 2000 when the state settled an American Civil Liberties Union lawsuit charging discriminatory failure to get minorities into challenging programs like AP. AVID began to work closely with the College Board, the huge nonprofit that sponsored both the AP and SAT programs. That opened more sources of funding for school districts that wanted to involve more low-income students from noncollege families in challenging courses.

Then came Texas. AVID's growth was stimulated by starting in the nation's most populous state, with a government eager to encourage more college preparation for minorities. It was first adopted in San Antonio, full of low-income Hispanic children like the AVID students of its San Diego County beginnings.

By the 1980s, Texas was a national hotbed of education reform. In 1984, four years after AVID was born in California, the Texas legislature passed a $2.8 billion education package promoted by billionaire Ross Perot and officeholders in both parties. The law created a state preschool program for low-income children with disadvantages, dictated more funds for districts full of disadvantaged students, raised academic standards, created proficiency tests for teachers, and raised teacher salaries, linking them to performance. It also required students to pass all of their courses or be banned from after-school sports and other activities, known as the "no pass, no play" rule.

Texas reforms expanded in the 1990s, including annual tests for all students to gauge how well each school was doing. George W. Bush, governor at that time, used the Texas experience to craft the No Child Left Behind law that became national policy in 2002 after he was elected president. Texas reforms were better funded than in other parts of the country, both because of the state funding and the interest shown in public education by several Texas entrepreneurs.

San Antonio adopted AVID in 1997, beginning in eight high schools. In 2001, the program expanded to three middle schools, and by 2006, all middle schools in the district had AVID.

"From there we had a variety of champions across the state," Gira recalled. The most important were Michael and Susan Dell, computer billionaires whose foundation had become a leading supporter of raising achievement for low-income children. "We approached their foundation staff and said, 'Look, maybe you could help us spread this program in the center of the country.'" They agreed to fund the creation of a central division of AVID, headquartered in Texas. Gira said the program also got strong support from state senator Florence Shapiro, a Dallas Republican and influential chairman of the education committee.

By the mid-1990s when Gira arrived at AVID, it had a small western division for schools outside its home state, and an eastern division that had materialized when Eric J. Smith embraced AVID as school super-intendent in Newport News, Virginia. Gira called him Hurricane Eric. Beginning as a science teacher in Florida, Smith developed an aggres-sive approach to students in poverty that included emphasis on AP and IB, and rigorous preparation for minorities similar to what AVID was attempting. Gira noticed when he presented his first strand on adminis-tration at the 1994 summer institute that the session was full of principals and assistant principals from Newport News. Smith then moved to the huge Charlotte-Mecklenberg district in North Carolina, then to the Anne Arundel County schools in Maryland, and eventually became education commissioner in Florida. At every post, he expanded the number of stu-dents taking AP and IB, and used AVID to prepare more students for that.

"The fact that AVID really connected with AP was the key thing," Gira said. School districts and states that encouraged AP and IB, like Boise, also encouraged AVID. Even before Smith became commissioner, Florida was a major AP and IB state. It provided subsidies to schools that expanded those programs. "Those huge school districts, like Duval and Orange and Hillsborough, were looking for anything that could bring coherence to their work, anything that you can get people speaking the same language and having the same worldview," Gira said. The emphasis was on raising achievement for low-income children. That fit AVID's model. The program rode the waves of national school reform, and avoided much of the criticism of No Child Left Behind made by teachers because AVID focused on encouraging inquiry in ways that teachers and their organizations approved.

COLLEGE READINESS FOR MIDDLE AND ELEMENTARY SCHOOLS

Shortly after Gira arrived, AVID began moving into junior highs and middle schools, particularly seventh and eighth grades. Schools for early adolescents were in trouble. High schools had some incentive for rigorous classes because many of their students were going to college and needed transcripts that showed they could handle demanding work. Middle schools lacked that motivator. Few, if any, middle school courses counted for college. American middle school educators tried to engage students with intriguing lessons, but demanded little work.

It was an itchy stage in life, teachers told themselves. Middle schoolers, many said, should not be burdened with too much rigor. If students were struggling with a subject, teachers' instinct was to make it easier. "They'll get that in high school," they said. Urban middle schools, like urban elementary and high schools, had always been a problem. Even middle schools serving wealthy families, like Scarsdale Middle School (New York) or the Sidwell Friends private middle school in Washington DC, were said to have problems.

This made no sense to AVID educators teaching ninth graders just a year older than their middle school siblings. They saw how much those children could do if given more time and encouragement to learn. A College Board project called Equity 2000 had shown that school districts requiring all ninth graders to take Algebra I produced more students passing that subject than the number of ninth graders who took Algebra I before it was required. Why not have most students take Algebra I in middle school? Why not strengthen the thinking, reading, and writing skills of average students before they got to high school?

Such changes would be difficult to make for entire middle schools. But introducing AVID might work because it would involve just a portion of the kids. If the note-taking, tutoring, binder checks, Socratic

Seminars, and other devices worked for them, then more teachers might be trained and more students exposed to rigor.

The idea of AVID in elementary schools took longer to develop, Gira said. Some districts with AVID middle school and high school programs had asked for something for younger children. The Cherry Creek school district in Colorado completed a pilot study of an AVID elementary school program in 2006. "That's what you do when you are stalling: you do a pilot," Gira said. He thought the elementary curriculum they designed was good, "but we hadn't figured out the infrastructure, and we hadn't figured out the professional development," he said.

The initial idea for elementary schools was to make it easy: have the curriculum and the training ready for anyone who wanted it. But that did not sound like the AVID way. It was not a complete, integrated system. Middle and high school programs were all the relatively small AVID organization could handle, so it backed away from elementary schools until the late 1990s, when some districts with successful AVID high schools said they were ready to try.

That new version of AVID in elementary schools focused on college readiness. Although AVID elementary was offered as early as kindergarten, it usually began with fourth graders. College was reality for them. They had older relatives who talked about it. The point was to help them see how to get there. Much of the elementary program focused on time management. When they went home from school, should they watch TV or do their homework? If they were writing a report in school, how should they organize their time?

Starting at that age also helped ease the imbalance between girls and boys in the high school AVID program. Many urban educators had noticed that fourth grade was the point when once cheerful boys eager to please were drawn into neighborhood conflicts and other male pursuits that clashed with school rules. Finding ways to engage them in academic work could be beneficial in future years. That was the thinking as the AVID elementary school experiment proceeded.

Under Gira's supervision, AVID also developed a postsecondary program in a few colleges and universities. The classes taught time management, study skills, and inquiry-based learning to college students who needed it but had not had AVID programs in high school. It forced college advisory offices who usually handled students in academic trouble to work more closely with the professors who were teaching the courses. AVID tutors in college, just as in high school, needed to know what was being taught in the college classes in order to help AVID students. The two sides had to communicate.

No Lockstep Curriculum:
Flexible Strategies for Reaching the Vulnerable

Gira had thought a long time about AVID's refusal to include the most troublesome students on high school campuses, even though they needed the academic discipline of AVID the most. "We say we don't bring the gang-bangers into AVID, and we don't want to bring in kids who are super discipline problems initially," Gira said. "In order to win faculty support, we have to start with a targeted group of kids who you know would move pretty quickly to develop a scholarly identity. The bottom-performing kids and the top kids, you can start to bring them in once you have launched AVID and have had success on your campus, but you don't want to start with them.

"When I was a principal, I recruited a kid for AVID who was a gang member, a very influential gang member on our campus. We practically had to bring in a SWAT team to get him out of AVID because he was poisoning the program. His influence was extremely powerful. He wasn't interested in academics. He was interested in exerting his influence. He saw AVID as a way to see what kind of influence he could have, and it was very negative. That was my fault.

"We do see lots of examples where later on you can bring in kids who don't exactly fit the profile, but since one of the things we look for is special circumstances, you may have a kid who is a high-performing kid but lives in his car, or has a single parent at home. That kid may be performing, but with such a strain he is killing himself. He doesn't have the support structure.

"You can take just enough to keep the standards high to do what you do best, and not be overwhelmed by lots of problems, like what happened when the charter school organization Green Dot took over Locke

High School, one of the lowest-achieving schools in Los Angeles," he said. "You've got to create an environment which is manageable because if you have created that culture, you can bring in more kids."

That depended on the teachers whose training had been one of Gira's specialties. He said he thought teachers reacted positively to the summer institutes and the atmosphere created by AVID teams because "we are treating them with extreme professionalism and a belief that the teaching profession is first and foremost. The folks that come to the institutes are not all top performers. They want to get better. They all get a tool box when they come to our institutes and conferences. They can come back and right away implement it."

One of AVID's most important assets in developing teacher skills was the appointment of Aliber Lozano as director of professional learning in 2007. Lozano's parents were migrant farm workers who raised five children. Lozano worked hard in school, participated in sports and other activities, but even then, he said, "Somehow I fell through the cracks." At the end of his senior year at Edinburg North High School in Texas, he revealed in the AVID educational journal *ACCESS*, "I had not applied to any colleges, had not completed any financial aid forms, nor had I taken any college entrance exams."

The memory of that moment and what happened next, he said, continues to inspire him as he helps AVID teachers learn how they can be most effective with students whose backgrounds are similar to his. His older sister Arminda, who would earn two master's degrees and become an administrator in an AVID school, had been his inspiration for years. "Every grading period, I would open my mother's tin box where she kept our school report cards, certificates and ribbons," he recalled. "I would pull my sister's report card from the same grade level and ensure that I not only matched her grades, but surpassed them as often as I could." When Lozano's high school failed to get him ready for college, Arminda—by then an English teacher—took charge. "She helped me apply to our local university and complete the necessary paperwork to receive financial aid." He began to realize, once he arrived in college in 1992, how little had been done in high school for low-income students. During his first college semester, "I sat in an auditorium full of hundreds of primarily Hispanic students, taking the ACT residual" exam, he said. "Most of us had not taken a college entrance exam which was needed to take any classes beyond the 12 hours (a full class load) most of us were taking first semester."

With educators like Lozano who have a gut instinct for what will work and what won't, AVID teachers can be creative, Gira said. "Ours is not a lockstep curriculum. It is a strategy they can apply and then expand on."

Gira noted the AVID emphasis on collegiality. "There is a team of people. Teaching is a very isolating business," he said. "One of the genius aspects of Mary Catherine's work was when we developed our summer institute, we put them in a joblike situation part of the time, but the rest of the time they are in a team situation. They have to sit and reach agreements on what they are going to do. If you train them in that way, you can get real change when people will agree and come to a consensus."

At the core of the training of AVID teachers were the tutorials, something that education schools rarely address, as inquiry-based tutorials are so rare. Gira looked for ways to make tutorials more consistent and more powerful. At its beginning, AVID tutoring was nothing more than an obvious way to handle a difficult situation, but eventually it proved to be one of the best ideas ever.

Asking Rather Than Answering Questions

Tutoring is common in America. Many students fail to grasp the material in class. They need personal, step-by-step assistance to understand the concepts and master the skills that will allow them to meet their teachers' standards and advance to the next level.

Usually classroom teachers don't do much tutoring, unless they are making extra money that way after school. The students most likely to have tutors are the richest and the poorest. Affluent parents can afford the $60 or more an hour. They tend to have the greatest desire that their children earn grades good enough to get into selective colleges. Students from low-income families in big cities have access to free tutoring programs set up just for them by nonprofit organizations preparing such students for college.

Kids in the middle appear to be the least likely to get tutors. But those were the students Swanson was trying to reach when she started AVID, so hiring tutors was one of the first things she did. They became so vital to her success that she took unusual steps to make the exchanges between her students and the tutors she hired as effective as possible. She turned tutoring into something never seen before in public high schools.

Her method is still so rare that there is no well-known term for it. AVID calls it inquiry-based tutoring. Some of the educators who encourage it call it question-making. The idea is for the tutors *not* to tell students the answers but to guide them through a series of questions to do the thinking that will get the students there themselves. Attached to that is an even more radical rule: it is the students in each tutorial, not the tutor, who are supposed to ask the questions that lead each stumped student to the truth.

The Challenges of Inquiry-Based Tutoring

In fall 1980, with thirty-two mostly low-income students in her first AVID class, Swanson needed to ensure that they could handle the rigor of the advanced courses in math, English, science, social sciences, and foreign languages in which she had enrolled them. Her AVID class was the place where they sought help with confusing and elusive concepts. The University of California and California State University systems required that applicants successfully complete certain honors courses at their high schools. Those were the classes the AVID kids were taking, eventually called the A through G requirements.

Swanson knew well the tutors she hired. They had all been in her classes at Clairemont. They all attended University of California, San Diego (UCSD), a hilly campus of eucalyptus trees eleven miles from the high school. She paid the minimum wage of $3.10 an hour. "That was less than a lot of them were earning in other jobs, but they were very dedicated to coming back to the school and helping me," she said.

Anticipating the costs of tutoring, Swanson had submitted grant applications to several organizations that might support raising the achievement level of the students from the poorest neighborhoods of south San Diego. She had gotten a Bank of America innovation grant of $7,000, enough to get started. "But I did not know a good tutoring system," she recalled. She went with her instincts, laying down rules for her tutors. "You could be friendly but not familiar with the students, because they were so close in age. They came in each Tuesday and Thursday," because homework assignments were often given out on Mondays, and often there were Friday tests to prepare for.

On tutoring days, students went to a grid on a side blackboard where all their names were listed, along with all the advanced course subjects. They put an X next to their name in the box for the subject that they needed help with that day. "As it worked out, the tutors stayed and had lunch with me on those days, so we were in regular contact about what was going on with the students. I think that was really helpful because when things started to go poorly, we could correct them immediately," Swanson said.

The first crisis came in October, when she gave her tutors a week off so they could focus on their midterm exams. "I thought my classes could still run very well that week," she recalled. "I would just go from study group to study group on the tutoring days, from math to science to whatever they were doing and they would continue on. But I was wrong.

"What happened was, particularly in the math and science groups, they were saying, 'We can't do our math and we can't do our science if the tutor isn't here,'" she said. "I saw they had become dependent on a tutor, rather than understanding how to study better themselves. So when the tutors came back the following week, we all sat down at lunch as we usually did and I said, 'We've got a real problem. This isn't going well. Talk to me more about what is happening in these tutoring groups.'

"I found out I had not observed them as closely as I should have," she recalled. "I was doing the tutoring myself for kids who had trouble with history and English, so I was pretty occupied during class. I found out what they were doing. They would have approximately seven kids in a tutoring group, and they were giving them answers. The kids would ask questions, and they would say, 'Here is the answer and here is why.' And so the kids thought, 'I can't do this on my own, but my tutor will give me the answers.'"

She told the tutors, "You can't give them the answers anymore. You have got to fashion good questions and ways that will lead them back to the textbook or back to their notes to find the answers."

It was immediately apparent, as the college freshmen tried to obey her instructions, that this would not be easy. "Fashioning good questions, especially when you know the answers but cannot give them away, is very tough," Swanson recalled. "It took us over a semester to get that down to any kind of a system in which kids were doing better in note-taking and the tutors were doing really good questions." Socrates was right to teach his students by asking them questions, but his methods had not had much impact in the millennia since except in some law schools. Tutor Nina Manzi's suggestion that Swanson teach the students how to take Cornell notes helped improve the tutoring process by emphasizing the importance of distilling what they were hearing or reading down to key questions, but it was still tough going.

Swanson thought the system they had developed was better than anything she had encountered. At the beginning of the second year of AVID in 1981, she had the tutors come in a week before school started so that all of them, including some new ones, could practice question-making. She tried to tell other teachers about it, but that did not always go well. Few other teachers taught that way. They would ask key questions, then quickly give the answers and move on if their students did not respond. Swanson started with Clairemont teachers who taught the advanced courses. Because the AVID students were doing so much better on homework and exams than was expected for low-income students, "my kids were being accused of cheating pretty often, and actually that was a very hurtful thing for me personally," Swanson said. "I had been at that school for ten years. It wasn't that I didn't know the faculty. I did. I was the English Department chair, so I was known for rigorous learning and all that kind of thing, and they actually were accusing me of developing a cheating scheme with the kids."

At her urging, her students invited the Clairemont faculty in February 1981 to an after-school session to see firsthand how the program worked. The idea was "to show them what we were doing so they would understand that we take notes and we study from the notes and this isn't some kind of a cheating scheme," Swanson said. She told the students before the gathering that they would have to obey an important rule: "You can never ever in these conversations accuse any teacher of being unfair in any way," she said to them. To the teachers she was inviting she said, "We need to listen carefully to the kids, and not be accusatory toward them."

LISTENING CAREFULLY TO STUDENTS AND EXPOSING CLASSROOM INADEQUACIES

All teachers were invited, but not all came. "I did pinpoint some of my friends who were leaders and asked them to come, and of course they did, which was helpful," Swanson said. "It was really interesting because I had never done anything like that before. I think this is done a lot more now. Back then teachers didn't listen to kids. Teachers had the answers. We had all gone to college. We had learned how to be teachers. We knew what the kids ought to be doing. Why should we listen to kids?"

Inviting teachers to talk to her students "was a pretty revolutionary thing to do," Swanson said. "From that, some teachers wanted me to come into their classrooms to show some of the methods. That was terrific. It went well. However, I would still hear complaints from kids in the tutorial groups about teachers not listening to them. If one kid says this teacher isn't letting us do this and I can't learn, it's the kid's problem. But when twenty kids tell you the same thing, it's probably a teacher's problem."

Swanson developed ways to investigate such complaints so that she could try, if possible, to alter the teacher's approach. If that didn't work, she could make sure her tutors knew they had to give extra attention to that teacher's students. "I would go to that teacher where none of the kids thought they could succeed very well, and I would always blame the kids," she said. "I would say the kids are really having a difficulty with this subject, and I would be very specific about the content. I would say, 'Would it be all right if a tutor came into your classroom to take notes on that part of the lesson so we can tutor them better?'"

Swanson continued, "The teachers interpreted that as having an expert sitting in the room. Of course that wasn't it, it was just a college student, but they taught better. Eventually I would ask if they would come to my classroom and see how we did things on tutoring days. Some of the teachers would say, 'Well, you can do that, but I can't.' And I said, 'What do you mean?' And they said, 'Well, your kids aren't organized. They are all talking.' And I said, 'But you need to go from group to group and listen to what the conversation is, listen to what they're talking about.'"

The tutors who took notes in the classrooms of other teachers told Swanson what they observed. "It was usually the teacher didn't explain very well at all or just moved on with the content before the kids got it," Swanson recalled. "We also had in those days no laws about what degree you had to have in the subject you were teaching. When the homemaking department lost enrollment, for example, they always switched the home-making teachers to math or English classes. But they didn't know how to teach those subjects. They didn't have a clue. That happened a lot. You can't do that anymore, thank goodness."

Eventually it dawned on some Clairemont teachers that they were dealing with a unique situation. "I told them to come by the AVID classroom anytime," Swanson said. "See what we are doing. And they would see the grid on the sideboard where the kids would sign up for tutoring help in specific subjects and specific teachers. Their names were there. And the teachers would say, 'You mean you know what I do in my class?' And I would say, 'Yes, because we have to work with it. You have our students in there, and we have to tutor for your class.' Before, they thought they were anonymous, and now they knew they weren't."

Some of the teachers with general credentials who had not been trained to teach their subjects asked Swanson for help. "I couldn't do it because I had my own classes," Swanson said. "I still had English classes besides my AVID class. So what I did was I used the Bank of America grant money to back the tutors for extra hours so they could go into those classes. They were just college students, but I had trained them very well, so they could teach those classes using our methods."

Swanson had a rule to make sure this would have the desired effect. She told the teachers that they couldn't leave the classroom while the tutor was there. "They had to stay," she said. "They couldn't learn what they needed to know in the faculty lounge. They couldn't take the period off." That was not, however, the explanation for her rule that she gave the teachers. "The excuse I used for it, which was true, was that it was illegal for them to leave. You had to have a credentialed teacher in charge. I did *not* tell them I wanted them to learn from the tutor. I said legally you have to stay."

The experiment worked to Swanson's satisfaction. No teacher ever complained that Swanson was interfering with his or her teaching. She only dealt with teachers who asked for help. "I can't say everyone was a convert," she recalled. "They weren't. But nobody was openly aggressive about it. The principal had promised me that if there were issues I couldn't solve, he would do his best. We had a geometry teacher, the only geometry teacher on campus, who was an alcoholic. He was out of his classes most of the time. The kids just partied. I said I can't do anything about an alcoholic teacher. I went to the principal. He got someone else to come into that classroom, and he wrote the guy up and took care of it." Unfortunately, that principal's successor didn't like Swanson or her program and refused to remove further obstacles, which was one reason why she left Clairemont in 1986.

GETTING ON THE SAME PAGE: ALIGNING AVID INSTRUCTION WITH COLLEGE EXPECTATIONS

The tutoring program and its exposure of classroom inadequacies took her deep into the pathologies of other prestigious educational institutions, including UCSD. She began to explore an old issue: the colleges would sometimes indicate that new students were not well prepared, even those who had gotten good grades in high school.

In 1982, the California State Academic Senate, composed of faculty representatives from both the University of California and California State University systems, had published a report on competencies expected of entering freshmen. The professors described the skills they expected the high schools to teach in English, mathematics, science, social studies, and a few other areas. "The report was sent to all of the high schools in the state, and they went to the principals' offices and were promptly filed, and nobody ever read them," Swanson said. "I am sure that happens almost everywhere. There was no program behind it. It was just UC and CSU telling the high schools what to do, and that was it. So I went up and met with the head of the commission in Oakland at the UC president's office and I said, 'You know, what is the plan to carry these out? Could we put something together to make these points really live in the high schools, so that the high schools understand the colleges better?'"

In effect she was asking, "Are you willing to spend some time and money explaining exactly what you mean and helping the high schools improve their teaching?" She got her answer. "They weren't interested," she said.

This issue was important to Swanson. If she was not preparing her students for college in the right way, then AVID was in jeopardy. Keeping her program going was exhausting, but Swanson had great reserves of energy, so she added another project to her schedule. She created a coalition of freshman-level college instructors from UCSD, San Diego State, Point Loma Nazarene University, and Mesa Community College, along with Clairemont High teachers who shared her concerns. They organized discussions of what high school kids had difficulty with in college.

"The rule was, no finger-pointing," Swanson said. "You can't say the kids are not doing well in your class in college because high school teachers don't know what they are doing, and we won't finger-point at junior high teachers, and so on."

She had the high school teachers read the freshmen competencies report. "We thought we were teaching what they were asking us to teach, but in truth our kids going to college, especially the minority kids, didn't do very well," she said. When the high school teachers tried to find out from the college teachers what their students were doing wrong, "We discovered we had no basis of commonality on what constituted something that was done well and what wasn't," Swanson said.

To clarify the difference, the group decided that at their second meeting, the high school teachers would bring in samples of what they thought were top-notch papers, and the college people would bring in what they thought were top-notch papers, in English, science, or whatever. It was quickly apparent to Swanson "that we did not agree on what was top notch."

"What we in high school thought were A papers, the college people said, no way is that an A paper," she said. "Let's take history. We weren't teaching them how to write a paper as a historian would. That was what they were expecting in college." If the topic was the causes of the Civil War, a good high school paper would explain that some people thought the war was caused by the state's rights issue, and others thought it was about slavery. The students would quote historical figures with different views, John C. Calhoun versus Harriet Beecher Stowe, and get an A. The college instructors pointed out the absence of any citations from scholars and their research. There was not much analysis of what state's rights meant in the nineteenth century, or the religious roots of the abolition movement. The papers lacked any analysis, backed by citations, of which cause, slavery or state's rights, had the greater impact.

"It was a revelation," Swanson said. "We were so glad to know it." The point had not been made in the state universities' freshman competencies report. To cure that disconnect, Swanson's group did its own research and found that UCSD scholar Charles Cooper, a former high school teacher, had written much on instruction in writing for high school and college students. "We put together a series of writing documents for various subjects, twelve different domains," Swanson said. "It was how to write a good science paper or how to write a good history paper and so on. The kids had to learn how to ask questions and then take a position and get evidence."

That fit well with the question-making that had become part of the AVID tutorials. It helped spark the AVID Socratic Seminars, where students argued their positions based on research. Swanson found that her efforts to improve writing instruction in her English classes, as well as in AVID, helped students become more thoughtful in their preparations.

ABANDONING INEFFECTIVE TRADITIONS: HELPING STUDENTS HELP EACH OTHER AND THEMSELVES

Swanson hated the three-paragraph essay form that had become standard in high school, particularly when teaching students how to answer exam essay questions. The first paragraph introduced their point, the second defended their point, and the last reiterated their point. This evolved into what was called the five-paragraph essay—an introduction, three paragraphs of defense, and a conclusion—but Swanson thought it, too, was stilted and archaic. "Every paper read the same," she said. "It was awful." Professional writers, including some teachers and parents she knew, agreed with her, but it was hard to get administrators to criticize the traditional practice. So she abandoned the tradition in her instructions for her students and hoped other teachers would catch on.

She was a devotee of the National Writing Project. It emphasized thought and vivid expression over form. The approach required that students do several drafts, sometimes submitting drafts to other students—called peer readers—for comments. Swanson showed students how to nudge classmates in the right direction without sounding like one of their teachers being annoying. If a student's sentences were too long, instead of saying "I'm falling asleep before I get to the end of your sentences" or "Faulkner may write sentences that long, but you're not Faulkner," the student was taught to emphasize the positive: "You have so many great phrases in every sentence, but do you think they would stand out more clearly if you broke the sentences down so each idea had its own period?"

That was good practice for asking leading questions in tutorials. To prepare students for the AP English Literature exam, the first to be given at Clairemont, Swanson acquired from the College Board some AP free-response questions that had not been used. They were ideal class material. She handed them out on Fridays and had students discuss how they should be approached. Their individual answers were due on Monday. "That became very good for inquiry-based questioning," Swanson said.

Swanson kept nudging her school toward better teaching. In the 1982–1983 school year, with help from Cooper, the writing instruction expert, she arranged for freshman-level instructors in English, science, and history from UCSD to come to Clairemont and teach in relevant courses for a while "so our teachers could actually see how they wanted it done at the university." They got a good sense of how college teachers assessed student work. High school teachers needed to demand more examples and more scholarly attribution to reach the college standard. But the high school teachers discovered that in high school classrooms, the college teachers were surprisingly inept at motivating students and presenting their lessons with depth and clarity. "Many of the instructors they sent to our classes were former high school teachers," Swanson recalled. "They had gotten their PhDs and went on to teaching at the university, and they weren't very good. We at Clairemont finally said to each other: the reason they left high school teaching was that they weren't good teachers there."

Swanson was particularly disappointed in the college instructors' style of dress. In the 1980s, teachers still dressed as if they were working in an office. "I wore heels and a dress every day," Swanson said. "That was not unusual. We respected the profession, and we dressed professionally. These instructors from UCSD would wear cutoff Levis and so forth." They acted as if the students were lucky to have them. "They expected all of the kids to be in awe and listen," Swanson recalled. "It doesn't work very well when you are dressed like a slob. The kids are going to treat you that way. They expected the kids to be at attention, and they weren't. They didn't know how to handle it."

Yet when Swanson attempted to follow through with the other half of the planned teacher swap, having Clairemont teachers conduct a few classes at UCSD, the university wasn't interested. Swanson saw that as snobbery, but she continued the contacts with the university because they had so much to offer her program, even if the universities had no appreciation of their power to improve instruction in high schools. The secret, Swanson said, was not the college instructors who came to Clairemont to give sample lessons. The best university instructors were her former students who came back to Clairemont to tutor.

Few other instructors in college or high school had tried to teach adolescents the way Swanson was teaching AVID. It was difficult for some students to see how binder checks and Cornell notes could serve them in college. "It looked like baby stuff to them," Swanson recalled. "I heard that all the time." The college students who came to tutor gave the AVID students a different message. "We know how much you guys hate taking those notes and keeping those binders and calendars, but we have got to tell you it is what keeps us getting good grades in college," one visiting college student said. She said other UCSD students would see her taking Cornell notes at lectures and ask how they might learn to do that.

WATCH CLIP 3: I LIKE BIG BINDERS
AVID teacher Ben Solomon raps to students about how much well-organized binders mean to him.

www.wiley.com/go/avid3

Swanson underlined the point when she took Clairemont students on college campus visits. She recalled a San Diego State lecture hall where her students sat in the back so that they could see what the students at the lecture were doing. Many of the college students were reading magazines or other books, not paying attention. They were not getting all they could out of the lecture. The AVID students noticed something else. "My kids had to take notes on that college lecture," Swanson recalled, "and when they got back to class they would say to me, 'We understand that lesson. We understood what that professor was saying.' I would ask them questions, and they would say, 'It is right here in my notes.'" They knew that when they went to college they could do the work even better than many of the college students who were already there.

It was not entirely clear to them until they got to college that the tutorials they had become accustomed to, with all that question-making, would be something that they had over most other college students. Thirty years after Swanson began forcing her students to create questions, such teaching was still uncommon in the United States. AVID had grown in part because of Swanson's insight that students need to learn how to help themselves find the essence of difficult concepts. That not only brought students to a new level but also lured some of the brightest and most energetic teachers to AVID, because they, too, realized that Swanson was filling an important gap.

Bringing the Power of Tutoring to El Cajon High

Lauren Ramers was five years old the first time she tutored a student. She grew up in Yreka, California, a rural town in northern California. In kindergarten, she knew a classmate named Andy, who had some physical and learning disabilities. He lacked full control of his body. He drooled, and dragged one leg when he walked. Other students made fun of him. Ramers appointed herself his protector and friend. He loved it, and so did she.

At Gold Street Elementary School, when everyone else went to recess, Ramers stayed in the classroom and helped Andy with his schoolwork. She said years later that she could not remember if this was her idea or a teacher's, but she embraced it. Andy was smart, but had trouble moving a pencil, so she would help him with his preliminary attempts to learn to write.

Years later when Ramers enrolled at Yreka High School, tutoring became one of her prime activities. It was an important step in a sequence in which she would eventually become AVID's leading expert on tutoring, the most radical and powerful part of Swanson's program.

TUTORING AND RELATIONSHIPS

Ramers was the academic star of the Yreka Miners class of 1992. She also was a cheerleader and ran cross-country and track. When she had an open period and could not leave campus, she tutored three students with Down syndrome. "It brought me great joy every day to walk into a room and have these kids be so excited to see me work with them," she remembered. That inspired her to ask the town's director of the juvenile detention center if he needed anyone to tutor students there.

She learned that the most important thing a tutor could do was develop a relationship with the student. There had to be a high level of trust. You couldn't just launch into the activity or homework that needed to be done. On bad days, if you tried to start that way, they wouldn't do it. They would shut down. They would say things like, "I don't know, I don't get it, I can't do it."

It was better to start by talking about how they were feeling. What's going on in school today? Are you having any fun? If the student was upset, as he often was, she let him vent. She would listen. At some point she would say quietly, "Are you ready to start?" and the tutoring could begin.

She did best when she broke each tutoring session into chunks. They would work for fifteen minutes, then the student could get up for a drink or a snack. "I let them know exactly what steps we were going to follow, to finish their homework or solve the problem they were having," she recalled. "They knew what to expect." That seemed relevant to her when she encountered the similarly organized tutoring system at AVID. The AVID system of making questions that focused on concepts made sense to her. When she tutored in college, she found that learning progressed more easily and went deeper if she could apply the concept being learned to something tangible in the student's life.

Still, it took Ramers a while to seek a career as a teacher. When she enrolled at UCLA, she majored in political science. She wanted to be the first woman president of the United States. Then she took government courses at UCLA and realized that politics as practiced in the real world was too cynical for her. "I just didn't like the people I was in those courses with," she recalled. "I realized they were going to be my peers in whatever political and government work I chose, and I didn't feel I could trust them."

When Ramers worked as a counselor at a UCLA alumni camp, a couple of graduate students there recommended she try some education courses. The teaching course she took her sophomore year was enthralling. She remembered how much she liked helping kids. When she was asked to tutor in the same course the next year, she grabbed the chance. "I loved designing lessons. I loved developing curriculum. I loved working with students," she recalled.

She graduated from UCLA with a major in English and a minor in education. She got her master's degree and teaching credential at Stanford in 1997, taught a year at Milpitas High School in the Bay Area, then followed her new husband to San Diego. She had only one job offer, from El Cajon High School. They could only offer a part-time assignment, three classes. "I can't," she said. "I am putting my husband through med school. I need more money than that."

"OK," the administrator said. "We'll call you back." The word went out that they had a teacher they wanted to hire but needed two more classes for her. She was willing to teach anything. Paul Dautremont, the AVID coordinator, needed someone to teach two classes. Ramers said she had heard of AVID. She didn't know much about it, but would take the job.

They sent her to the AVID Summer Institute in San Diego. She was mesmerized. "I had never attended anything like it," she recalled. "I thought I had a great education coming out of Stanford and UCLA. My professors were outstanding. But I have never been as inspired as I was at my first summer institute. I had outstanding staff developers, William DeJean and Sandra Martinez. They not only taught me so much about how to work with kids in an inspiring learning environment, but they challenged me to be a better person. I was overwhelmed."

They showed her how rigor and depth did not have to be just for kids in wealthy neighborhoods. Public school traditions of mediocrity could be overcome. Many low-income students at El Cajon High could be raised to the level where they not only got into college but did well. "The institute gave me a sense that I could really make a difference in the life of kids," she recalled.

NEVER GIVE THE ANSWER: LEARNING BELONGS TO THE LEARNER

For Ramers, the AVID approach to tutoring was galvanizing because it was both so similar and so different from the way she, a tutor since age five, had been doing it. She was accustomed to doing the hard work. She would get the kids engaged, keep them focused, explain how to solve whatever problem had stumped them. But she was giving them the answer. At

AVID, that was not the way tutoring worked. The staff developers emphasized the difference repeatedly. The job of the AVID teacher was never to
give the answer but to have the students do that work, to figure out the
root of each stumbling block in each course, analyze it, and suggest lines
of inquiry.

El Cajon had one AVID elective class for each grade. The classes met
every day, with tutors coming Tuesday and Thursday. The tutors were former El Cajon students now in college, at San Diego State, UCSD, or one
of the community colleges. Every day, they turned standard tutoring systems on their head. The tutors were trained that "tutoring was not about
a tutor standing up at the whiteboard telling you how to solve the problem," Ramers recalled. "They were trained to ask really good questions
and more importantly, have the questions asked by the other students in
each tutoring group."

Each student arrived in class with a tutorial request form they had
filled out. There was a key question on it, what some schools would come
to call a "point of confusion." It reflected the homework the student had
done the night before. Students focused on where they were stuck. They
did not see how to do the next step in a math problem or did not understand an explanation in history. They would write that on the form, noting at the top which subject their problem pertained to. The AVID class
teacher collected the forms and sorted them into groups. The students
with science problems would be in one group, the students with math
problems in a second group, those with English problems in a third, and
so on. Math problems tended to predominate. Often there would be more
than one math group. AVID recommended that no group be larger than
seven students.

The tutors were assigned to subjects in which they had the most
expertise. Ramers recommended that they start the session the way she
had when she was tutoring in high school. How are you doing? How are
things? If two questions were similar, the tutor would arrange to have
them discussed at the same time. The tutor started with whoever had the
question most likely to address a weak area for many students.

Desks were shoved together for each group. The student picked to
begin would move to the front and hold up a small whiteboard where he
wrote the question to be addressed. In Swanson's original class in 1980, the
Clairemont students had divvied up different sections of the blackboards

on the walls, but by the 1990s, the whiteboards had taken over. They were portable, manageable, and not as messy as the old chalkboards.

The tutor sat in the seat vacated by the student at the whiteboard. She kept quiet while writing on the student's point-of-confusion form the questions and points other students were making. The student at the whiteboard would start with what was called the thirty-second speech. He would explain his problem and define key vocabulary words. Then the critical thinking began.

WATCH CLIP 4: TUTORIALS
In this inquiry-based tutorial, high school students help each other by asking specific questions. Rather than giving students the answers, the AVID tutor guides them through which questions to ask.

www.wiley.com/go/avid4

The term *critical thinking* had already become a popular piece of educational jargon, so overused that in some contexts it had become meaningless. In the best circumstances, it was a search for weaknesses or contradictions in what one is learning, and a means of getting to the conceptual foundation of the lesson. Efforts to promote critical thinking often stopped short, with only a question or two at the end of a textbook chapter. AVID's inquiry-based tutorials seemed to Ramers very different, and very difficult, but closer to what advocates of critical thinking were encouraging.

"We were very conscious of that fact that in learning, the learner had to be doing the action," she said. In traditional tutorials, when a student got to a sticking point, the tutor would step in and show how to get the answer. In an AVID tutorial, getting to the sticking point was only the beginning of the process. The other students in the tutorial would be required to ask questions of the student who was stuck, not only nudging him in the direction of enlightenment but also helping them see their own ability to move past points of confusion if they just thought about them more.

Math was usually the subject that generated the most difficulty. Ramers loved the way students learned to unravel knotty problems. One student explained to the group, "I am at the point in the equation where the variable is on the left side, but I have to divide both sides of the equation by a negative number to solve it, and I don't know how to do that." The students often began tentatively. Sometimes they did not know the answer themselves, but had been trained to look for the best ways to attack confusion. There might be an error in the rendering of the problem. It might be similar to a previous problem, or it might be entirely new, untethered to anything the class had been taught. "Do you notice anything unusual about the equation?" one student asked, not sure yet what the issue was.

"Do you think the result is going to be negative or positive?" said another, underlying the fact that working backward from a possible answer sometimes helped.

"Have you tried doing another problem, an easier one, that also requires division by a negative?" said another student. "What is the result of 1 divided by negative 1?"

The student might see the answer. He might not. The tutor noted on his form all the questions asked and his answers. If the student needed further help, he could see his math teacher and be much more ready to understand what he was told because he had done more of his own thinking, urged on by the group.

THINK, QUESTION, AND REFLECT: POWER IN PUZZLE SOLVING AND PEER GROUPS

Two important things happened during such exchanges. Both were keys to college success and almost unknown in American high school classes. First, the students were practicing well-worn ways to unlock intellectual puzzles. There were many ways to find a missing answer, and AVID teachers would have them listed on the board. But those methods didn't work for most students unless they practiced them. Such puzzle solving in most schools was reserved for homework time, the worst possible arrangement. Many students didn't do their homework, or went through it quickly and only recorded the answers easiest to come by. In most cases, homework was graded, if at all, for completion, not mastery. Getting students to practice critical thinking had to be done in class if it was going to work.

That was one of the insights that had led to the rising interest in "flipped" classrooms. Students absorbed the lesson, the equivalent of watching the teacher explain a concept on the blackboard, at home online. In class the next day, they worked on solving knotty problems with the teacher to guide them. The system broke down if they didn't do the online work at home, but it guaranteed that problem solving would be addressed in class, although usually not through inquiry-based tutoring.

Ramers noticed that although her students paid attention during tutorials because they needed to finish their homework or prepare for a test, those student concerns were not the reason for the AVID tutorial. The idea was to get them used to thinking for themselves. When Ramers was tutoring in the traditional way and found that a student was confused, "I would explain it to them again and again and again until they got it. That was not what the AVID tutorial was about," she said. In college, they would be less likely to have tutorial help. They needed to learn how to ask themselves their own questions.

The second key dynamic of the AVID tutorial was difficult to understand without familiarity with adolescent culture. In high school and college, like other stages of life, peer groups are powerful. The inventors of Facebook made billions of dollars out of that truth. Attacking a problem with a group of school friends was exciting in a way that traditional class sessions were not. Teenage bonding in AVID tutorials led students to pay closer attention and appreciate more the value of what they were doing.

WATCH CLIP 5: SOCRATIC SEMINARS
Angela Hessom, a sixth-grade AVID teacher in San Diego,
discusses the benefits of having students work together in small
groups during Socratic Seminars.

www.wiley.com/go/avid5

At the end of a tutoring day, Ramers watched the last quiet flourish of the AVID method. Each student composed on the bottom of their form a reflection, again something rare in American high schools. "They wrote what they learned, how they got past their point of confusion, how they gained greater understanding, how their new learning connected to previous learning, and how they planned to apply it to the future," she said. She read each student's reflection. "I could tell by the quality of the reflections if they actually benefited from the tutorial session and if things were going well."

It was not easy to teach students how to think, ask questions, and reflect, Ramers learned at El Cajon High. It took much time and practice for her students to grasp what questions to ask. But once they did, they were in possession of a powerful tool. When they were enrolled in college, they gravitated toward study groups and knew how to use them. They told other students where they were stuck, and joined their friends in asking questions that would get them where they needed to go. As AVID spread through California, educators often said that question-making was the part of the program they liked best. But not every school in the Golden State was so impressed with Swanson's big idea.

Santa Barbara Rejects AVID

In 1998, her second year as AVID's California state director, Judy Lookabill got a call from the coordinator of region 8, which included Kern, Ventura, San Luis Obispo, Santa Barbara, and other counties near the central coast. There was a problem. The Santa Barbara city school district had started an AVID program, but wanted to do it their way. This was not unexpected from a city that had long thought of itself, with its ocean vistas and millionaire estates, better than the rest.

The regional coordinator, new to her assignment, asked Lookabill to help sort out the problem. Visiting the rapidly growing AVID regions and districts was the most important part of Lookabill's job. She was the program's first California director, having been hired in 1996 with a portion of a million-dollar appropriation from the state legislature. As Lookabill saw it, AVID's rigorous curriculum and insistence on data appealed to conservatives, while its emphasis on educating low-income minority children pleased liberals, so it was popular throughout the state capital.

TROUBLE IN PARADISE: FORGETTING THE ESSENTIALS

Lookabill at age fifty-six was a wily veteran of California classrooms and California education politics. She had grown up in Indiana, fallen in love with France and its language, and been recruited as a French teacher by the Fremont school district in the San Francisco East Bay region in 1967. She became an assistant principal in the district in 1980 and then principal of Hillsdale High School, across the bay in San Mateo, in 1986. She became director of curriculum for the San Mateo County Office of Education in 1992. While in that job, and then as assistant superintendent for curriculum and instruction in the neighboring Santa Clara Office of Education, she helped start several AVID programs, including the Los Altos classes that would have such an effect on the life of Kande McKay in Madison, Indiana.

When introduced to AVID by educators who had first encountered it in Southern California, Lookabill saw that "it addressed things that everyone talked about—closing the achievement gap, raising academic standards, getting more nontraditional kids prepared for college." But it was clear, when she became state director, that not everyone understood how AVID worked. District leaders were accustomed to adopting programs and then doing whatever they wanted with them. It was unnerving to some administrators to discover that AVID was not only collecting data on their progress but also insisting on compliance with its rules. One of Lookabill's tasks was to inform districts when their sites were in danger of losing their status as a certified AVID school.

Lookabill found that some districts saw the program as little more than a way to quiet critics who said they had not done enough for minorities. AVID told schools that careful recruitment was important. The program wanted kids in the middle, with average grades and test scores, who had the potential to go to college but whose parents had not done so. Lookabill told district officials that the ethnic balance of the AVID program should not be dramatically different from the ethnic balance of the district. "But many schools just wanted to put all of their African American kids in the program," she said. "It wasn't supposed to be a dumping ground, but that is what people wanted to do."

"If you don't meet the criteria, you won't get the results you want from the program," she warned them. Often the district officials told her they didn't have time for careful recruitment, or they didn't understand the rules, or their bosses wanted to use AVID to show they were supporting minorities, so they were being ordered, in effect, to ignore Lookabill and her rules.

That was what appeared to be happening in Santa Barbara. Lookabill flew up from San Diego, where she worked in the AVID headquarters with the rest of the small staff. She did what she always did before meeting with district educators: she visited some schools. At a junior high school, everything seemed fine. Students were doing Cornell notes and keeping their binders in order. Inquiry-based tutoring was thriving. Then she drove to Santa Barbara High School, a beautiful campus of mission-style stucco buildings on a hillside overlooking the distant ocean. AVID at that school, she discovered, was a quiet disaster.

"It was just a glorified study hall," Lookabill recalled. "The students had their assignments, and they were working on their assignments. I didn't see any instruction. There may have been tutors, but they weren't there that day, and clearly they weren't using tutors in the way we wanted them to. They even told me they weren't comfortable with tutors as a rule." The regional AVID coordinator told Lookabill that what bothered the high school administrators the most was the AVID rule that they had to provide data each year on how they were doing.

Lookabill convened a meeting in a district conference room. Nearly a dozen people were there, comprising her, the AVID regional coordinator, a couple of school district officials, and several educators from the high school and the junior high she had visited. The Santa Barbara people began to enumerate their problems with what AVID called the 10 Essentials, later becoming the 11 Essentials.

They did not like AVID's focus on preparing students for four-year colleges. Every AVID student was supposed to be enrolled in the honors courses that the University of California and California State University systems required for admission. The Santa Barbara educators said that the rule should not apply to them because Santa Barbara City College (SBCC), the local two-year community college, had such a good reputation. Their students didn't need to get into four-year colleges. They could do all of those challenging courses at SBCC.

Lookabill never raised her voice. She had dealt with unhappy school officials for many years and knew that a professional tone was essential. She told them that throwing out the four-year-college requirement would be shortsighted and would limit student choice. "What kids decide to do at the end of their high school career is really up to them and their parents," she said. "Our goal is to say to this kid, 'When you graduate, you will have choices. If you want to go to a four-year college, you are prepared to do that. If you want to work for your father for a few years or join the military, whatever, you have choices. If you are just going to a community college and you don't have to pass all the UC requirements, that makes it a lot easier. But you are not prepared to go to a four-year college.'"

There was an undertone in the complaints that Lookabill had heard elsewhere in affluent districts such as Palo Alto, where she had lived for many years. It was a privileged, this-is-not-for-most-of-our-kids attitude. They would say "We just have a few students who need this program."

As the coordinator had mentioned, what bothered the disgruntled Santa Barbara administrators most was the AVID data-gathering requirements. "You've got to turn in data," Lookabill said.

"But how are you going to use it?" one administrator asked. "Against us?"

"We're not going to use it against you," Lookabill said. "It is the way we certify our program. It is what we do. It is how we maintain our quality control."

After two hours, the meeting ended. Lookabill had given the Santa Barbara people her basic response to complaints about AVID: "No one is holding a gun to your head. If it's not the right program for you, don't do it." But she had a responsibility to respond in full in writing so that they had all the facts when planning their next move.

THE SANTA BARBARA MANIFESTO: KEEPING AVID STANDARDS HIGH

The letter Lookabill wrote became famous among AVID staffers as the "Santa Barbara Manifesto." Neither she nor current staffers have been able to find a copy of it, but Lookabill remembered its content when interviewed in 2013. The letter got a big reaction from her colleagues because no one at AVID had ever before written such a detailed description of a district's AVID failings, then actually signed it and sent it to the district. It was the first such letter she wrote, but not the last. During her six years in the job, there were five or six occasions in which a district had strayed so far from the AVID model that she wrote a detailed notice telling them to do something about it or drop the AVID label.

In the letter, she pointed out which of the 10 Essentials Santa Barbara was violating. At least six were in jeopardy: no. 3, commitment by participants to fully implement all components; no. 4, implementation of a rigorous course of study in AVID classes; no. 5, rigorous writing and reading activities as a basis for instruction; no. 6, inquiry as a basis for instruction leading to critical thinking; no. 8, AVID-trained tutors leading Socratic-method tutorials; and no. 9, analysis of all sorts of data to foster data-driven instruction.

"My feeling was that maybe there was someone at the district office who thought AVID was a good idea, but it was forced on others. It was not a collaborative decision by the people at the site. It was like everything else. People are going to resist, and it was my sense it was forced on them," Lookabill recalled. "I said if it is not the program for you, there are many other study skills programs that you can engage in and embrace and get good results from. But we can't call this AVID and do AVID if you are not going to do it the way we require. This is how the program works. When it is done right, it works, and that is just the way it is."

In the letter, she told them "what I observed and what we talked about and what they would need to do to become a valid AVID program. And I sent them the letter and never heard anything back."

Swanson loved Lookabill's letter. She thought it was exactly what needed to be done to keep the program's standards high. Swanson had been dealing with backsliding schools since she left Clairemont High in 1986. There were several ways that schools diluted the program, and these might not have been noticed if AVID had not insisted on the data collection that Santa Barbara found so troublesome. "It was not uncommon for some schools, those that didn't think these kids could really succeed, to give a highfalutin title to a class that was still remedial," Swanson said. "It was not an advanced class at all. That's deadly. That's really bad."

There was also the problem of districts like Santa Barbara that found it burdensome to prepare all AVID students for four-year colleges, but pretended they were doing it anyway, much to the detriment of kids not encouraged to meet the standard. "We found that some of the schools were getting kids to the junior year, but they were missing credits. They did not have enough to qualify for four-year colleges, so the AVID program washed them out. They just got rid of them," Swanson said. They would no longer be in AVID and got no AVID help in getting into college. In some cases, they might be so low on credits that their high school diploma was in jeopardy.

That was not how Swanson had handled the problem of AVID students without enough credits at Clairemont High. "I was all over them," she said. "They had to go to summer school to make up the credits. If there wasn't summer school in the district, they had to go to community college, which they could do after they were sixteen years of age. They had to stay on track, and if that meant they had to take more than the usual number of high school courses, so be it. That's what they were going to do."

During her travels, Lookabill had found several schools that weren't complying. She tried to reach out to people in the district who could, at least, be honest with her about what was going on, and give her a hint as to what she could do to get them back on track. She was a former principal, so she knew how to talk to those people. "Once I went to a principal after I had observed her school," she said. "I walked into her office and I shut her door and said, 'Tell me about rigor in your school.' That was a pretty up-front question. She said, 'I'll tell you that we don't have it. We don't have it in the school at all, and one of my goals is to work on that.'"

Students were also good sources. Lookabill was once meeting with AVID students at an Orange County high school, talking about AP. One girl said, "I went into the AP English course. They had put too many kids in it. There wasn't room for all the kids in the classroom. So the teacher said she was going to have a test the next day. Within twenty minutes, at least ten of those students were in their counselors' offices trying to drop the course because they weren't ready to have a test."

That girl said she stayed in the class, however, and took the test. Lookabill asked her why she didn't drop it. "Because I learned in AVID that I had to stay," she said.

In 2002, just before she turned sixty, Lookabill retired from AVID to help her ailing mother in Indiana. She kept track of the program and did some consulting. She was happy to hear that Santa Barbara eventually resumed the program, and not sorry at all that she had sent them a manifesto telling them to either get going or go away.

THE IMPORTANCE OF AVID SUPPORT SYSTEMS FOR SUCCESS

Santa Barbara County school officials did not have clear memories of Lookabill's memorandum when asked about it in 2013, but the superintendent, David Cash, said he did recall the 1998 disagreement with AVID and what the district did about it. He was then principal of Goleta Valley Junior High School and was responsible for implementing AVID at that school, as the individual schools did not have their own AVID coordinators. He said it was true that the district felt that Santa Barbara City College was a fine alternative to sending students to four-year colleges, and resisted AVID on that point. But he said district leaders had not rejected the collection of data, as they thought the numbers were very valuable. What they objected to, he said, was "the way AVID required the data to be submitted . . . as it required us to collect and reformat it to AVID's needs." He said, "The AVID supports we needed were the incredible professional learning opportunities in their summer conference and throughout the year."

After being told to shape up or leave the program, the district's leaders tried an AVID-like program of their own called REACH. "There was a fundamental local belief that we could do it without the support of the state AVID organization," Cash said. The AVID-style approaches they kept were "tutors, note-taking strategies, college awareness and preparation, and critical thinking strategies necessary to be successful in rigorous secondary courses," he said. They did not collect the data AVID had wanted.

The REACH program lasted two years, Cash said. The district leaders concluded that it "was unsustainable without the support that the AVID statewide organization provided," he said. "Shortly thereafter, Santa Barbara secondary schools adopted AVID again, and within a short time after that, elementary schools did as well."

District officials said that the AVID program at Santa Barbara High School was performing better in 2013 than what Lookabill found fifteen years earlier. Aaron Harkey, the district's AVID coordinator, said the school had 257 AVID students in seven sections in the 2012–2013 school year. Each of the district's three high schools and four middle schools had an AVID program, for a total of 1,068 students. Nine elementary schools were also using the AVID elementary school program, encouraging younger students to develop good work and thinking habits. Harkey said that the middle and high schools had the required tutorial days, and at least two tutors in each class were college students.

In 2013, 87 percent of AVID seniors in the Santa Barbara district completed all requirements for entry into four-year state colleges, but Santa Barbara's preference for two-year colleges persisted. Forty-nine percent were accepted to four-year schools, but only 23 percent enrolled in one. Sixty percent enrolled in two-year colleges.

Cash said district leaders remained committed to Santa Barbara City College and did not see the relatively low numbers of students heading to four-year colleges as a problem. "The district's high schools had and continue to have a great pathway for students" to reach four-year colleges through the city college's dual-enrollment courses and transfer programs, he said.

Santa Barbara still liked AVID, and would keep it, but retained its traditional community pride, particularly when it came to the local college, and would continue to do so no matter what AVID said. Its AP programs were strong, which became an increasingly important measure of how well AVID was doing.

"Our Teacher Said We Couldn't Take the Test"

One spring at El Cajon (California) High School in the late 1990s, Lauren Ramers asked the seniors in her AVID elective class who were taking AP European History if they had signed up for the AP exam. She was the school's AVID coordinator, still in her twenties and new to the job. She was puzzled by their response.

"Oh, Mrs. Ramers, we're not allowed to take that test," one girl said.

Ramers knew that the college-level course was the greatest academic challenge they had ever had. AVID had been designed to prepare average students for such courses. This was a radical departure on many campuses. If a student's parents had not gone to college, that student was usually not invited to take AP. AP exams were unlike anything in the regular school curriculum. They were about three hours long. Regular high school finals rarely lasted more than an hour. The AP tests included not only multiple-choice questions but also several questions that required long written essays, also rare in high school.

The AP exams were written by college professors and other experts. They were graded by experienced AP teachers and college faculty at summer reading sessions. The readers did not know the names or high schools of the students they were grading. By contrast, high school finals were usually written by the teachers of the courses. They could be watered down if the teacher feared too many students would fail. AP exams and their grading rubrics were compared to those of introductory college final exams to make sure they were not diluted. That made them much more difficult than high school finals, but that was the point. Even if students struggled with AP exams and failed them, they were better prepared for college than they would have been without that challenge. They had gone one-on-one with the academic equivalent of LeBron James and had lost, but henceforth knew what they had to do to play at that level.

Ramers assumed that all of the El Cajon AP teachers agreed with her that AP courses and AP exams were good for any student who wanted to go to college. Because the purpose of AVID was to prepare students for college, AP was right for everyone in AVID. She did not understand why her students thought they weren't allowed to take the AP exam.

Maybe, she thought, they misread the rules. "Of course you can take the test," she said, "Anyone can take it. You don't even have to take the course to take the AP test." She knew this from personal experience because she had taken the AP Government and Politics test when she was in high school even though the school did not teach that course. It had seemed to her a necessary thing to do, given that she had wanted to be president of the United States. She had read everything she could about American government. She felt herself well prepared, course or no course. She scored a 4, the equivalent of a college B, on the exam, and got the college credit.

Everyone Takes the Test: Meeting Resistance with Insistence

Later Ramers realized how silly and naive she had sounded to her kids. They tried to drag her back to reality. "No, no, Mrs. Ramers. Our *teacher* said we couldn't take the test."

She told them she would check this out. The truth had still not dawned on her. She thought it was some misunderstanding. The AP European History teacher had been there a long time. He wasn't as familiar with AVID as the teachers on her team. She would fix it. She walked up to him in the outdoor courtyard and said, "Hey, I heard that you told my AVID kids that they can't take the AP test, and they can. Maybe you don't know that they can, but anybody can sign up for that test."

He became very angry very quickly. She was questioning not only his professionalism but his intelligence. "Who do you think you are? You've never taught an AP class. You just got here," he said. "These students are not going to pass the test. You do a disservice to them by having them take a test that they are not going to pass."

She paused for a moment, having suddenly discovered what the problem was. It was standing in front of her. She took a breath. "Well, actually we have evidence, and a letter from UCLA, saying that even sitting for the test leads students to do better in college, even if they don't pass. Just sitting for the test and having that rigorous experience is good for them."

The AP teacher became more upset. "It's a waste of money," he said.

"Well, they are not paying much money," she said. "They are getting waivers from the fees because they are low income. They only have to pay five bucks or something." She could see that only made him angrier. Every point she raised only reminded him of the temerity of a teacher just barely out of college questioning his judgment.

She excused herself and went looking for backup. The teacher who had been mentoring her since she arrived was also the AP coordinator. "Rick, I don't think this is right," she said. "I know that my kids can take this test. I want them to take this test, and I don't think it's right that this teacher is preventing them from taking it."

"Sign them up," he said. She did so. Within a year, a memo from district headquarters went to all the schools saying that if students were enrolled in an AP course, they should take the AP test. But that did not end Ramers's unpleasant conversations with the AP European History teacher. He was a traditional instructor. He gave lectures and assigned reading, but did not provide much support to students who needed more help. That job fell to AVID—to Ramers and her teachers and tutors. The European History teacher not only tried to keep some students from taking the AP exam but also thought that the best way to help students who were struggling was to remove them from the class. If their quiz and test scores were low, he would drop them. He did it in the first week of class if he thought they had not done all of the reading he gave them for the summer. If they missed a class or two, he would also try to get rid of them.

When that happened, Ramers went to the counseling office and spoke to the scheduler. "These AVID kids are not being removed from this course. They are going to stay in it," she said. The school had agreed to follow AVID procedures. Removing students from challenging courses because they were having trouble with the work was a no-no. The right response was to identify their difficulty and work with them on it.

The teacher lacked the power to remove AVID students from his class, but he could complain to Ramers about it. "Why are you keeping a kid in a course where they are getting a D?" he asked.

"I would rather they get a D in a challenging course than get an A or a B in a course where they were not getting that challenge," she said.

Ramers taught at El Cajon High five years before moving to North Carolina, where her doctor husband had obtained a residency at Duke and she became a consultant for AVID.

When she left, she recalled, there were two going-away parties. One, which she attended, was organized by the teachers and administrators who mourned her departure. The other, to which she was not invited, was a celebration by a small group of El Cajon staffers, including the AP European History teacher, who were pleased that she was leaving. In their minds, she had gone too far forcing them to teach kids who, they felt, were not good enough for their classes. They thought she was wasting their time and kids' lives. But by that time AVID had gained national recognition, and their point of view would be challenged at many more schools than El Cajon.

AVID ON *60 MINUTES II*

The image of a rumpled, bearded man wearing a green T-shirt and speaking with a thick Texas accent flashed on television screens nationwide the evening of January 30, 2002. His name was Wayne Dickey. He was addressing his students, calmly but firmly: "I'm not asking you to get to class on time. I'm telling you to get to class on time." No AVID teacher had ever before been featured on a national TV show. The program was the CBS news magazine *60 Minutes II*, a spin-off of *60 Minutes*. The televised report, called "Making the Grade," would quickly define AVID for millions.

Producer Janet Klein's TV crews focused on AVID classes at Sam Houston High School in San Antonio, where Dickey was not only an AVID teacher but a legendary basketball coach; at Spring Valley Middle School in San Diego; and at Fallbrook High School in Fallbrook, California. Klein had twenty years' experience in TV news. Her team spent two months developing the segment. They worked hard to find dramatic personal stories to enliven the statistics that often made education stories too dry for most viewers.

The correspondent was Scott Pelley, who would eventually become anchor of *CBS Evening News*. His interviews with AVID teachers and students were often personal and emotional, but he began with a broader, more analytical slant, putting the program in the context of the recently passed No Child Left Behind law:

Last night in his State of the Union address, President Bush praised Congress for passing the biggest education reform in decades. But he said there is more to do to prepare our kids to read and succeed. So how do we prepare kids to meet the new higher standards in mandatory testing? Well, recently we heard about a fresh idea in education that may be the answer. It's called AVID. AVID changes the way public schools teach.

It works so well that AVID has spread to twelve hundred schools in twenty-one states. AVID gives struggling students intensive tutoring, and it revolutionizes the role of the teacher. An AVID teacher is a coach, a cheerleader, and a cop, who pushes kids to be more than they ever thought they could be. Today, kids who were lost in remedial classes are now making the grade because of teachers like Wayne Dickey down in San Antonio.

Dickey appeared on the screen, being interviewed by Pelley at his school. Dickey would be the star of the show. His athletic success was not mentioned, but Pelley called him Coach Dickey. Dickey showed that his motivational skills extended far beyond the basketball court as he described struggling students. "Too often we see them in the back row, and they are down here like this," he said, crouching a little. "First impressions from a teacher is he's a knucklehead who is not going to be able to do anything. So we teach him, you know, to sit up. Don't go to that back row. Look the teacher in the eye."

In a voice-over as the screen showed the teacher in action, Pelley said: "Wayne Dickey is the AVID teacher at Sam Houston High and for his students AVID is a last chance at college. They are kids in the middle making C's and even D's. Kids like Lucy Allen [the screen switched to a slender young woman] who is struggling and working nights because as a senior in high school, she's a mother."

> *Allen:* I didn't have confidence in myself and I didn't think I could do anything.
>
> *Pelley:* You were skipping class a lot?
>
> *Allen:* I skipped a lot.

The scene changed to another young woman serving dinner to an older woman in her kitchen. Pelley's voice-over said, "Charlotte Bates planned to drop out. Since her dad died, she's been caring for her disabled mother."

> *Pelley:* Were you going to go to college?
>
> *Bates:* No.

Pelley: Had no intention of going to college?

Bates: No intention.

The screen shifted to Pelley talking to Dickey: "A lot of these kids just don't believe you when you tell them they're going to go to college."

Dickey: You have to realize a lot of these kids have been told all their lives that they can't do this, they can't do that. If you are told something constantly, even though you might have great will power, staying power, eventually you're going to believe that.

Pelley (voice-over): AVID changes that belief by changing the way kids are taught in public school. First, AVID transfers students like Charlotte out of remedial classes and into advanced courses like chemistry and calculus. That would be a formula for failure if it were not for the AVID class itself.

The screen showed a college-age tutor telling a student, "It is better if you break it down."

Pelley (voice-over): AVID meets one hour every day and it is largely about tutoring. If a student has trouble in any subject, they get help in AVID class, help from Dickey, from college students trained as tutors, and from each other.

Pelley appeared in a classroom with four students working on a calculus problem during a tutorial.

Pelley: All four of you are working on the same problem.

Student: Yeah.

Pelley: Each of you has got a piece of this puzzle.

Student: Yeah.

Pelley: So you are teaching each other.

Student: Yes, and trying to be twice as effective.

Pelley (voice-over): But even more effective than the tutoring, AVID revolutionizes the way teachers teach. Here's the difference. Dickey's job is to watch over his students' entire day. He monitors how they are doing in algebra, history, English, everything. And if they have trouble with schoolwork, he finds them help. If they have trouble with teachers or classmates, he intervenes, always working to keep the class on the straight and narrow.

Dickey: People, I'm not asking you to get to class on time. I'm telling you to get to class on time.

Pelley (talking to Bates): Tell me about the first moment you met Coach Dickey. You thought what? What have I gotten myself into now?

Bates: I was like, I think I'm going to get out. I don't want to be in here with him because I was like, he thinks he's gonna run me? He's not gonna run me.

Pelley: And so what turned you around?

Bates: Him talking to me personally, showing me that he cares.

Mary Catherine Swanson appeared, answering Pelley's questions.

Swanson: Every one of these kids has some huge something missing in their home and their community, and that's why they are not doing well in school.

Pelley (voice-over): Mary Catherine Swanson started AVID twenty-two years ago in San Diego. She believed then that underprivileged kids were falling behind because no one showed them how to succeed.

Swanson: What they need is stability. They need family, they need somebody to whom they are responsible, and that's what the AVID teacher becomes.

Pelley: You think one of the places where American schools fail is because the English teacher isn't paying attention to what is happening to the child in history class, and the history teacher doesn't care how well he's doing in algebra class. There's no connection.

Swanson: There's no connection. One of the problems in America today is our schools have become very large and students slip through the cracks of anonymity.

Pelley (voice-over): In 1980, she convinced a group of those anonymous kids to volunteer for her experiment.

The screen showed old pictures of the classes at Clairemont High. Some of her first students appeared, being interviewed two decades later.

Pelley (voice-over): Josefina Pelayo told us the most important lesson from AVID, the lesson that changed her life, was to believe in herself. She said she needed that when her alcoholic father wanted her to quit AVID.

Pelayo: One time I had a term paper due, and when I was ten pages into it, he picked it up and he just tore it up, page by page in front of me.

Pelley: You know, a lot of kids would have quit.

Pelayo: I don't think so. I think when you have somebody telling you, that something you dream about, that you can actually accomplish what you set out to accomplish, it doesn't matter where it's coming from, because no matter what, if Mary Catherine Swanson could help us, she would. So as long as she believed that I was not wrong to believe in myself, I was not going to give up on myself.

Pelley (voice-over): AVID's system, teacher acting as coach, the daily tutoring, is now being used with younger kids like these at Spring Valley Middle School in San Diego. Here twelve- and thirteen-year-olds are learning how to take notes like college students, how to manage their time. Javier Lopez is graded on how well he keeps his stuff in order.

Lopez (opening his binder): Then I have two highlighters, a glue stick, a calculator, and four pencils.

Pelley (interviewing Swanson): You're teaching middle school students time management?

Swanson: Absolutely. It's the way all successful people get through life. They don't just let life happen to them. They learn how to organize and control life. And that's what we teach in AVID.

Pelley (voice-over): And it's a lesson that AVID says comes cheap for most school districts, about a dollar a day per student. When AVID arrives at a new school, there are inevitably teachers who think that it's too good to be true. That was Connie O'Connor. She actually kicked the AVID kids out of her Advanced Placement or AP English class, and was forced by the AVID teacher to take them back.

Pelley (interviewing O'Connor at Fallbrook High School): How do they do now compared to the best and the brightest?

O'Connor: They not only pass the AP test along with my other students, but more of them pass the AP test. They are setting the curve in the classroom, which makes my regular honors students work more to their standard, which is really an incredible feat.

Pelley: Wait, you're saying that the AVID students are bringing the honors students up?

O'Connor: I am. I am.

The screen showed Javier Lopez saying, "I was a D-average student."

Pelley: And what are you doing now?

Lopez: I am an A/B student.

Pelley: God, that must make you feel great.

Lopez: Yeah.

Pelley turned to another student in the group: "First A on your paper. What was that like, Joselyn?"

Joselyn: Well, for math it's really different. I stink at math. AVID gives me that hope. And I went home and I was cheering again. It feels good to succeed. I think I am the smartest person in my house, I think.

Pelley: Javier, did your parents go to college?

Javier: No.

Pelley: Michael, did your parents go to college?

Michael: No, my mom didn't go to college.

Pelley: How about you, Joselyn. Did your parents go to college?

Joselyn: No, my mom didn't go to college.

Pelley: Who's going to college? *(All five students raised their hands.)* Everybody's going to college.

The screen showed Dickey talking to Pelley: "All they have to do is have somebody pushing them. Somebody telling them, 'Yeah, you can do it. Hey, you've got a chemistry test on Friday, tutoring session on Tuesday. Take your rear end home and let's study. Bring it in.' We'll do whatever we've got to do."

Pelley (voice-over): It is hard work, and not everyone succeeds. In San Antonio, all twenty-three students in Coach Dickey's senior class graduated, and of those, eighteen are now in college. That includes Lucy Allen, the teenage mother.

Pelley: Would you have ever believed that about yourself when you were younger?

Allen: No, I didn't think I would. I didn't fill out any college applications. It's amazing.

Pelley (voice-over): What's amazing, with the support and encouragement of AVID, these kids are able to overcome all sorts of obstacles. Charlotte Bates, who wanted to drop out, was diagnosed with pancreatic cancer in her junior year, but with Coach Dickey she stuck with AVID, and now she's in college, too.

Bates: None of my parents graduated from high school. I am going to be the first one that graduated from high school, with honors.

Pelley: Are you more now than you ever thought you could be?

Bates: I'm stronger now. I can do anything now.

Pelley: What pushed you over the top? What made you the person you are now?

Bates: AVID.

Pelley (voice-over): AVID says 95 percent of its students go on to college, as opposed to about 63 percent for students nationwide. It's a lesson in success that is changing the lives not only of the kids but also of a lot of teachers who are showing them the way.

Dickey (speaking to Pelley): I tell you what. You get to a point where you really, you get attached to these kids, and you care about them as people first. You want them to succeed in anything they do, so there's a lot of book victories, but in AVID there are also an awful lot of individual stories about these kids overcoming things.

Pelley: You're proud of these guys.

Dickey: Very much so. They are *(voice breaks)* . . . they're my kids.

Years later, viewers, particularly teachers, would recall the hopeful impression left by the *60 Minutes II* piece. But it would be only that, a quick image. Teachers would eventually embrace the program, and quadruple the number of AVID schools, because of how closely its methods aligned with what they knew worked best in classrooms, particularly with disadvantaged students.

Changing the Mess
at Bell Gardens High

Bell Gardens High School was already a problem for the growing Hispanic community in east Los Angeles County when science teacher Liz Lowe arrived in 1989. She thought the campus was a mess, overflowing with kids, trailer classrooms, and graffiti. More than three thousand students crowded into school buildings surrounding a concrete quadrangle with patches of grass and some trees. Gangs were active. Not much learning was done.

"It hurt my soul that here were these wonderful students who were very, very capable, but they were expected to be the working poor," Lowe recalled. They needed an opportunity to go to college, but that goal was elusive.

AVID's introduction to Bell Gardens High began in 1994 when the school's principal sent Lowe to check it out. The principal liked Lowe because the teacher had had success with a basic science course. She had turned it into a popular exploration of sea life, with dissections. The principal thought Lowe might be able to determine whether AVID was as worthy a reform as advertised.

Lowe signed up for the summer institute in San Diego. "I thought it was one of the best things I had ever seen," she said. "The whole piece was about making things comprehensible, and I didn't know how to do that. I had to be able to figure out how to teach them, and I didn't know how to do that."

"The Cornell notes were a big part," she said. "I told the principal we needed to do this." But the principal found no support for the idea and was soon replaced. Lowe believed that the people in charge thought the best that could be done with Bell Gardens was to keep students moving to graduation, even if they were getting mediocre grades in easy courses.

AVID AS A PROGRAM FOR THE MIDDLE

In 1998, as AVID began to pick up state funding, Bell Gardens assistant principal Janet Johnson decided to give it another try. She had done her homework. She sent a team, not just one teacher, to the summer institute. The new Bell Gardens site team recruited thirty-six ninth graders for the first AVID class. Twenty of them graduated four years later. That was not bad, the AVID teachers thought. But it was nowhere near what such a large school was capable of.

Juan Herrera, later the school's principal, was then an assistant principal in charge of state funds coming into the school. When Johnson told him about AVID, the first thing that came to mind was his work at Schurr High, a somewhat more affluent school in the same district, Montebello. He had been a student and a teacher at Schurr. He had started a chapter of MECHA, an organization devoted to building pride in Hispanic students. He thought that the school focused too much on the top students, often the children of the most financially secure parents, and ignored those who were disadvantaged and struggling in their classes.

Herrera's father had been a janitor and his mother, a seamstress. He had difficulty with his courses in high school, having to take remedial reading and writing. He had no desire to go to college. He enrolled at East Los Angeles College (ELAC) only to pass the time until he was twenty and old enough for the police academy. But a professor at the community college told him that he had talent in math. Why not become a teacher? He did so well at ELAC that he got into UCLA and launched a career in education, a surprise for him.

What struck him about AVID, he said, "was that it was going to target those kids in the middle, like me. They tended to be left out. There were programs for the top kids and programs for the kids at the bottom. And the kids in the middle need that extra push."

Lowe had not been part of the AVID site team. She was not sure why. But when the AVID coordinator decided on a career change in 2001, Johnson asked Lowe to take his place. "Sure," Lowe said. "I have been waiting for you to ask me."

The initial AVID team included middle school teachers, so Lowe had the luxury of dealing with ninth graders who had already been in middle school AVID. She also had the support of committed principals and a school board that saw AVID as a promising solution for the low standards at Bell Gardens. The new state funding financed an office in the Los Angeles County Office of Education that watched over AVID in Montebello and other independent districts. It was similar to the arrangement in San Diego County when Swanson first took AVID beyond Clairemont High.

Lowe could not get a reliable count of how many students would enroll in AVID each year until late summer, but her principals did not mind. They could count on funding, no matter how many kids showed up. By 2013, Bell Gardens High had a $100,000 budget for tutors.

In 2012, however, California governor Edmund G. (Jerry) Brown cut the designated funding for AVID out of the state budget. He said that he thought the program was strong enough to prosper on its own. Swanson shrugged it off. Removing AVID's name as a recipient was not the same thing as cutting the funds. The money was still being sent to schools and would be spent on AVID, as it was so well established.

Demographically, Bell Gardens was one of the least diverse schools in the country, very different from Clairemont High with its mixed incomes and races. By 2013, the enrollment area for the school was more than 98 percent Hispanic. In a half century, the high school's population had shifted from primarily non-Hispanic white to almost entirely Hispanic. According to the 2010 census, non-Hispanic white students were just 1.5 percent of the student body. Blacks, Asians, Pacific Islanders, and Native Americans constituted .5 percent. More than 93 percent of the school community spoke a language other than English.

The education level of parents was the lowest of any community of similar size in the state: 55 percent had not graduated from high school, 27 percent were high school graduates, and only 17 percent had some college. More than 92 percent of students were from families that qualified for federal lunch subsidies. The median household income was slightly more than $30,000.

Yet from 2005 to 2012, the AVID program grew vigorously, as did the high school's academic standing. In 2005, the Bell Gardens High Academic Performance Index (API), the 1,000-point scale used by California to measure test score success, was 511. By 2012, it was 686, a 34 percent gain. Attendance was robust, a rate of 94.6 percent in the 2011–2012 school year, according to the school.

By 2013, Bell Gardens demanded that all students complete the courses required for admission to the University of California system. It offered seventeen Advanced Placement courses, open to all students who wanted to be challenged, and required for AVID students. The school consistently placed on the *Washington Post*'s Most Challenging High Schools list, with a rating in the top 7 percent of all US schools in 2013 based on participation in AP exams.

The AVID program at Bell Gardens grew from 29 freshmen in its first class in 1997 to 566 students, about 18 percent of the total school enrollment, in 2013. The school had eighteen AVID elective sections. Herrera had become the principal. AVID was growing, he said, "because everyone here believed in the program, and it was our goal to service more students. The biggest part was leadership. We were recruiting teachers. We were sending teachers to training. The word was out with the middle schools and the parents. The middle school principals were recruiting and telling parents about the AVID program."

No One Is Turned Away

The school did well enough to win AVID National Demonstration School status in 2004, although it almost lost the designation in 2010. The AVID teachers and math tutors, trying to be creative, had decided that their students did not have standard math algorithms, such as the multiplication tables, sufficiently imbedded in their brains. It took them too long to make simple calculations without calculators. So the AVID team ordered algorithm warm-up drills at the beginning of tutorial periods. The AVID inspection team did not like that. They appreciated the effort to improve students' calculating abilities, but suggested that the school find another way to do it. Tutorial time was precious. It was the core of the AVID method. No warm-up activities were allowed.

Lowe and her teachers complied, even though Lowe still thought the idea had been a good one. Her kids started at a lower level than many AVID schools. At Clairemont, she said, Swanson had had a significant number of middle-class students in advanced classes who helped set a higher standard for the AVID kids. Bell Gardens had almost no middle-class students, so she needed every advantage to raise the bar.

That was obvious when she recruited eighth graders. About one thousand moved up to ninth grade at Bell Gardens each year. She sent invitation letters to about 450, with a goal of getting 200 into the program. Usually she got about 150. "That is because of this urban myth about AVID," she said, "that you have to work too hard in that class. They say, 'I would rather take auto shop or wood shop or something like that.'"

With almost all Bell Gardens families low income, the parents were distracted by the strain of making a living. They usually lacked the educational background and language skills to see the importance of AVID. In most cases, Lowe found, it was the students, not their parents, who were deciding whether they would join the program. In middle school, all of their courses were chosen for them. They dreamed of going to high school and having some fun electives. AVID did not sound like that.

Lowe had never had to turn down anyone for AVID. "If all 450 of them wanted to come, the administration would make it happen," she said. Other schools turn down students whose parents are college graduates, because the AVID rule is that they are not kids in the middle. "We don't have anyone like that," Lowe said. Other schools decline to take students whose grades are too low and whose habits too erratic to do the work AVID requires. Lowe said she didn't do that, and cited a recent documentary, *Boys in Peril*, that profiled some Bell Gardens students who would not have been welcome in other AVID programs. "If the kids sign up, we keep them," she said. "Many times they will come to me and want to get out. I say, 'You know? You need to hang on a little bit longer.'"

The secret to growth at Bell Gardens, Lowe said, was the district's adoption of an AVID program for the elementary schools. Fifteen of the district's eighteen elementary schools had AVID beginning in fifth grade in 2013. Three had AVID beginning in fourth grade. "They have binders, they have binder checks, they have agendas," said Aida Hinojosa, the former Montebello district director for AVID. The new classes meant that many more teachers went to the summer institutes, where AVID habits and principles were instilled to last.

THREE DAYS
AT THE SUMMER INSTITUTE
A Crash Course in AVID

The Windsor room of the sprawling Town and Country Hotel had a high ceiling and excellent acoustics. There was enough space for a small high school prom, or twenty-nine women and twenty-nine men at ten tables trying to learn how to be AVID teachers.

On July 30, 2013, when social studies teacher Mike McColl strolled in for the first day of his first AVID Summer Institute session, the tables were covered in plastic pink, orange, purple, blue, green, and yellow tablecloths. Five or six teachers were at each table. The participants' ages ranged from twenties to fifties. They wore shorts, jeans, polo shirts, and sundresses, sitting and chatting, the noise rising.

A poster on the outside of the conference room's big door said "Welcome to H.S. Implementation with Brett and Bruce. Today became great when YOU got Here!" The letters were done with green and yellow markers by English teacher and AVID staff developer Brett Tujague, an Oakland Athletics fan using his team's colors.

McColl, thirty-seven, from Mount Vernon High School in Mount Vernon, Washington, filled out a sticky note with his name and school. He put it on a wall poster that sought to gauge the experience of the participants. There were no stickers placed on the top choice, "I am totally avidized." Seven chose "I wicorize my lessons." More than twenty said "I use some AVID strategies." Twelve said "I've heard of AVID." One chose the bottom space, "AVID what?"

McColl picked "I use some AVID strategies." He had been teaching fourteen years at his big brick school on a hill. It was one of the 2 percent of AVID schools with National Demonstration School status. He had never taught an AVID class before, but his selection to be one of the AVID elective teachers in the 2013–2014 school year meant that he had earned the respect of the principal and AVID coordinator. He was known for motivating students by getting to know them well, particularly those most difficult to motivate. Mount Vernon was one of a tiny number of schools that looped its AVID classes; in other words, the AVID ninth graders McColl taught in fall 2013 would still be his AVID students the following years when they were sophomores, juniors, and seniors. He had learned some AVID methods and was looking forward to the institute session, thought by many AVID teachers to be the best professional development they had ever had.

The two staff developers introduced themselves from the front of the room, where a large screen was ready for a series of PowerPoint slides. Tujague, who had been teaching AVID for fourteen years, was tall, with a goatee, gray dress shirt, and black slacks. His colleague Bruce Varela, an AVID teacher for five years in Wheeling, Illinois, was short and clean shaven. He wore a white polo shirt and tan slacks. On one of the side walls was their agenda for Day 1:

> Materials Management/Curricular Overview
> Community Building
> Social Contract
> AVID Student Profiles and ID
> AVID Agreement/Contract
> Intro to WICOR
> Costa's Levels of Thinking
> Focused Note-Taking
> Binders and Student Panel
> Phil Chairs
> Learning Logs

It was quite a load. They described a mountain of books and videos that each teacher would receive, with all the secrets of AVID. The three days of presentation would be only an introduction. They had a great deal of material to absorb and would only get the high points from Tujague and Varela.

What Makes AVID AVID

A PowerPoint slide announced "The 3 Non-Negotiables," the AVID trinity, the three features most important to success and most difficult for students to get used to: binders, tutorials, and Cornell notes. "It is a lot to cover today," Tujague said. "If we are talking too fast, write down your question on a sticky note." The teachers were asked to pull out the three-ring binders in their conference bags and add the papers they had just been given for the Implementation strand. A torrent of clicks rolled through the room as teachers unsnapped and resnapped their binders.

"So what do we do in AVID?" Tujague said. "Later on in the week, we are going to give you a CD with the whole curriculum on it."

As happened throughout the session, the staff developers asked each table to take a moment and share thoughts with each other. For the first round, everyone had to take turns telling their table mates where they taught, what they taught, what their dream vacation was, and what they hoped to get out of the summer institute. McColl named his high school, said he taught social studies and that he would like to go to Bora Bora, and told them "I am excited to be able to do something to make a difference in education."

Over the hubbub Varela shouted, "If you can hear my voice, clap once." The voices quieted. They moved on to the social contract, the web of relationships between students and between students and teachers that would in theory give AVID the power to move everyone to a new level. "The AVID classroom should feel like a protective barrier," Tujague said. "This is different from regular classrooms."

The staff developers recommended that teachers begin by asking students for rules of engagement, ways to treat each other in the class. They should write suggestions on the board or overhead and see which ones everyone could accept. These included being courteous to speakers, being mindful of time, and being open minded. A teacher asked, "Does everyone have to agree on the social contract?"

"If there are students who say 'I cannot adhere to that,'" Varela said, "you should say 'Well, let's talk about that and find out why and seek a solution.'"

The staff developers went over what they called "developing AVID goggles," identifying students who fit the program's profile. The principal characteristics were average-to-high test scores, grade-point averages between 2.0 and 3.5, college potential, and a sense of desire and determination. They might also have at least one of a secondary group of characteristics, such as parents who did not go to college. They might also be from an underserved group or low-income family, or have special circumstances such as a physical handicap.

"What happens if a student drops below 2.0?" a teacher asked.

"They have to want to do better," Varela replied. "You can't just stick them in there."

"But there are middle-class jobs that don't need college," said another teacher.

"AVID focuses on college," Varela said. "At least you have taught them something. Ninety-three percent of AVID graduates go to college. If they decide to go somewhere else, you have still done your job."

The staff developers recommended that the teachers have students already in AVID interview the applicants. "They can tell if the kids are there just to go on field trips with their buddies, or really want to go to college," Tujague said.

One teacher said, "We find kids that meet all the criteria but cannot read or write at our level." Tujague replied: "Without a doubt when I recruit, I don't look at the reading. We can build that up. I look at the math score, because they will have a real problem if they are below the 50th percentile."

Recalcitrant students can hurt an AVID program, the staff developers said. "The idea is that I am in this class to go to college," Tujague said. "If the person next to me doesn't do his Cornell notes and doesn't do his work, that attitude will spread like wildfire through the rest of the class." Someone asked what happened if a student didn't keep up with AVID rules and standards. Tujague warned against ejecting anyone at midyear "unless they are beyond disruptive." There were several ways, the staff developers said, to coax better performance. The idea was to make sure the student was improving, even if she had not yet reached the mark. "If they don't turn in their Cornell notes, they can be suspended from all school activities, such as sports, for the week; or if they have not done the Cornell notes, you can have them come in and copy another student's notes," Tujague said.

A good AVID teacher will talk to the student and find out why he wants to leave the program, they said. It is best to consult with the rest of the AVID teachers on the site team, talk to the parents, and always remind the student that he signed a contract to do his work. "Remember that leaving AVID should be hard," Tujague said. "I say, it is like an act of Congress to get students out of our class."

After a quick break for another team bonding exercise, the session moved into a presentation of Cal State Sacramento education professor Arthur L. Costa's three levels of questioning, one of Swanson's favorite tools. The idea was to find ways to advance students' question-making, as some questions were deeper than others. The Pledge of Allegiance was used as an example. Level one is defining, naming, listing, and observing, such as asking, "What is a pledge?" Level two is analyzing, contrasting, and synthesizing: "Why is it necessary to pledge allegiance to the flag?" Level three consists of hypothesizing, evaluating, and predicting: "Is having the word 'God' in the pledge a violation of the separation of church and state?"

THE DEVELOPMENT AND PHILOSOPHY OF NOTE-TAKING

Next came Cornell notes. "This is a huge part of the writing piece," Tujague said. "You are going to start teaching Cornell notes in the first two weeks." He quoted Swanson: "You really don't know what you know until you see what you write." Students have to learn to take the disparate facts and concepts in a lecture or piece of writing, summarize them, and derive the key questions to answer before they understand the lesson. Through that act of analysis, they are also more likely to remember what they have learned.

The staff developers presented a short lecture on the development and philosophy of note-taking, including the work of Cornell notes inventor Walter Pauk. The teachers were required to take Cornell notes on what was said. McColl's summary at the bottom of his page of notes said, "We take Cornell notes in order to implant the content in our memory by writing it down and then thinking about it enough to summarize in our own words. We teach the process by modeling it in class and having them do it again. We punish those who don't take them."

"What if one of their teachers lectures until the bell rings? How can they complete the summary?" a teacher asked. "The note-taking phase is a twenty-four-hour process," Tujague said. "When they get back to the AVID class, they should find another student and compare notes. They can write their summaries then."

For McColl, Cornell notes were key. "The biggest thing that I thought of when I saw what the AVID people were doing was that I had never been taught how to take notes," he said. When the staff developers asked if any of the strand participants had been taught note-taking, "there were like five people out of sixty in the room who raised their hands," he said.

The staff developers looked embarrassed as they put another Power-Point slide on the screen and explained why the slides were not among the items in their teachers' workbooks and conference bag. "We are not allowed by AVID Center to share the PowerPoint at all," Tujague said. "It is not our rule, it is the AVID Center's." He gave the traditional teacher's shrug for all inexplicable, lawyer-driven acts by people at headquarters. He welcomed the teachers to pull out their cell phones and iPads and snap as many pictures of the slides as they liked. Many did. (AVID officials told me the policy was needed to keep any outside groups from replicating their training, which had taken much time and money to develop. They said they would make sure that information on the slides vital to the training was in the materials given to trainees.)

In the midst of a detailed discussion of how to assess Cornell notes—"the goal is student growth, not giving a grade," Tujague said—a hush fell over the crowd. Living, breathing AVID students had arrived.

This was always a high point of summer institute Implementation sessions. The organizers had invited four students from southern California high schools who were part of an AVID student leadership group. In the midst of the training on how to get kids to take Cornell notes and keep their binders organized, the three girls and one boy went from table to table giving short speeches illustrated with real binders—big, beat-up, three-inch-thick blocks of paper of which they were proud.

Danielle Covington, a tiny senior with a sharp wit, pointed out that her binder included just one semester's work.

"Where are your previous semesters' binders?" someone asked. "On my dad's desk," she said. "He was the one who wanted me to take AVID, so I thought he should see the consequences." Like the other three students, she acknowledged that the work was hard and that not all students complied. Danielle said, "I didn't fight the system because I knew I wouldn't win."

Philosophical Chairs:
Learning to Think Persuasively through Debate

They left, and the teachers got a chance to be students. The topic was Philosophical Chairs, the intricately structured format for debate in AVID classes. "The purpose is to experience their learning in a discussion-based activity," Tujague said. "A question is posed, and each student has to make a decision"—which side to be on? "I think it is a huge piece," he said, "because it has our students thinking in a persuasive mindset."

The rules were different from the standard classroom bull session or a formal debate-team event. The teachers listened carefully because they were going to do their own Philosophical Chairs in a minute. The topic would be: "Parents should have to pay a fine when their kids skip school." Each participant would pick a side and line up on the proper wall, pros on the left and cons on the right. Each speaker would have to begin by summarizing the remarks of the previous student. A student who had spoken would have to wait for three more speakers before chiming in again.

Tujague said several times that Philosophical Chairs was too tricky an exercise to try early. "Wait for two months until a community feeling has been established," he said. "We don't want them to bully or single out individuals because that would hurt what we are trying to build."

A teacher named April, the first to speak from the pro side, said; "I think that ultimately as a parent you should be responsible for your children and are accountable for them."

The next speaker said, "What I heard April say is that parents are responsible for their child, but my school is a Title I school [full of low-income families] and it is a big burden to charge a fine to those parents."

McColl lined up against the proposition. He felt strongly about not doing anything to disrupt the sense of community he and the other Mount Vernon teachers had forged with their students and families, particularly the 67 percent of them who were low income. Since he was hired in 1999, he said, "morale has gotten steadily better. Our school is now compared to what it was when I started as a better place to learn." The growth of AVID had something to do with that, as well as the increased participation of students in the most challenging courses. "My first year we maybe had one AP class, and now we have AVID and have added much more AP."

The session ended with a brief discussion of learning logs, another way of forcing students to think about what they have been listening to. "If my kids didn't take Cornell notes in another class," Varela said, "they have to do learning logs for that class that day. It is an expression of what you understand and what you don't understand about a topic."

They broke for the day.

WATCH CLIP 6: PHILOSOPHICAL CHAIRS
AVID students in middle school and high school demonstrate Philosophical Chairs debates in both "Classic Style" and "Jury Style."

www.wiley.com/go/avid6

TUTORIALS: KEEPING FOCUSED ON QUESTION-MAKING

Next morning, they were back tackling the heart of AVID: tutorials. Every teacher present was given a question to answer, along with an answer to a different question. Each took turns pretending to be a student in a tutorial presenting their point of confusion. The pressure was on the other teachers at their table, pretending to be the students who had to ask questions that would lead the student toward the answer. Several had difficulty with the assignment. "It is a great challenge when I already know the answer," McColl said. "If it is hard for us, it is going to be hard for them."

Tujague described the consequences of not keeping students focused on question-making. It was hard, he admitted. "The first time I did this activity I felt stupid," he said. "It is a tough process, but the minute you give up, AVID will turn into just another study hall." He had visited schools where the coordinators did not understand that. "They think they are running AVID, but they are running AVID Lite."

Varela pointed out that tutoring filled up 40 percent of AVID class time. "Step one, in other classes they are taking Cornell notes. Step two, at home they look over their notes and fill out the TRF [Tutorial Request Form]. This is their homework Monday and Wednesday nights," he said. "As they enter the class on Tuesdays and Thursdays, they hand the form to the tutor. Some don't have it done on time. We have those kids sit out in the hallway and do it, or lose five points for not doing it in time. Some who persist that way don't stay in AVID."

"They have to understand that there is no exception to this rule," Tujague said.

Each student gave a thirty-second speech to his tutorial group presenting the problem, then the questioning began. He might not get his question answered, the staff developers emphasized. He would be urged to discuss the problem with other students in the same class, or with the teacher. "Sometimes I personally walk the student to the teacher and say, 'He has a question for you,'" Varela said.

It was intense work, Tujague said. If an AVID teacher worked under a block schedule where each class was eighty minutes long, they would spend no more than forty minutes on the tutorials. McColl made a note of that. His school had a block schedule with eighty-five-minute periods.

And don't start the tutorials too early for students unaccustomed to them, Tujague said. "We don't have tutorials for freshmen until about Halloween," he said. "A month minimum." (AVID officials said they recognized that AVID teachers had to improvise in difficult situations, but they did not support Tujague's recommendation. AVID guidelines given to all teachers say tutorials should start in the third week of school for ninth graders. They said they would be emphasizing this in future trainings of staff developers.) Tujague displayed a PowerPoint slide summarizing the tutorial process. A crowd of teachers with iPhones and iPads moved to the front to take photos.

College students made the best tutors, Tujague said. But in the California districts where he had worked in recent years, he said, there had been no money for tutors, so adult volunteers and advanced high school students had been used. He said outside unpaid tutors could be unreliable. (In conversations with AVID Center staff, they clarified the organization's position on tutors. College students are the expected standard for well-functioning sites, but could be augmented with peer tutors. In fact, a secondary school AVID site can achieve minimal certification status by using peer tutors.) Next year, Tujague said, all of the teachers in the room should return to summer institute and enroll in the Tutorology strand. "Don't do anything else," he said. "You must do that and then you can go back and train your tutors."

Buying into AVID Strategies

The third and final day of McColl's strand covered critical reading strategies, Socratic Seminars, and the steps of the writing process. Some time was also set aside for the participants to talk to each other and start their own planning, with the staff developers there to answer individual questions.

Asked a month later, a week before his school started, what he had learned at the summer institute, McColl said that with those three days and the online materials, "I feel like I have the bare bones, skeleton outline of what the class should look like. I just need to fill in the details."

He said, "I think the biggest part of AVID that was not touched on in the Implementation strand is the human aspect. How do I best build relationships with and motivate my students to achieve their potential? It makes sense that it wasn't addressed, because each teacher and student is different, but I will put a lot of thought into the human aspect of the job and not just the strategies. The strategies will only work if I show my students that I believe in them, care about them as individuals, and have high expectations of them."

Most of the Implementation strand participants interviewed afterward said they appreciated the intense sessions, although one teacher said she was bored by icebreakers. "We are all professionals," she said. "We don't need the icebreaking exercises. I would like to brainstorm with the other teachers on practical ways of teaching these lessons."

McColl thought the AVID training was one of the two best professional development experiences he had ever had, tied for top spot in his mind with Link Crew, a freshman orientation system by the Boomerang Project of Santa Cruz, California. "For one, AVID is giving you specific information," he said. "They are going quick, and I am going to have to spend a lot of time going back over things, and rereading and making it my own. But [in three days] they are giving you an entire system of how to run a class . . . That's a lot. They are not wasting time. They are going right for it. It is all quality stuff that can be used. It's practical. I really appreciate that. Not every professional development opportunity is like that."

The packets of information McColl took home were several inches high, not to mention the CDs. "I don't think there is going to be any end to how I can use these in new ways in my classes." A week before school started, he was eager to get back with students, whose own stories—like the ones he heard at the Implementation session—were going to be better than anything he could learn from staff developers.

"I Don't Care If I Have to Haul You Down There Myself"

It didn't take long to figure out that Jonathan Brown, a new ninth grader at Shoemaker High School in Killeen, Texas, was trouble. He was nearly six feet tall and weighed 230 pounds. Like that of many foster children, his life had been chaotic. He had lived with families in Kempner, Bartlett, Jerald, and a few other places he forgot. In school he talked back, was disrespectful, ran away, and never listened to reason.

His mother had abandoned him and his brother, Joshua, in a public park in Lampasas, Texas, when they were five and three years old, respectively. She had been abusive and neglectful. She used and sold drugs. When two policemen asked the little boys what they were doing in the park, Brown said they had run away from their babysitter. "Where do you live?" one officer asked. Brown pointed to a big oak tree in the middle of the street. That was their home, he said, apparently hoping the policemen would go away. Their mother never regained custody.

When he was ten, he was placed with Keith and Mercedes Brown, where he stayed until he finished high school. His foster father was a retired soldier. His foster mother directed a day-care center on the army base at Ft. Hood. They were strong and encouraging. They recognized that their new foster child was quick and bright, capable of doing good work. His foster parents clashed repeatedly with him over his bad grades. He could do so much better than that, they said. He ignored them. He picked fights with his teachers. He insulted the principal. He blew off schoolwork.

At one point, however, his grades improved, and the school recommended he be put in the gifted-and-talented program. When told about this, he pointed out that none of his friends were in that class. He began to sabotage his own grades to end the conversation.

117

PUSHING THE CAPABLE TO REACH FULL POTENTIAL

But the year before he reached Shoemaker High, he encountered a math teacher named Amy Reynolds, later Amy Armstrong. He liked sitting in her classroom at Palo Alto Middle School because she was a soccer fan and welcomed the students at the school who, like Brown, were devotees of that sport. He resisted accelerated math, just as he had resisted the gifted-and-talented class, but Reynolds put him in her eighth-grade algebra course. She would not take no for an answer.

"She was constantly pulling me into her class and out of the hallways," Brown recalled. "She said, 'You need to take my class.'" She was the one teacher who could get him out of an angry mood. He liked hanging out in her classroom, so he eventually agreed to take the accelerated course. He found algebra fun and easy. "She was really good at kind of showing me different ways to do things, and it kept me busy all the time," he said. The basic algebra lessons were a breeze for him, so she gave him harder stuff. "It was challenging to me, so I never got time to fool around, as I usually did," he said.

Once Reynolds had him in that good mood, she pressed her advantage. He wasn't doing much over the summer after eighth grade. She suggested to Brown's foster parents that he take the summer geometry course she was teaching for high school kids who needed to catch up, and younger kids who could be accelerated. The foster parents were eager to see their recalcitrant ward realize his potential, so they said yes. Brown himself was happy to spend a summer with Reynolds. He continued to work hard in math.

"Geometry was fun as well," he said. "I wasn't very good at it at first. It was something new and different, which frustrated me." He sometimes felt those old feelings, the desire to get out of anything that required effort and might label him a smart kid. But it was Reynolds's class, so he stuck it out.

That made him a candidate for AVID. For a while, Brown resisted that, too. He had been asked to enroll in his middle school's AVID program, but had said no. "I thought it was for the dumb kids," he said. "They said a lot of the kids in AVID were really smart kids. But I didn't want to be a dumb kid, and I also damn sure didn't want to be a smart one. If I was just in the middle, then I could be cool and be me."

He said the same thing when a ninth-grade teacher suggested he join the AVID program at Shoemaker High. He tried to finesse the offer. "Yeah, yeah, yeah," he told the teacher. "I'm going to do it." Then he threw the application away. The teacher, an expert in student evasions, found the crumpled application and gave Brown a new one. "You are going to go to this interview," he said. "I don't care if I have to haul you down there myself."

Following the path of least resistance, Brown did as he was told. The interviewer was the ninth-grade AVID elective teacher, Paige Tallman. She was as smart and as tough as Reynolds. She got Brown to open up in ways he had never done before with teachers. "I told her I was a foster kid and I didn't think I was going to have a future," he recalled. She offered a different view. He could go to college. Because of the potential everyone around him saw that he had, if he applied himself, that could be the road to his future.

"In talking to her about college and what it was like," Brown recalled, "I began to get the idea of college being my next foster home. I knew colleges had cafeterias, so I would be able to eat. I knew they had dorms, so I knew I would be able to sleep. After that conversation, college seemed to me the next logical step."

He still carried a lot of resentment. He joined AVID in the middle of his freshman year and quickly discovered that he was going to have much more schoolwork than before. "I felt they tricked me because you had to do all this work in the advanced classes on top of the work in the AVID class." He had coasted in middle school. He worked hard only in math because Reynolds demanded that, and he liked it. He got an A in Spanish because his foster mother was Panamanian. But in ninth grade, once he joined AVID, he was forced to take advanced English and advanced history, as well as Algebra II, since he had completed geometry in the summer.

Even worse in his view were the key AVID requirements. He loathed doing Cornell notes. He did enough of them to get by when his AVID teachers checked his binder, but he didn't like it. (He only took Cornell notes seriously when he got to college and discovered, belatedly, that they were a godsend.) Binder checks also aggravated him. He was accustomed to stuffing all his papers in his backpack. He dug through the crumbled mess at the bottom to find anything. But he had agreed to be in AVID. He needed college as his next foster home. So he kept a neat binder and was surprised, and then amused, when non-AVID teachers began to compliment him for being so orderly, when he was only doing it under duress. The big problem was, he recalled, that "I had to get used to the fact that I had to carry this big three-ring binder and everyone would see me go by and say: you must be in AVID."

Brown was also irked by his foster parents' attitude toward his AVID status. They usually had four or five other foster children staying at their big old two-story house in the Willow Springs neighborhood. Every child had chores. If he had not done the dishes the night before, his foster father would wake him up at 4 a.m. to get them done. But when it came to schoolwork, he was treated differently.

They expected A's and B's from him after he joined AVID. "It was frustrating for me because my foster brothers would bring home C's and that was OK with them," Brown recalled. "I said, 'Why are you so hard on me?' Even when I got a B, they would say, 'That's good, but you can do better.'"

More Than Organizational Skills and Time Management

As he struggled with the extra homework for the advanced classes, the Cornell notes, and the binder checks, he discovered that there were other AVID features that were, astonishingly, a blast. The Socratic Seminars and Philosophical Chairs "were what kept me going," he recalled. "I was the kind of kid who could never shut up. I had to put in my two cents." The only problem was that the two AVID styles of debate were very structured. He couldn't open his mouth unless he held the Koosh ball, the symbol that a student had the floor.

Brown realized that his AVID elective classes were full of bright, opinionated students who wanted the Koosh ball as much as he did. If the discussion got hot and Brown was fidgeting in his chair, classmates would tease him by telling each other, "Don't pass Jonathan the Koosh ball."

One of Brown's biological parents was black; the other, white. Like Barack Obama, he accepted the societal assumption that he was black. Shoemaker was a predominantly black school, but there were other ethnicities. Some of the better AVID discussions tapped into that. "One of the topics was, if an African American male wore a Malcolm X T-shirt, could a Caucasian kid wear a White Power T-shirt?" Brown recalled. "I had to play devil's advocate. I had to be on the other side, which meant yes, he could wear the White Power shirt."

That contrarian instinct, and the AVID emphasis on cogent and well-sourced arguments, forced him to think much more about what he was saying. "It helped me learn how to organize my thoughts and organize my arguments," he said. "That and the speech class turned me to the track I pursued in college."

In Speech Communication his junior year, he was the star pupil. He had a deep, resonant voice. He yearned to put forth his views on nearly every topic. One day his teacher, Ms. Card, told him something that surprised and thrilled him, and changed his life. "You can get paid to talk," she said.

The AVID tutorials also helped him. The tutors were former Shoemaker students who had gone to college, mostly Central Texas College in Killeen. He listened to their stories of life at what he thought of as his next home. College was more than cafeteria food and dorm beds. There were courses in speaking for future communicators like Brown. There were also sports, a Brown obsession.

His usual school attire was polo shirt, blue jeans, and Michael Jordan sneakers, covered by various athletic jackets and insignia. He arrived at Shoemaker accomplished in soccer, and lettered all four years. In his junior year, the football team, a perennial loser, needed a place kicker. He tried out for the job, but when the football coach saw him, a muscular 250 pounds and five foot eleven, he talked him into being a defensive lineman. Brown thrived. The team had its first winning season.

The tutoring, debates, and academic orderliness of AVID all worked for Brown, but its most important contribution to his life was time management. His foster parents had already trained him to go straight home from school or practice. He was not allowed to go to friends' houses or have friends come to his home. There were plenty of chores. Often he would come home late from practice, tired, and want just to have dinner and go to bed. If he had homework, he would tell his parents he didn't. The AVID calendars put a stop to that. The grid log calendars had to be filled in with all of his assignments. When he said he had no homework, his foster father would say, "Show me." If the calendar showed an assignment due and Brown couldn't produce it, he had to stay up and get it done.

FINDING A HOME IN COLLEGE AND BEYOND

He was unhappy when he didn't get into Texas Tech, where he thought he could make the nationally prominent football team. Instead he went to South Plains College and then transferred to the University of Texas of the Permian Basin (UTPB) in Odessa. He studied TV production. He interned with a reporter at ESPN and began to do some inspirational speaking. His speech before a big business-sponsored conference on education reform got a rave reception. That led to a job with AVID, taking its principles of learning into colleges. At UTPB he earned both a bachelor's and a master's degree.

He had graduated from Shoemaker High School with a 3.5 grade-point average. In college he used Cornell notes in every class, something he had not done in high school. He talked to his instructors after class about points of confusion. He formed study groups. He graduated with a 4.0 and began a career as both a speaker and a college teacher on AVID methods for college students who needed the same support he had gotten in high school.

College was the home he had hoped it would be, but he didn't need a home anymore. Much of the anger that had underscored his life stemmed from being a foster child. It felt like a prison sentence he could never escape. Through elementary, middle, and high school he was known as Jonathan Grant, carrying the last name of the mother who did not want him. But in his senior year of high school, something happened that would later be one of the highlights of his speeches, and a moment he would treasure.

Keith and Mercedes Brown had been tough foster parents. But they never treated him as anything but their own son. No matter how much he lied or complained, they never said, as foster parents often did, that he could leave if he didn't like it. "I knew what to do and what to say to get foster parents to say that," he recalled, "but they never would say that."

One evening during his senior year at Shoemaker, they called him down to the living room for a chat. Mercedes Brown said to him, "We want you to be a part of our family."

"Mom, I am part of the family."

"But we want you to be a Brown," she said.

Jonathan Brown recalled years later, "I never cried so much. It was the coolest thing in the world."

Once they had the paperwork ready, they all got into the family's blue Econoline van and drove to Lampasas, where the Browns officially adopted him. The park where the police had found him was still there, along with the big tree in the street where he had said he lived. But from then on he had a real home in a big old house in Killeen, where he knew he belonged forever.

LOSING IT IN ATLANTA

At the AVID Summer Institute in Atlanta in 2004, Kande McKay threw a fit.

She was thirty-one years old, in her third year as AVID coordinator for Madison High School in southern Indiana. She had given it her all. She was taking care of an infant and a young husband who had had a stroke, while building the program in her hometown high school. AVID, she thought, gave her students a challenging curriculum that would prepare them for college much better than she had been prepared when she attended Madison.

She knew her school was remote from the rest of the AVID universe. The only other AVID program in Indiana was at Lawrence Central High School near Indianapolis, 150 miles to the north. Lawrence's AVID coordinator was supposed to be the AVID state director and make sure she got the support she needed, but she had not heard from him. Her messages had not been returned, so she focused on her kids and looked for ways to improve. Her only contact with AVID administrators was at Summer Institutes, which she found very helpful until that summer of 2004.

She was conducting a site-team meeting with the rest of the attendees from Madison when an AVID official came in and asked why she had not turned in her certification forms. "You should be certified at this point," the woman said. She seemed offended that Madison had not done this, as if Madison were some hick town that couldn't get it together.

McKay was not sure what was happening, but she didn't like it. Three other members of her team were there, as confused as she was. There were five other site-team meetings going on in the hotel conference room. McKay felt herself getting upset. She hated that. She had a stressful life. Losing her temper was not going to help her cope any better.

"I had been trying my hardest to do the program the way I understood it should be run," she recalled. "I thought we were making great strides. By that time the freshmen we had started with were juniors.

They were just starting to get why they were taking Cornell notes and why they were doing the stupid binder, and I had done the juniors, too, and they were starting to get it. I am going to Summer Institute and am getting ready in the coming year to send the seniors to college. This was going to be our first real class of seniors."

The AVID official wasn't interested in that. She was a staff developer, a role that McKay would fill in future Summer Institutes. This staff developer was attending to AVID and its rules. She was earning some extra summer money making sure all the schools at the Summer Institute had their papers in order.

"You should have your self-verification," she said to McKay. "Where is your self-verification document?"

"I don't know what you're talking about," McKay replied. She felt herself slipping out of control. She explained that the district director at Lawrence Central was supposed to be telling her about what she needed to do, and hadn't done it.

"No, that can't be right," the woman said. "You should know this."

"No, I don't know," McKay said, her voice rising. "Nobody told me. What are you talking about? I did my site-team plan at the last Summer Institute. I don't know anything about verification."

The staff developer did not seem to have heard her. "Well, this affects your certification."

"What are you talking about? You mean we can't be an AVID school anymore?" At that point, at least as she remembers the moment, McKay lost it. She raised her voice. She made demands. Known to her friends as the queen of niceness, McKay's tantrum may have seemed no more than mild consternation to those watching. However she looked and sounded, she had never been so upset at a professional gathering.

She started to cry. "I have no control over it whatsoever, and it was embarrassing," she said. "I was so frustrated and so mad. I was busting my hind end to try to do what's right, because I always thought from day one that AVID was the way to change education, and now they were telling me I'm doing it wrong."

REPAIRING BREAKDOWNS IN COMMUNICATION AND
STAYING OUT OF THE WAY

The staff developer appeared stunned. She said she would get someone who could help. McKay took several deep breaths. She tried to get back to the discussion with her team. After several minutes, another woman walked up to the Madison table. She asked to speak to McKay in the hall.

The official, whose name McKay eventually forgot, seemed sympathetic. "Tell me what's been going on," she said.

"Where do you want me to start?" McKay said.

"Just start at the beginning, and when you get to the end, stop."

It took a while for her to explain how AVID had begun at her little school, how she had been told that the coordinator at Lawrence would be her supervisor, how that official never got in contact with her, and how she had been working as hard as she could to get her school up to AVID standards, mostly based on the paperwork she gathered and the strands she attended at each Summer Institute.

The woman listened. When she was sure McKay had wound down, she apologized. "Wow," she said, "we didn't even know that was going on." It appeared, she said, that AVID Center had assumed that Madison was part of the Indiana AVID state organization, but did not know it was so far from the other Indiana school. AVID administrators did not know she was getting no guidance from the person listed as the state AVID director.

"She was very AVID-like, very good at calming me down," McKay recalled. "I have seen that happen with participants now that I am on the other side." When organizations grow, they often become unwieldy and clumsy, and suffer breakdowns in communication. The AVID official knew that the only thing to do was to listen and fix the problems as soon as possible. "She was very good at it," McKay said.

The official said, "I think what's happened is that the person who was supposed to be your contact person is no longer with us, and you have been lost in the shuffle." AVID national had just established its central division, where Indiana was supposed to be, but that change added to the confusion.

So McKay was appointed district director, with responsibility for just her high school, as it was the only AVID school in that part of her state.

She gave the AVID officials her address. The mountains of material that went to hundreds of other district directors would start coming to her, too. She was given the name, telephone number, and email address of a central division official based in Texas. That was the person she should go to if she had questions.

But her troubles weren't over. She got no more pay than other teachers at Madison for being an AVID teacher. She was similarly uncompensated for her new duties as district director. AVID depended on teachers doing much extra work for free. But becoming a district director, McKay was told, was going to cost her district an extra $10,000. That was the approximate cost of staff development, transportation, and lodging for the four training sessions in Texas she would have to attend. "My district can't afford that," she said. "They have no money. They are not going to fund it. They are already paying the licensing fee, and for the Summer Institute. They are not going to pay an extra $10,000 to send me to Texas."

She told the AVID officials what she had been doing the last three years. It was on-the-job training for district director. She knew what she was doing, even if she had not completed all the necessary paperwork she hadn't known about. She should not have to do the Texas training. They were convinced. They waived the training fee and introduced her to George Buss, an AVID staff developer from Illinois who became her friend and counselor.

"He came to Madison and spent the day with me," McKay recalled. "We went through everything. He told me what I needed to do. He got me in the right direction. He went over all the certification stuff with me. And that got us in the right direction."

The core of Mary Catherine Swanson's management philosophy had always been to find great educators with a passion to help kids, make sure they know what works, collect data on what they are doing, and stay out of the way. McKay's summer meltdown in Atlanta revealed that that sensible approach was not always executed perfectly. But as long as AVID educators wrestling with administrative breakdowns kept their focus on helping children learn, they could work it out, even if there were some angry words and tears. The tutors they trained were a particularly important part of that effort to overcome mistakes and entropy.

INSIDE TUTORING

At the core of the AVID program at Bell Gardens High School were its tutorials. Many of the tutors were Bell Gardens graduates, and most were students at one of the California State University campuses in the area. Their tutees ranged from ninth graders to twelfth graders. The tutors and students had varying degrees of experience with a method they all found strange when they started.

A LITTLE PRODDING FOR NEW PROCESSES

In a class for ninth graders on an April day in 2013, AVID teacher Mirna Underwood was moving around room 402, intervening in several tutorial groups to make sure her students and their tutors were not letting standards of inquiry slip. The students had been participating in the process for several months, two days a week, but Underwood knew it took a long time before it became second nature.

"I am going to stop you," she said to one freshman who was presenting a math problem. "What are you missing on your board?" The student had not recorded the steps she was taking on the whiteboard she held up for the students in the tutorial to inspect. She added the needed words: "Steps: 1. Write expression. 2. Factor numerator and denominator."

The tutor, embarrassed that the teacher had to prompt him, said to the group, "How can you help your classmate?"

One student gave it a try. "What is the difference between these equations, so what are you missing?"

The student looked confused. The tutor chimed in: "What do your notes say?"

The student reached for his point of confusion form. "No, your notes," the tutor said. He wanted the student to look at his Cornell notes in his binder. The student tried a new approach, but the tutor said he was on better ground before. The student had to erase some of his work.

"Do you understand why you had to go back?" the tutor asked.

"I had the right formula but the wrong numbers," he said.

Underwood saw a student in another tutorial erasing work on his board. "Martin, what are you doing right now? Why did you erase it?" she asked.

"Because it didn't work."

"So are you trying another way?" The tutor in that group took notice and nudged the student forward. The class was still full of students uncomfortable with the process and needing to be prodded.

In Margaret Pedregon's room A108 class for AVID seniors, the students were much more assured, even though the math problems—as always the prime subject for tutorial sessions—were tougher.

A student at the table for calculus students wrote on her whiteboard: "If the position function of a particle is $x(t) = \sin^2 t$, $t > 0$, find the distance that the particle travels from $t = 0$ to $t = 2$." Her point of confusion was: "What should be my first step?"

There were five boys and two girls at the table. Two of the boys were having a rapid discussion of how to solve it. "Just use the formula from A to B," one said. The tutor decided this was a suggestion on a way to proceed, not the answer. He let it go. The student with the question began to write equations on the board, and described her steps: "1. Get the absolute value of the equation. 2. Integrate the velocity equation from A to B."

The two boys were punching numbers into their graphing calculators. "I don't think the integrating is right," one said.

"Let's start all over," the other one said. The student began to erase her board.

The tutor nodded. "They can do the problem," he said to a visitor. "But they have to describe the process in a way that will help the student do it in the future."

TUTORING AS MOTIVATION, NOT BABYSITTING

Brittni Kimura, an international business major at Cal State Dominguez Hills, started tutoring at Bell Gardens in 2011. The training course took a day. "The most important thing we learned was we are not these students' babysitters. We are their motivators. We are their support system when they are struggling. We are their second chance at getting that understanding," she said.

"I think the students were kind of leery of having a college student teach them," she said. "I had to be tough, and intrusive." She had never been exposed to inquiry-based learning before. It was not offered at Los Altos High School in Hacienda Heights (different from Los Altos High School in Northern California), which she had attended. There was no AVID program there.

It has been difficult to keep up the standard, she said. "I don't want to just give them the answers, because once you give, they take. You just have to keep quiet and force the questions on them, so hopefully they will really think about it. They really need to think," she said.

If her students did not offer questions in a tutorial to help the student dealing with a point of confusion, Kimura would call on them and insist they come up with something. The tutor needed to pierce a thicket of doubt and shyness. "Today I had a math question," Kimura said. "It was geometry, and one of the students was asking, 'Well, what do you know about arc angles?' The student said, 'I don't know anything,' and the student asking the question fell silent." That was a common dodge. Kimura had to give the other students a pep talk. "OK, what other questions can you guys ask? What do you guys know that he doesn't?" It worked, but she was sure she was going to have to do it again.

Mario Martin del Campo was a Bell Gardens tutor as well as a graduate of the school and its AVID program. One of his older sisters had been in AVID, so he got an early impression of the program before he was in it. He had been a motivated student. He knew he was going to college. But he also saw he needed the support AVID would give. Some of his friends said they didn't need that stuff. His answer was, "How do you know, and why not take advantage of it?"

The inquiry-based learning "helps me now as a college student," he said. "If during office hours I want to go ask a professor a question, I ask it in just the same way as I would have asked a tutorial question."

He had been a regular note-taker in high school, but was not keen on Cornell notes. Making questions and summarizing the point seemed too much to him. Once he got to college, he began to understand. "It helps me a lot when I annotate a book where there are questions I am trying to answer. It motivates me to get both the source material and my own notes to figure out the best conception of what I am learning," he said.

He also found binder checks an annoyance. He thought he was fairly orderly in high school. He always brought his pens and papers and whatever else was required. In college, he was more likely to follow the binder concept because there was so much to absorb from every class, although he used folders, not binders.

PURSUING INQUIRY: AVID'S GREATEST GIFT

Pursuing inquiry, the process del Campo was taught in high school and that he taught as a tutor, struck him as AVID's greatest gift. "The first thing most students who aren't in AVID say is, 'Well, I don't get it.' And they will go ask, 'How do I do it?' rather than say, 'I don't know how to do it. I'm going to try it and see how far I can get,' so they can finally say when they ask for help, 'This is the point where I just don't understand it.'"

He attended California State University, Northridge as an English major. He wanted to be a writer. He planned to seek work in journalism, "but a big dream of mine is to be a comedy writer. Right now I just do stand-up comedy a little." The inquiry method had gotten him through difficult times. "I wasn't an English major at first," he said. "I was a physics major, and I would have a lot of trouble. Sometimes I would look at problems and say, 'I just don't get it,' and I could feel the AVID student in me saying, 'You can't just settle for 'I don't get it.' You got to try it, you got to see how far you can get. You get to the point where you know you can't go on, but you also know you can figure it out." That lent confidence and impressed professors when he appeared at office hours and sought help.

As a tutor at Bell Gardens, del Campo said, he found that the difficulty of the work depended on the age of the students. "The trouble with seniors is they are about to graduate and they have all these events, such as prom and college visits, and it is difficult to keep them on task. Sometimes they don't want to do the work. If they aren't prepared, I take off points. I still make them do it. There are a certain number of points you get for each tutorial. If they can't perform to our standard, they still have to complete the work, but they just don't get the points."

In the 2012–2013 school year, he specialized in seniors. He worked with them until the bell rang and then conducted tutoring in algebra. He worked all day every Tuesday and Thursday. He was paid $12 an hour and worked fourteen hours a week, starting at 7:15 a.m. His mother used to work in a factory, but was laid off in 2008. His father was a retired coffee delivery man. He needed a job to get through college. At first he worked at a television station, but decided he preferred the hours at Bell Gardens. He doesn't have to work until 4 a.m. as he did at the TV station. He lived with his parents in Montebello.

Tutoring the Algebra I students was different from tutoring for AVID. He walked around the classroom as they did their homework and saw who needed help. They often were not AVID students. They did not have to work their way to a point of confusion. But he pushed them in the AVID way. He asked questions rather than immediately showing them how to get the answer. "I want to see how much they can do on their own," he said.

"Don't Give Me That, Akila"

Robert Quinlan had only two years' experience as a full-time teacher when he flew to Atlanta with several veteran colleagues from his New York City school to do his first Summer Institute in 2009. His principal, Margaret Lacey-Berman, and assistant principal, Iris Chiu, wanted to start AVID at the Brooklyn High School of the Arts. They knew Quinlan was relatively new to teaching, but they liked the energy and imagination he showed in his ninth-grade Global Studies class.

He had read the AVID materials, helped recruit the first AVID students, and researched the program on the web. Still, he was not prepared for the wave of AVID enthusiasm, almost cultlike, that hit him when he arrived in Atlanta.

"It was unlike anything I ever experienced," he recalled. "It was literally nine to five nonstop. It was intense. It was interactive. We were sharing ideas, collaborating, veterans interacting with people like me. It was a great experience. You learned in icebreaker sessions with students. We had an idea of what we were getting into, but the passions, the paradigm shift, I was just awestruck. I was taken by the trainers' enthusiasm. There was no way you were going to tell them that AVID doesn't work."

The staff developers were paid to excite and teach the attendees. Quinlan realized that some of the words had to be hyperbole. But he found it hard to discount what he heard in the speeches by AVID students. They did not read from a script. They were telling him what had happened to them and how that could help his kids.

Pulling Academics from the Sidelines

Quinlan grew up in West Islip, Long Island. His single mother, Christine, working multiple jobs, gave him much responsibility in helping raise his younger brothers, Patrick and Ryan. He babysat, coached lacrosse, helped with homework. He majored in American history education at New York University and looked forward to teaching.

His first two years at the Brooklyn High School of the Arts went well. The students were admitted based on auditions—vocal, dance, instrumental, fine arts, and theater. The student body was about 80 percent black, the rest mostly Hispanic, with a few whites and Asians. They yearned to develop their talents. Academic work was unfortunately often a sideline. Quinlan wanted his ninth graders to be excited by history. Making that happen was hard work.

By the end of the Atlanta Summer Institute, Quinlan thought he and his colleagues were ready to AVIDize the world. He wanted to fly back to New York and give everyone a binder.

———————

Brooklyn Arts, like most public high schools in New York City, did not have designated middle schools that fed students into their ninth grades. Ninth graders arrived without the high school's having received much information about them except for state testing data and socioeconomic status. The Brooklyn Arts students were from middle schools all over the city. In regular high schools, AVID teachers visited the local middle schools that fed into their school and gave their recruiting pitch to the eighth graders and their parents. Brooklyn Arts couldn't do that, so the principal and staff decided there would be no AVID elective class in ninth grade. They would start with tenth graders and move steadily up to eleventh and twelfth grade.

The previous spring, Quinlan had visited ninth-grade history classes with the school's guidance counselor, David Kosoff, to recruit students for AVID. "Raise your hands if you would like to go to a four-year college," Quinlan said. Many students did so. "How many of you feel you are disorganized and that you need a structure that will help you improve your grades, that will help your performance in class?" Many hands went up. "If you feel frustrated with school, raise your hands." Many acknowledged they felt that way. "We've got the program for you," he said, and showed the *60 Minutes II* video.

He was disheartened to find that some students he thought were perfect for the program were difficult to persuade. Akila, one of the first students he asked, said, "I'm not going to college. I'm not going anywhere. I don't want no AVID. It's not for me. No thank you."

"You really need to do this," Quinlan said. He could see, behind her dismissive attitude, a brilliant writer. She had much more than just singing talent. But she had no structure in her academic life. She didn't know how to organize her time or her work. "Don't give me that, Akila," he said. "You are going to college. You have already told me you are into fashion, that you want to go to the Fashion Institute of Technology or you want to do law. So you need to do AVID." He called her mother. "We have this new program," he said. "It will be great for her." The next day Akila grudgingly gave him a completed application.

Zaivon, a student with learning disabilities, presented a different challenge. AVID was looking for average students with grade-point averages between 65 and 80 percent. A student scoring in the 90s did not have as great a need for AVID's tutoring and time management lessons. A student scoring in the 50s usually lacked motivation and for the moment was beyond AVID's reach. Such students often acted out in class, wasting instructional time that the other AVID students needed. Zaivon's grade-point average was 55. Quinlan thought he would be a poor risk for the program. The student was disengaged and on the brink of dropping out. He was a poor writer and regularly disrupted his classes.

But when Quinlan was recruiting tenth graders for the eleventh-grade elective class, Zaivon came to him and asked to join. "Why do you want to join AVID?" Quinlan asked.

"I think it would really help me," Zaivon said. Even significantly delayed students were susceptible to natural maturation processes, Quinlan knew. They would suddenly begin thinking about their futures. That didn't mean that Zaivon was right for AVID. But his disability seemed manageable if he was given extended time to complete assignments and tests. "So," Quinlan said, "please come back tomorrow with a writing sample saying why you want to be in AVID."

Quinlan would never forget what the student handed him the next day. "I believe that you probably don't think I am serious and you have doubts about me," his writing sample said, "but trust me, if I am given a chance, I will excel." The kid had read his mind, Quinlan thought. How did he do that? Almost all the words were spelled correctly. Zaivon was in.

Teaching Honors Like AVID and Getting Real Results

In the first year of the program, Quinlan taught the tenth-grade AVID elective and two sections of tenth-grade Global History reserved for AVID students. He also had two more Global History sections for non-AVID students, one of those labeled an honors-level course. Such distinctions were required in the New York City schools, but the Brooklyn Arts AVID teachers ignored them. He taught all five sections as if they were AVID classes. All of his students had to take Cornell notes. They all had binders. If he picked one up, shook it, and saw papers fall out, that was a grade of zero for that binder check.

Students quickly noticed. A Global History tenth grader named Malcolm asked Quinlan in class, "Hey Mr. Q, why are you teaching us like you teach the AVID class?"

"Well," Quinlan said, "their grades are going up, and your grades are going up, so let's just roll with it." They bought it. The honors class ate it up. They did Cornell notes and binders as if those unusual features were one of the privileges of being in honors. "The class was not called AVID," Quinlan recalled. "I didn't care. I was teaching it as AVID."

This led the next year to Quinlan's teaching AP World History to eleventh graders, and pulling as many AVID students into that course as he could. In 2011, he had only eight students in AP World History and fourteen in AP English Literature and Composition. In 2012, he had 150 students apply for AP World History.

Teaching students how to criticize in an academic way, a difficult part of AP, was encouraged by the AVID Philosophical Chairs approach. "You have the kids come in and you give them a thought-provoking article," Quinlan said. "The students evaluate the article and come up with questions, and take a side. A generic example might be smoking in restaurants or abortion."

Those for the proposition would stand on one side of the room, those against on the other. "If you wanted to say something against it or for it," Quinlan said, "you had to cite the article, give the name of the peer you are responding to, say what the peer said, and then say why you agree or disagree. If you change your mind, you simply get up and change sides. It is like musical chairs, but with a rigorous article instead of a tune."

After the discussion, the students had to write a reflection paper. What had they learned? They had to cite two peers and cite their own thesis and use excerpts from the article as well.

At the beginning, Quinlan wondered how this would work when it came time for his Global History students to take the citywide final exam. It was a test written by experts. Quinlan had no influence over how difficult the questions might be. In the past, the school's passing rate had been abysmal, often under 50 percent.

Quinlan allowed himself to hope for better when he saw his students celebrating as they left the exam. One of the essay questions had asked them to describe two individuals in global history and tell what impact they had had on their society. "In previous years our city kids tended to pick people like Martin Luther King Jr., which was erroneous since the test specifically said not to use examples from US history," Quinlan recalled. But in 2009, after the first year of AVID at Brooklyn Arts, they were citing Martin Luther or Gutenberg or Gandhi or Stalin.

The school's teachers graded the exams. The team handling Global History gathered after school and entered the scores as they worked their way through each answer sheet. They didn't think about the overall result until one teacher, looking at the scores on the spreadsheet, said: "Holy shit." One of his students had gotten an 88, another a 95. There were two 99s. This had not happened before. His two-word exclamation was repeated several times as other teachers scanned the sheet and saw the scores of kids they knew well. All ten of Quinlan's students with learning disabilities had passed the exam. Akila, the girl who had tried to avoid AVID, got a 98.

The class average for Quinlan's AVID students was 95. The non-AVID class got 90 percent. Close to tears, Quinlan put the results in his pocket and waited for his students to stop by for their report cards. He loved the looks on their faces as he delivered the news. "You got a 96!" "You got a 97!"

Eventually Quinlan became the AVID coordinator. The principal's plan to AVIDize the school proceeded. By 2012, nearly half of the faculty had attended a Summer Institute or other AVID training. Conversations around the school were full of AVID jargon. Quinlan began to think of ways to extend the program to the ninth grade, even with the troublesome admission system. "I want AVID to permeate all corners of the building because it has become the building block for AP," he said. "Then we can better prepare our students for more rigorous courses and colleges. My students embraced AVID as a means of academic and socioemotional improvement."

Such change was hard to implement, Quinlan acknowledged, but it was working. "Three years ago when we started, I bought into it even when I didn't know what it was," he said. "Now it is a mindset, and pays tremendous dividends."

LOOKING FOR MORE MR. SEARCYS

Granger Ward, later to be one of AVID's national leaders, would have qualified to be an AVID student when he was in high school if the program had existed then. He was bright, poor, and confused. It took him a decade after high school before he discovered how smart and capable he was. He was one more example of what happens in American school systems that don't recognize their students' potential.

SEEING AND SURFACING UNTAPPED POTENTIAL

Ward was born in 1953 in Manhattan to Jamaican parents. His father was an alcoholic who never held a steady job. His mother was a postal worker. When he was eight, either through inattention or poor training, an enrollment staffer at a school he had just transferred to in the Bronx concluded after a five-minute test that Ward couldn't read. A teacher eventually saw that was wrong and moved him to a top class. But he still didn't learn much.

His junior high honors class of thirty-six students was heavily Jewish. The teacher tried to push all of them to greater achievement, but Ward was shy and unmotivated, and he did barely enough to get by. He liked reading on his own. He developed a passionate interest in birds. He would wander down to the Bronx River or take the subway to Central Park to see if he could spot interesting species. School to him was a chore.

He had dreams of being a pilot because his father, who sometimes wore a bomber jacket, had served in the Royal Air Force during World War II. Ward applied and was admitted to Aviation High School, an hour subway ride to Long Island City. It was a huge boys' school. He learned to handle rivets and sheet metal and do some math and physics, but as usual he didn't work very hard or think much about the future.

Then he met an English teacher named Roland Searcy. "He forced me to apply to college," Ward recalled. He did not take the SAT, but

Searcy knew his grades would get him in as long as he had at least one extracurricular activity. The teacher told the very shy student to sign up for the school speech competition.

"I told him absolutely not because I don't speak in public," Ward recalled. "He called home and talked to my mom, and I was in the competition." As AVID teachers would do years later, Searcy saw potential that Ward wasn't living up to. He could write well in English class, but he couldn't bring himself to stand up and talk to people. Force was necessary. Ward's topic in the contest was Martin Luther King Jr.'s "I Have a Dream" speech. His heart was pounding in his chest. He thought he would fall apart. Instead, he won.

Searcy, one of only two black teachers at the school, appeared to be the only person at Aviation High who thought the withdrawn son of Jamaican parents could handle higher education. When, on Searcy's orders, Ward went to his white counselor to seek advice on the best colleges for him, the man said: "Don't bother applying. You'll never get in."

Searcy did not give up. He called Ward's mother frequently to make sure the college application paperwork was getting done. Ward's interest in birds and biology led him to apply to just one school, the State University of New York (SUNY) College of Environmental Science and Forestry, a little-known campus in Syracuse. He had no idea what he was getting into. College was alien territory. He planned to major in biochemistry, but had never taken a biology course because Aviation High didn't offer one. He had never taken an AP course.

His reaction to the move from his mom's apartment to a dorm in Syracuse and a college full of strange people was "complete and total shock," Ward recalled. He tried to get home every other weekend at least, hitchhiking or taking buses. The academic demands "hit me like a brick wall," he said. Organic chemistry his sophomore year almost killed him. "I was shattered," he recalled. "I didn't know how to study. I was on academic probation and stopped going to class. At the beginning of second semester sophomore year, I realized I was in way too deep."

FROM DROPOUT TO SUPERINTENDENT

He remembered that time vividly when years later he got involved in AVID and saw the power of regular tutoring and academic advising. There was no support for him at the SUNY campus. "They suggested I study harder and go to the library," he recalled. "Tutorials and organized study groups didn't exist then." Halfway through sophomore year, he quit. It would be a decade before he got back on track.

He applied for work at a Syracuse hospital. They said he was overqualified, but gave him a job as an operating room orderly, prepping patients and cleaning up the mess after surgery. He did part-time work as a radio DJ. He met a young woman attending law school who liked his show. He began seeing her regularly. She suggested they move to Albuquerque. There he got odd jobs—security guard, newspaper deliveryman, and eventually heavy equipment operator. They married and had two daughters. His wife was working for legal services. She did not pressure him to go back to school, but he began to see that doing so might be a good idea. He took the 3-p.m.-to-midnight swing shift at work so that he could take a few biology courses at the University of New Mexico, not certain what he would do with them.

His wife persuaded him to move back to Syracuse to be nearer her family. He looked for jobs in steel plants, but the industry was in trouble. A former SUNY professor recognized him at a supermarket and encouraged him to go back and finish his degree. He was older and wiser. He felt he could do it, so he went full-time and finished in eighteen months. He worked summers in wildlife refuges. He liked explaining animal behavior to young visitors, so with his biology degree he got a teaching job in the Syracuse city schools.

Very soon he realized he had found his calling. For fourteen years, he was a teacher and then administrator in Syracuse. His first job was at Washington Irving, a last-chance alternative high school for students with discipline problems. His students were mostly black males. He loved the challenge. His biology classes were full of eye-catching if somewhat gruesome exhibits that appealed to boys, like taxidermied animals and road kill. He had to be a tough disciplinarian. His memories of what Roland Searcy and his mother had done for him inspired his firmness. He also had the advantage of being a husband and father who had seen much of the world, knew what the job market was like, and had been a union steward.

He taught six classes a day. The principal was smart and encouraging. He let Ward occasionally run the school for him when he was away. Ward got to know the district superintendent, Lionel "Skip" Meno, who took him into the central office, gave him research projects, and made him the district's liaison with the state government in Albany. Ward earned his administrative credential and became principal of Corcoran High School, a socioeconomically diverse collection of black and white kids. He was transferred to another school with similar discipline problems. He managed to bring it under control with his calm, strong approach to kids and parents.

In 1996, New York City schools chancellor Rudy Crew hired Ward to be the superintendent of Manhattan's forty-nine high schools. Ward learned how to handle many problems at once. Then he took a job on the other side of the country as superintendent of the Grossmont district, twenty-five thousand students in eastern San Diego County.

It was 1999. AVID had been in existence for nineteen years, but Ward had never heard of it. It was not yet well known on the East Coast, but was widespread in San Diego County. Ward introduced himself to his new district by wandering its classrooms at random. In one ninth-grade room, he found a teacher supervising a band of college students who were conducting tutorials where the high school students, not the teacher or the tutors, did most of the talking.

The teacher gave Ward a brief introduction to the program. Ward the New Yorker pronounced its name with a long *a*, as in *aphid*, rather than with the correct short *a* as in the English word for enthusiastic. The teacher said, "Ask the kids how many are going to college." The room was mostly Hispanic and black students. Ward did as he was told. Every hand in the room went up. "I really didn't believe it," he recalled. He remembered his counselor not thinking he could go to college. It was too much of a stretch, he thought, for every child in that room to have that dream.

But as he kept bumping into the program, he decided to investigate it. "I saw an engagement with kids and an enthusiasm among kids and teachers, and I frankly said to myself, 'So what? I am glad they are happy, but what are the results?'" One AVID teacher told him that 90 percent of her students the year before had been accepted into college. Ward was dubious. The teacher said that that was also the percentage of her AVID kids who went to college the year before that and the year before that.

THE AVID PUSH: A SYSTEM AND STRUCTURE FOR SUCCESS

An AVID activist heard that the new superintendent had been asking questions. That teacher and a group of other AVID partisans asked for a meeting. Ward said he could give them thirty minutes. "Two hours later, they had me convinced," he said. "You sense the emotion, but they also brought the data. They said here is how the structure works, here is how we support the kids, here is how we do the training. It really hit me that this is the thing that I have been looking for. I wished I had known about it as a principal and a superintendent back in Syracuse and New York City because it has substance to it; it has structure to it. Mr. Searcy saved my life, but I was only one kid, and here was something touching thousands of kids, with the same kind of impact and effort."

He told his visitors a bit of his story. "This is what we need," he said. "This is the kind of systematic approach to helping lots of kids because there are many kids as smart as I was who never had Mr. Searcy. And they didn't get that push."

"So what are you going to do, Mr. Ward?" one asked.

"We are going to make this bigger and better than it is."

He found that the principals of Grossmont's eleven high schools were split on the subject. "I had some saying, 'I would love to do this. How do I get the money to do it?' Others were going, 'Well, I don't know why we need to expand this. What's the point?'"

It was no surprise to him that there were so many barriers to students, even affluent white students, getting into top-level courses. If educators believed, as many did, that their schools were there to help only a select group preordained to go to college, with maybe one or two lightning-bolt low-income minority exceptions, then those were the kids you supported, and the other 90 percent you forgot. As some of those high school principals said, what's the point?

To principals who said they didn't want to do AVID, Ward's answer was "That's not an option here." Getting more students into rigorous courses, prepared to succeed, was nonnegotiable. He published a set of metrics that every school had to meet: more rigor, more students participating in rigorous courses, more students succeeding in rigorous courses. "If any of you can show me something that has the same impact," he said to his principals, "you can go ahead and do it. I will not bother you again."

None had an alternative in mind. They all went with AVID, grudgingly in some cases. The district was getting millions of dollars in federal money under the Elementary and Secondary Education Act to help low-income students, but "we were basically throwing it away into remedial courses," Ward said. "We were doing nothing for kids who mostly did not graduate because we gave them fourth-grade work. We needed to put our dollars into things that would have an impact." Ward noticed in a data report that only 3 percent of Grossmont secondary school students were in AVID. "I said, wait a second. That's not the middle. We have way more kids than that in the middle."

He visited a high school on a day in spring when 150 AVID students from the local middle school were visiting the campus where they would be ninth graders. "This is great," Ward said to the high school principal.

"Well, we have just one AVID section for thirty of them," the principal replied.

Ward didn't react right away. It was no good to lash out at principals without thinking first. What he thought was, *We have 150 kids on their way in the right direction, with a college focus, and we're going to cut that down to 30?* He began to cut deals with principals: "I will put up money for a section of AVID if you will do the same, and if you do more, I will add more."

The results were obvious to Ward. "Over four years, we were able to increase AP enrollment and test-taking by almost 100 percent," he said. "We were able to diversify the classes. When I could walk into an AP class that reflected the demographics of the school, that was when I knew we were really winning. In fact, we went up in average AP score, from 3.7 to 4.1 . . . I had AP teachers who said four years before, 'Don't you dare put those kids in my class,' and now they asked, 'How do I get more of them, the AVID kids? They take notes. They do the work. They make the whole class better.'"

When Grossmont voters elected a school board not of Ward's liking, he accepted an offer to be AVID's California director. He later became executive vice president supervising all AVID divisions worldwide. Granger Ward, the obvious AVID candidate who never got to be in AVID, had finally reached a place of power and influence he had always had the talent for. He wanted to make sure that the thousands of children who had the same disadvantages he had had would not have to spend so many years overcoming them.

STRUGGLES OF AN AVERAGE
AVID PROGRAM

Rebecca Farley graduated from Foothill High School in Bakersfield, California, in 1993. She was one of the few students to go for the International Baccalaureate (IB) diploma at the sprawling school in a dusty, low-income part of town. She pursued her education at UCLA and Claremont Graduate University, then returned to Foothill in 2000 to teach English.

When she had attended the school, it had had many impoverished students. Some IB students could not afford the exam fees, so Farley and other students had helped sell spaghetti dinner tickets to raise the money. By the time she returned as a teacher, the number of low-income students was even greater, 85 percent. Eighty percent of the students were Hispanic. Setting high academic goals for students whose parents did not speak English well and never finished high school was a struggle.

When Farley was a student, the IB program was like a club. Only students whose parents were strongly committed to college and could afford the test fees were likely to be steady performers. When Farley returned to teach, that began to change. Some Foothill High faculty wanted the IB program dropped as too elitist, but the school went the other way. Like many other California school systems in the 1990s, Bakersfield adopted AVID and its college readiness focus. That meant it had to expand the IB program so that students could have the rigor in their courses that the AVID classes were designed to prepare them for.

Farley proved to be an extraordinarily energetic teacher. By 2005, she was serving as both the IB coordinator and the AVID coordinator for the school. Despite its heavy load of students in poverty, the campus was well maintained, with a central quad of concrete and grass with a few willow trees. The Foothill principal, Brenda Lewis, told visitors that Farley had saved IB. It became strong enough to avoid cutbacks when the recession of 2008 and 2009 hit school districts with deficits. It became what could be described as a typical AVID program, not at the top of the mark like Bell Gardens but somewhere in the middle, with weaknesses, such as inexperienced teachers, but also with measured improvement in student outcomes and college preparation.

CHALLENGES WITH STAFFING AND TURNOVER

By 2013, the Bakersfield district had eighteen comprehensive high schools, twelve with AVID. Ten of those AVID programs had been in existence since the 1990s, with two added more recently. One of the high schools, East, was an AVID National Demonstration School. Foothill was not yet at that level. In 2013, both AVID and IB at the school were improving, but Farley had to deal with the loss of some of her best teachers.

She had four AVID elective classes, two in the ninth grade, one for sophomores, and one for juniors and seniors. Farley taught the AVID elective for eleventh and twelfth grades. She had had a strong team of four AVID teachers, including herself, for eight years. But three of her teammates had been promoted to jobs in the district office. That left her with just one veteran AVID teacher (herself), plus one teacher with three years of AVID experience, one with two years, and one brand-new AVID teacher in the 2012–2013 school year.

The rookie on the team was Mike Biezad. He had a difficult assignment. "Your first year with AVID, you feel you really don't know what you are doing at all," Farley said. "There are so many things AVID is asking you to do, and you have so many goals and objectives." Biezad taught his first year of AVID without having attended a summer institute. He got that training in Sacramento before he began his second year.

Dealing with the ninth graders, as Biezad did, was particularly challenging. "When I taught AVID 9, I did it for eight years, and I was always overenrolling that class," Farley said. "I would try to get as close to forty as I could, thinking that the students were not always aware of what they were getting into, and I would always lose a few because they thought it was too much work. The Cornell notes—some would say, 'I don't want to do that!' Whatever it was, there would be some attrition."

She eventually split the large group of ninth graders into two sections, but sensed that she might be losing more ninth graders than usual. "We have been having discussions about how we can adjust that, and we are also talking about going back to the one ninth-grade section for budget reasons next year. We can have that one section and really work on our strategies," she said.

At the same time, she said, the quality of the tutoring had improved markedly. For years, Farley had to make do with peer tutors, advanced Foothill students who handled the sessions every Tuesday and Thursday. Many of them were juniors and seniors in the IB program. Neither Farley nor her AVID supervisors liked that option, but they were unable to lure students from California State University, Bakersfield in the west side of the city to Foothill in the east. It was also a strain on the IB students to add the tutoring job to their own demanding studies.

In 2012, Farley and Lewis managed to secure state funds to raise the tutoring budget. They could offer college recruits extra duties, such as tutoring math students after school, so that they would earn enough to make it worth their while to make the long drive. They were guaranteed thirty hours a week at $15 an hour.

To buttress the college tutors, Farley persuaded some classroom teachers, particularly in math and science, to come to her large classroom and help either during tutoring periods or during the morning snack break. The classroom teachers were paid extra for that time, at substitute teacher rates. Farley also used the popular Kahn Academy website to augment tutoring in math, which, as for most AVID programs, was the toughest subject for Foothill students.

ADJUSTMENT PROBLEMS: CONVINCING STUDENTS AVID IS WORTH THE TROUBLE

That did not ease Farley's greatest problem: convincing students new to the program that AVID was worth the extra time and work. She laid out the enrichment and assistance they would get if they stuck with AVID. She did not have the advantage of AVID programs in the two middle schools that fed into Foothill. An AVID middle school once sent students to Foothill, but the enrollment boundaries had changed. "Things were different when we had twenty kids a year coming from that middle school with dynamite preparation and we could start planning for college and doing research projects and hit the ground running, but now at the beginning of the year we get, 'You want to do what?'" Farley said.

Freshmen who enrolled in AVID had an adjustment problem. "Everything is a shock to them when they get here," Farley said, "and AVID is a very different mode from preparing for state multiple-choice tests, getting down to an *a, b, c,* or *d* answer. AVID is hard. That is not the type of testing that we are training them to respond to."

The primary intake event was a spring showcase at the high school. Eighth graders and their parents were invited to sample special academic programs and activities, including AVID. Farley had AVID students answer questions from the eighth graders while she talked to parents. When she found students who were interested, she sent them to a table where AVID students conducted interviews. They sought contact information. They demonstrated by their own conduct that this was an important program with articulate students.

Farley encouraged new recruits to take Health, an undemanding freshman course required for graduation, in summer school before ninth grade so that they would have an opening in their schedule for the AVID elective class. In the second week of summer school, Farley organized an ice cream social for incoming AVID ninth graders so that they would feel comfortable with what would be happening in the fall.

Farley generally followed the rule that students with college-educated parents were not eligible for AVID, but there were exceptions. If a parent came in and made a case for a student, Farley might say OK. "We have had two sisters who made it through our process," she said. "One is a junior at Foothill, and one is in junior college. The mother came to us—she was also an educator—and said, 'My girls need this support. Will you please put them in your program?' She has been an advocate for our program and her girls have done well, although she was right. They did need that support, that extra encouragement."

By the same token, Farley subscribed to the AVID policy that the lowest-achieving students were likely to be overwhelmed by the challenging courses. "Let's say a ninth grader is scheduled to go into Foundations of Math. That is a remedial course three levels below algebra. At that point we generally say the AVID elective is not a good idea for that student," she said. But she would accept some low-scoring English language learners if they were motivated to build their language skills so they could succeed in advanced courses. "We don't want them to get behind," she said, but if their level is too low, "they are not likely to be considered."

The path to completing the A through G requirements, the honors courses state universities required of applicants, began in ninth grade. All AVID students enrolled in what Foothill and many other California schools called English GATE, a course for gifted and talented students. GATE used to be just for students who scored above a certain level on an IQ test in elementary school, but that approach overlooked so many children ready for advanced courses that the rules faded away. Other advanced courses at Foothill were labeled college prep. AVID students were assigned to them also.

Farley, as both IB and AVID coordinator, struggled with the failure to get more students achieving the IB diploma, which required good grades on six IB exams, a four-thousand-word research paper called the extended essay, and a "Theory of Knowledge" essay. In 2012, only seven students got the IB diploma, an honor in addition to the school diploma that all IB seniors in AVID received. Farley was particularly bothered by the poor record of boys in IB. "We just had a deadline for the extended essay and Theory of Knowledge paper," she said. "We had four young men who declared in November they would be diploma candidates, but they did not turn in those last two pieces to complete their diploma candidacy, so we have just three males left. Of the twelve students attempting the diploma this year, only three are males, and two of those males are AVID students."

UNDERMINING RESISTANCE TO HARD WORK

Joan Herman's counseling duties at Foothill included AVID students. She spent much of her time undermining their resistance to hard work. She emphasized the difference between getting to college with AVID and getting to college on their own. "Sure," she said to them, "you have college prep courses to prepare for college, but college is a huge leap. It is sink or swim. They treat you like adults. You are on your own to get the resources and help that you need, whereas if you are in AVID, you get that support."

She did not mention it directly, but most of those students lacked parents with college backgrounds who could help their children adjust to more challenging programs. "With AVID having a built-in tutorial, and intervention for all its students, we have the structure they need," Herman said. "We talk about the interventions we have and how AVID provides them in the classroom as well as after school or at lunch, if they need it." The new money to pay college student tutors was crucial to meeting that promise. "I describe it as a safety net, that is what AVID is, a safety net to give them all the tools they need, and catch them earlier. The binder checks and everything else happen on a schedule so they cannot get too far behind without somebody knowing and saying, 'OK, you need the tutoring.'

"When I explain the long-term benefit, there is rarely a pushback," she said. But demands like the extended essay, rare even in affluent US high schools, were so daunting that Foothill AVID students, despite regular encouragement, often didn't go all the way to the IB diploma. The IB teachers couldn't be too hard on those who dropped the essay, as AP students in other schools also didn't have such long writing assignments. The students who opted out of getting the diploma were still enrolled in IB courses. They would look just as good to colleges as students taking the same number of AP courses.

Students who tried to leave the AVID program altogether were treated more sternly, Herman said. "We will not let them out without parent permission," she said. "They should know what their children are taking. Sometimes the students want out because they want to take it easy, just coast." If the parents said no to leaving AVID, the teachers had more influence with that student, particularly in the Hispanic neighborhoods that surrounded Foothill. "AVID has a feeling of a community in the midst of a larger community," Herman said.

There was a pecking order of Bakersfield AVID schools. In a school of 2,000 students, only 120 Foothill students were in AVID. That was fewer than in AVID National Demonstration Schools like East High, yet better than the 80 percent of US high schools that didn't have AVID at all.

It was the same with IB. "I serve on the board of the California Association of World IB Schools," Farley said, "and there is a bit of a stigma. Some schools will say, 'Well, we locked in a hundred diplomas last year,' and they will ask me, 'Rebecca, how will you do?' and I will say, 'Well, we had seven, but we had 194 kids signed up to take at least one IB exam, and I am so proud of that.'"

Farley recalled her initial contact with the state's GATE program, which had its own pecking order. "At one point I was our GATE coordinator and went to the district meetings, where each of the coordinators would receive their list of all the kids who would qualify based on their test scores. I would see reams of papers piled in front of them, then they would bring me one sheet of paper that had eleven names on it, and I would think, 'Oh goodness.'"

Discontent with gifted designations grew so much in California that the Foothill faculty was allowed to put anyone they wanted in a GATE class. "Maybe they don't test very well, but it doesn't mean they are not talented," Farley said. Principal Brenda Lewis said, "When you look at our college prep kids, you have a wide range of abilities even there, so we are constantly raising the bar for our kids beyond the expectations they come to us with. They don't have to be designated GATE to be in a GATE class. We never say never. If a student is willing to challenge himself, that will do it. It is never a drawback to having them challenge themselves. Ramp up the rigor, we call it."

That created a divide between students in the highest-level classes like GATE and IB who were in AVID and those who were not. "Many of our kids are in GATE classes but not in AVID," Farley said. "They have been able to skate on just listening to the teacher and making mental notes of a few things. They haven't had to develop the study skills. Our AVID kids, even though they might not need them so much just yet, are much more ready for college."

"AVID is like boot camp," Farley said. "You do something over and over again because when you need it, you don't want to have to think about it. It must be second nature to you. We come to the first day of IB Physics and everyone's panicking, and have no idea what Mr. Halbur is talking about. The AVID kids know how to make a study group. They know how to ask each other questions. They know how to go to out-side sources. So they emerge as leaders. That is why 80 percent of the IB diploma kids last year were AVID kids."

By Lewis's reckoning, about half of the student body would qualify for AVID if she had that much money to support the program. Funds have been tight, the principal said, "so we have to be very creative. We may not be able to grow the program right away, but my goal is to be able to sustain it for now, to sustain what we have and not lose out."

This meant that Farley and the other AVID teachers had to focus on how well the new college student tutors were engaging their students. Alexander Salem, a twenty-three-year-old Cal State Bakersfield student, had a short beard and dark hair swept back. He wore dark slacks, a red polo shirt, a brown jacket, and Oxford shoes. The student he was tutoring before school wore a blue-and-gray-striped polo shirt, jeans, and sneakers. Salem asked many questions, trying to nudge the student past his trouble spots in math.

Salem: The first thing, what kind of information do you have at this point? This is going to be in what format?

Student: Fractions, percentages.

Salem: This is to examine probability. *(He opened a calculus book. He took out an iPad and wrote an equation with his finger, using an application that turned the screen into a blackboard.)* So you would do what?

Student: Divide the 3 by the 2.

Salem: And get what? *(He put more marks on the iPad blackboard.)* If I was to say, what is the other part that gives me 1.0, what would it be?

Student: Repeating decimals.

Salem: It is $4\frac{1}{3}$ here. What would be the probability of it being incorrect? . . . Are these two numbers as they play out similar to this example? . . . The first step is to do what? That gives you the probability. What did they do over here?

Three tutors including Salem had arrived at 6:50 a.m. in Farley's classroom. It was zero period, a time before school that teachers used to stretch the day to accommodate all they wanted to do. Farley used zero period for extra tutoring, counseling, and announcements. Her room, C-9, was twice the size of a normal Foothill High classroom, as it was the center of both her IB and AVID activities. Across one long wall in large letters was posted "Foothill High School: An International Baccalaureate World School." A back wall had the word "AVID" in large letters. The room had sixty standard desk-and-chair sets, some in rows and some pulled together in groups.

Tony, another tutor, wore glasses, a black T-shirt covered by a black hoodie, black slacks, and tan moccasins. Around his neck was a blue-and-yellow CSU Bakersfield ID band. He said to the early-arriving students: "Now that there are two of you, you can slap down questions for each other." They were struggling with a math assignment. He was there to help, but they were going to have to ask each other questions, too, as they would do later at the regular tutorial sessions.

Tony had a 24-by-12-inch whiteboard. Left-handed, he began to write with a red marker a question from the assignment: "Following off the graph, discuss what kind of function models can be used to make model behavior of the graph."

"This correlation has the ability to deviate," Tony said. "Did he specify?"

"He didn't explain what he meant," one student said.

Tony asked the student to do his best and address the question anyway.

"Maybe find the linear function?" the student said tentatively.

"What are your ideas?" Tony said.

"Estimate from the line and then plug in." He made a note on a sheet of AVID paper of what he intended to do. Tony wrote down the formulas from the assignment, a problem dealing with high-jump heights and world records. "If you guys are doing scatterplots . . . " he said, and stopped talking to see if the students would finish his thought.

"Like try to get the line that is closest, try to get the point that is closest?" one said.

More students came into the classroom, some checking computers while others sketched problems on whiteboards. Farley said, "Take a moment or two to finish the question that you are on." A minute later the bell rang. It was 7:24 a.m. More students arrived. A second bell rang at 7:27 a.m.

COLLEGE ACCEPTANCE: FINDING THE RIGHT FIT

Farley addressed the group in a happy tone. "Out of fifty-six thousand applicants to UC Davis, six Foothill students have been chosen. I don't want to be sexist at all, but this is girl power." There were applause and cheers. She recognized five female students in the room who had been accepted at the UC campus, a major achievement at a high school that sent most college-bound students either to community colleges or to one of the California State University campuses. The University of California campus at Davis would not be something to brag about at an affluent high school in West Los Angeles, but at Foothill it was the equivalent of Yale or Princeton.

One of the UC Davis admits piped up: "I got another one yesterday from San Diego [UCSD]." This brought more applause.

"UC Davis offers an opportunity to visit the campus," Farley told the class. "It is free to you, but you have to sign up. If you don't feel at ease at your college, you won't do as well." She recalled how much she preferred the intimate Claremont College campus, where she went to graduate school, to UCLA, where she was an undergraduate. "You have to send in your registration by May 1, so you have just a little time to decide what to do." She recommended that they try to stay with a friend, or a friend of a friend, on campus to get a sense of college life at night.

Another bell rang. "Zero period family, thank you very much," she said. "We'll see you tomorrow."

On a magnetized board hanging behind Farley's desk were the names of the twenty-six AVID students in the senior class, seventeen girls and nine boys, a 65-35 ratio typical of US high school programs that raise achievement of minorities and low-income students. There were columns labeled "Cal State," "UCs," and "Private schools." Alongside each student's name, magnetized tags had been attached with the names of the schools that had admitted them so far. If the tag was upside down, that meant word had not come yet.

A senior named Veronica, one of Farley's stars, had a big haul: her tags said CSUB (Cal State Bakersfield), CSULB (Long Beach), San Jose (San Jose State), CSULA (Cal State Los Angeles), UCI (UC Irvine), and UCD (Davis). Still upside down were the two most selective public universities in the state, UCB (UC Berkeley) and UCLA (Los Angeles). Jason D. had gotten into Cal State Bakersfield and UC Merced, but six other schools were still upside down—Cal Poly San Luis Obispo, San Diego State, San Jose State, UC Santa Barbara, UC Irvine, and UC San Diego. One of Foothill's academic stars, Jessica T., had been admitted to several schools but was still waiting for USC and Stanford, competitive private campuses that few Foothill students dared apply to. They needed the kind of top grades and scores that won not only acceptance letters but big financial awards.

Farley's next class was for AVID seniors. Fourteen were in the room. Not all of that group could make the class because it conflicted with an IB course or other classes crucial to their transcripts. Farley stuck to AVID basics. "We will have a binder check tomorrow," she said. "Anyone talk to Olivia yesterday? She was very sick. No one? I'll call her mom today and check on her."

She repeated the UC Davis announcement. "We are still waiting for UCLA and Berkeley," she said. "Remember, they send the notification on a rolling announcement schedule, so if you did not get it by the first announcement, that does not mean you did not get in. If you have not heard from a Cal State, you should contact them. You may have missed an email. Maybe you had a password problem and missed messages."

Several computer stations lined the left side of the classroom. The AVID and IB students could sign on to them and keep track of their college-related correspondence, as well as look for class assignments. Most of them had computers at home, but their machines sometimes broke down, and repairs were expensive.

"We want to see who offers you the most money," Farley said. "We also want to get you to those campuses to see what they feel like." If they had friends or relatives at schools that had accepted them, she said, "this is a great time to send them a text. 'Hey, I have just been accepted at your school. I wonder if I could come up and visit your school, take a tour, maybe stay with you?'"

It was tutoring day. She asked what subjects needed assistance. They were calculus, math analysis, algebra, English, and biology. Bailey Torres, one of the tutors from Cal State Bakersfield, worked with students trying to decipher seventeenth-century English poet John Donne's "A Hymn to God the Father." She said, "We need to define the words we don't know."

One of the classroom teachers who tutored for AVID was working with a math group. He did not seem as comfortable with inquiry-based tutoring as the students from Cal State. "This is *not* going to be linear," he said, violating the rule against answering the question, "but that is a linear model you have there. Maybe you need to open your math analysis book and go back."

On the blackboard was Farley's weekly schedule for her senior class, AVID 12:

Monday—"The Other Wes Moore," chapters 2 and 3. [This was a book by a successful writer and speaker from the Baltimore ghetto about his correspondence with a prisoner who shared his name.]

Tuesday—tutorials

Wednesday—College readiness activity: "Deconstructing a textbook chapter."

Thursday—tutorials

Friday—Finance Friday [talk and exercises on paying for college] and two learning logs due. [In learning logs, students write reflections, in this case on "transferable skills."]

As the class period came to a close, Farley issued a series of reminders. Many of them referred to IAs, internal assessments, which were papers required in IB classes. "If you are in Calculus, make sure you get your internal assessment in today," she said. "Other IAs are in? Bio is done? History is done? I want to make sure you are not on my MIA list."

Her afternoon AVID class for juniors had twenty students in attendance, five of them boys. They were all in the front seats, unlike the classes for ninth and tenth graders, where the students gravitated to the back. "I am afraid we have lost our momentum today," she told the juniors. A FedEx truck had crashed into the back fence of the school during PE, a distraction that delayed some students in getting to class.

"Have you updated your planners and your homework assignments?" she asked. She mentioned the upcoming annual campus visit by eighth-grade students and parents interested in AVID. "We will be conducting interviews with the incoming freshmen," she said. The juniors she was talking to would be evaluating the possible AVID recruits. "You are quite discerning. You will be able to tell if the student is ready and willing. Remember, AVID is about individual determination, not the mother's determination."

A Friend, a Teacher, a Mentor

When Isaiah Moore enrolled at Warwick High School in 2002, he was scared. It was a big, noisy campus in what many considered the least desirable part of Newport News, Virginia. Michael Vick, the football star, had graduated from Warwick, but most of its alumni were not very successful in life. The standard of instruction was low. To Moore, trying to negotiate the school's crowded halls, there were too many people and too much disruption.

Warwick did, however, have an AVID program. Moore had been in AVID since sixth grade at Gildersleeve Middle School. His father was an apartment building maintenance man. He lived with his mother, who worked at a Walmart. Neither of his parents had gone to college. They did not talk much about his future. But one of his older sisters had been in AVID and went to Norfolk State. He remembered the big binder she had to take to school every day. The program helped him be a better student, although at Gildersleeve it did not conform to AVID standards. The AVID elective class was only fifteen minutes a day, little more than a place to have binder checks and quick reminders of how they should be handling their classes.

AVID as Guide and Protector

At Warwick High, he enrolled in his first regular AVID elective class. As the year progressed, Moore learned that the AVID program would not only guide him toward college but also protect him from the worst chaos at Warwick High. As an AVID student, he was automatically enrolled in advanced and honors classes for students who wanted very much to get an education. It made a difference.

His freshman year went fine. He had trouble keeping his binder straight, but he was learning something. On the first day of sophomore year, he saw some friends in the AVID class, but no teacher. A short man

161

walked into the room, rubbing his hands. He looked too young to be the teacher. One of Moore's friends said that out loud. Moore cringed, expecting the kind of harsh reply that was typical of Warwick faculty. But this teacher smiled at the attempt at humor. He replied with another joke. All of them relaxed.

The AVID teacher said his name was Sam Logan. His voice was firm and deep. He told them where he was from, some details of his life. Something in Logan's introductory talk stuck with Moore. The teacher said, "I'm a Morehouse man." He was proud of being an alumnus of the college that had educated Martin Luther King Jr., Spike Lee, Samuel Jackson, Edwin Moses, Maynard Jackson, and several other prominent African American men. Fifteen-year-old Moore knew nothing about Morehouse, but the more time he spent with Logan, the more he liked the idea of attending that man's college.

There were many jokes that first day. Logan teased his students as they teased each other. He noted that Moore's friend Cal Rivera had such a full head of hair that his forehead looked small. Moore himself, the teacher said, had a very big head. After the bell rang, Moore got another taste of Logan's method. He stopped the boy and smiled. "You're funny," he said to Moore. "You're also smart. I can tell because you are witty. What do you want to do with your life?"

"I don't know," Moore said. "I haven't really thought about it." Years later he realized he had been stuck in the middle of the adolescent spectrum. He wasn't a good kid. He wasn't a bad kid. He could be pulled either way, and on some occasions was. He didn't know where he was going. He was just there.

Logan smiled. "Man, you're smart," he said. "You could be anything you wanted to be."

Moore headed for his next class feeling different about his future. "From that day on," he said years later, "I knew I had a friend, a teacher, a mentor, someone I could confide in and believe in and someone who could push me as well." Henceforth he always looked forward to his class with Logan, who was also his AVID teacher in his junior year. The man was tough and principled and would not let students slack off. "I was harnessed to steel, so to speak," Moore said. There he learned what critical thinking was. Logan taught his students to question what was obvious to them.

The teacher asked one day, "What is the color of that board?"

"It's a blackboard," several students said.

"Why is it black, Isaiah?" Logan asked.

"What do you mean? It's black."

"Who says it's black? And why is black black? Couldn't black be blue?"

The discussion touched on the character of light and reflection, but Moore got the deeper meaning: he had to delve below the surface of things.

Logan was not only a teacher but a preacher, a man of the Bible. His lessons on speaking would be models for Moore, who would become both a teacher and a frequent public speaker. "We were told we couldn't say 'uh,'" Moore recalled. "He said rather than saying 'uh,' we should just pause. It sounds way better. Also, when you are speaking in front of people, you are often kind of in a fast-forward mode. You rushed. You mashed words together. He said everyone in the crowd is still in normal mode, so if you talk slowly, that will seem normal to them."

Logan had his students write a great deal, more than in some of the advanced classes. He emphasized vocabulary. He had them do quick essays from the tops of their heads on something they had just read or something that was happening in the community. The topic of college came up often. Morehouse was a theme. Moore was impressed with what Logan said about his alma mater, but Moore had a problem: "I didn't want to be in an all-male environment," he recalled. "I am not a player, but I did want to meet females. I wanted a social life."

In his other classes, he did well in some and not so well in others. He got an A in English and an A in World Geography. He was strong in the humanities because he was beginning to read a lot, pushed in that direction by Logan. He got a C in Chemistry. His Algebra II grade was a B. Logan pressured him to do better. Moore knew that he was in advanced classes because of AVID and was expected to do his best, but once Logan began watching him closely, he realized he was not giving it his all. He began to study harder.

FROM THE CLASSROOM TO THE REAL WORLD

Logan had more planned for Moore and his friends. They liked to sit in the teacher's room before and after school, or at lunch, just talking in the place they felt most comfortable. Early in their sophomore year, Logan interrupted their conversation. "No, you are not going to just be in here," he said. He made them join the Chrome Club, a gathering for future scientists. "We did fun things," Moore recalled. "The activities showed how math and science were applicable to the real world. We had Busch Gardens, the theme park in the area, so we went there and talked about the science of roller-coasters."

Also at Logan's urging Moore joined Key Club, which emphasized public service. There was talk of self-esteem and leadership. He joined the Male Membership Club and talked about what it meant to be a man.

By junior year, he was taking AP classes in English literature and psychology. There he learned how much difference a good teacher made. The AP Psychology teacher did not push her students very hard. She was the opposite of Logan. "I could get away with whatever I could get away with," Moore recalled. The AP English teacher was not like that. "She told me she thought I had the makings of a good student," he recalled. "I worked very hard in that class. Later, she attended one of my speaking engagements."

Not all teachers at the school were supportive of AVID, Moore recalled. Some would take the students' notebooks at the end of each class so that the AVID teacher would not be able to tell what they were doing. More important, Logan would not be able to identify what topics they were struggling with so that he could organize the tutors properly. It required delicate negotiations to get teachers to let the AVID students keep their notes in their binders.

When it came time to apply to college, Moore had many options in mind. There was Morehouse, of course. But he also applied to Hampton, Old Dominion, Howard, Virginia Commonwealth, Oklahoma Baptist University, William & Mary, University of North Carolina-Greenville, University of North Carolina-Chapel Hill, and Louisiana State University. He worked hard to prepare for the SAT and the ACT, and took both exams twice. This was rare for a Warwick High student. Many students didn't bother with the exams. They were either not going to college or going to a community college that did not require them.

On the reading and math portions of the SAT, Moore scored over 1000, which put him in the elite of students in US inner-city schools. His ACT score was in the high 20s, also better than average. That was enough to inspire mailings from scores of colleges looking for bright black applicants, particularly males. The top black students in American cities were usually girls. Banneker Academic High School in Washington DC, one of the few magnets made up almost entirely of black students, had long been about two-thirds female.

Another Morehouse man on the Warwick faculty, Diron Ford, recruited Moore for the debate and forensics team. Moore was good at debating. He learned much from the AVID Socratic Seminars and Philosophical Chairs that trained students to present their ideas and opinions in the most effective way.

With such a resume, Moore was a prize catch. Five colleges offered him admission: Morehouse, Hampton, Howard, Virginia Commonwealth, and Old Dominion. His family could not afford to send him to any of them, but the AVID teachers were prepared for that. Since junior year they had been teaching how to apply for scholarships. One of their students' assignments was to fill out and submit the applications. They had a list of likely scholarships. Each student was given a minimum amount of money they had to apply for, based on their personal financial circumstances. Moore learned to fill out the FAFSA form for college financial aid. For every application for money, he had to record the deadline for application, the date he had applied, and the date he expected to hear from each donor.

He hit the jackpot, a Dell Scholarship, one of the best in the country. It provided $20,000 a year, plus a laptop and a printer, essential tools for the modern college undergraduate, yet unaffordable for a student like Moore. He also received money from the Newport News Redevelopment Authority, Omega 55, the Kappas, and other groups.

He chose Morehouse. It was to him the most prestigious of the schools that accepted him. His mentors, Logan and Ford, were examples of the caring, effective men the college produced. He wanted to be like them.

Morehouse was in Atlanta, far from home. It was hard for Moore at first. He was forced to grow up. "They had so many naturally talented and gifted young men in one place, and it forced me to focus," he recalled. He gave top priority to his studies, as AVID had taught him to do. As happened with many AVID students when they arrived at college, he found that the high school emphasis on Cornell notes suddenly made sense. His freshman year grade-point average was only 2.3, but at the end of that first year, he knew what he had to do to improve. When he graduated in 2011, his GPA was better than a 3.0.

"AVID showed me that anything was possible," he said. He had been a disorganized student living in one of the most disadvantaged parts of his city. His mother made only $6,000 a year. Within a few years, he was a graduate of Morehouse, a teacher, and a public speaker. His options were limitless. He had been frightened of Warwick High School, but nothing scared him much anymore.

CHECKLIST FOR AVID GREATNESS

Kristi Drake was a veteran social studies teacher who served as AVID coordinator for Mount Vernon High School in northwest Washington State. She wore vacation garb, a T-shirt and shorts, as she passed out to her table of mostly younger colleagues the school's application to renew its status as an AVID National Demonstration School. They were proud of the designation. Only 2 percent of the forty-eight hundred AVID schools bore that label. But AVID wouldn't let them keep it unless they had the data. On a couple of points, Drake thought they were struggling.

EVALUATING PROGRESS AND ADHERENCE TO THE AVID ESSENTIALS

The application included a seven-page cover letter seeking answers to four questions: What evidence do you have of progress? How have you affected achievement? What are you most proud of? Where do you plan to improve? This was accompanied by a twenty-six-page Certification System form that asked how the school rated itself on AVID's 11 Essentials.

AVID's 11 Essentials in Brief

Essential 1: *Student Selection*
- Students in the middle with academic potential

Essential 2: *Voluntary Participation*
- Students and staff who choose to participate

Essential 3: *Full Implementation*
- Commitment by participants to fully implement all components

Essential 4: *Academic Rigor*
- Implementation of a rigorous course of study in AVID classes

Essential 5: *Strong, Relevant Writing and Reading Program*
- Rigorous writing and reading activities as a basis for instruction

---

Essential 6: *Inquiry as a Basis for Instruction*
- Inquiry as a basis for instruction leading to critical thinking

Essential 7: *Collaboration as a Basis for Instruction*
- Collaboration among all AVID stakeholders as a basis for instruction

Essential 8: *Tutorials led by AVID-Trained Tutors*
- AVID-trained tutors leading Socratic-method tutorials

Essential 9: *Use of AVID Center Data System*
- Analysis of all sorts of data to foster data-driven instruction

Essential 10: *Available Site/District Resources*
- Funding, curricular, and professional development support

Essential 11: *Active, Interdisciplinary Site Team*
- Collaboration to achieve student access in rigorous courses

It was a revealing document. It showed what AVID considered important and required a school to rate itself, before the AVID inspectors arrived, on its strengths and weaknesses. American schools rarely did this. As Drake; her principal, Rod Merrell; and five of their AVID teachers discussed the forms at a round table in their San Diego hotel conference room in August of 2013, the pressures of being a top AVID school emerged. This was their site-team meeting, one of thousands being conducted by AVID schools at summer institutes throughout the country. What might have seemed like a minor detail, whether their tutors were enrolled in college or had just graduated, turned out to be important in the assessment of which schools were doing their jobs and which weren't.

"We can't be a National Demonstration School without having 2s and 3s in all areas," Drake said. On the face of it, Mount Vernon seemed to have no problem. It had four AVID elective classes in each of the first two grades, and three classes each for juniors and seniors. Fourteen AVID classes were far more than most AVID schools had, particularly those like Mount Vernon with just seventeen hundred students.

But as Drake led the group through the forms, she and her team found weak spots that worried them and AVID rules that concerned them.

The first few were easy. Essential 1 said, "Student selection must focus on students in the middle, with academic potential." Mount Vernon was a solid 3, the top score, with 100 percent of AVID students meeting the criteria, all documented. Essential 2 said that all program participants, "both students and staff, must choose to participate." That also got a 3, with documentation. Anyone reading the forms could see that AVID was big on written proof. Swanson had seen too many elegant scams in her early years to take schools' word for what they were doing.

Mount Vernon also got a 3 on Essential 3, "The school must be committed to full implementation of the AVID program." But at Essential 4, the school slipped to a 2. "AVID students must be enrolled in a rigorous course of study that will enable them to meet requirements for university enrollment," the certification document said. There were five separate measures of Essential 4. Mount Vernon got a 3 on only one of them, the requirement that 90 percent of AVID students be on track to complete the math sequence required for college admission. They received 2s in other categories because they had 100 percent of students enrolled in "academically rigorous courses" but not "the most rigorous academic courses" and had 70 percent, not 85 percent, of students getting at least C's in core academic courses.

"We have to make sure kids are getting the proper challenges," Drake said. One teacher said the problem was AP English. Students were in the habit of saying "I don't want to take AP English. AP English is a lot of work," so they would opt for a local college course that earned them credit in Washington state colleges but did not rate as high with AVID Center. Someone in the group suggested that the school urge students in the local college course to take the AP test anyway, since that might improve the school's rigor rating with AVID.

The school got 3s on the next three Essentials: no. 5, "a strong, relevant writing and reading curriculum; no. 6, "inquiry used as a basis for instruction," and no. 7, "collaboration is used as a basis for instruction."

Mount Vernon slipped to a 2 again on Essential 8, "A sufficient number of tutors must be available in AVID elective class(es) to facilitate student access to rigorous curriculum. Tutors should be students from colleges and universities and they must be trained to implement the methodologies used in AVID."

This weak spot sparked a lively discussion among the site-team members. Tutor supply was not a problem. Washington was one of the few states in the AVID universe that had an established budget line and pay scale for tutors, going from $13 to $18 an hour based on experience. Mount Vernon scored only a 2 because on average only one, not two, of the tutors in each section were "current college students." The prevailing view at the table was that complying with this Essential was difficult to arrange. Mount Vernon asked so much of its tutors that many likely recruits still in college didn't have the time, but once they were out of college, looking for a job to get started, they loved the opportunity. Why couldn't they be counted as college students, the site-team members asked, considering that they had all the necessary skills and depth of knowledge about college life?

The school also had to settle for 2s on the last three Essentials. They missed a 3 on no. 9 because 100 percent of seniors had not scored proficient or above on the annual state test and had not been accepted by four-year colleges. They scored a 2 on Essential 10 because all of their AVID teachers had not attended at least two summer institutes. The same happened on no. 11 because parents were not represented at site-team meetings and were not providing leadership in encouraging more students to do AVID.

CONTINUALLY IMPROVING: CHARTING OUT A COURSE FOR BETTERMENT

The site-team teachers agreed they needed to work harder to involve parents. They were not participating enough, some of the teachers said, and their preference for sending their children to local community colleges was one reason why the school did not have 100 percent acceptance to four-year schools. Getting to a 3 on no. 10, making sure everyone had done two summer institutes, was going to take more money. That might be difficult because the district was already spending $500,000 a year on AVID. Still, the program's popularity in the community, everyone agreed, was strong. "The school board is totally with us," Drake said. "The mayor comes by and visits."

In answering the four big questions at the beginning of the form, the strain of raising the achievement of so many students came through. "There is evidence that AVID students enrolled in rigorous courses struggle with the expectations related to the quality of work," said the response Drake composed. "We will develop an additional after-school program that could include intentional work sessions, reading and discussion groups, and computer lab time that will support AVID students beyond the tutorial."

She said the school would "continue to refine recruitment and enrollment of AVID students that reflect the demographics of our school. Males continue to be under-represented in the program despite intentional efforts at recruitment." Its other goals, the response said, included "being consistent with students who struggle to maintain the contractual agreements of AVID due to grades" and "refine the practice and strategies associated with our AVID probation program to support students toward success in all content areas."

The application said Mount Vernon had more AVID elective courses, more AP courses, and more AVID graduates than ever before. Toward the end of the San Diego session, the Mount Vernon team talked about how they could spread interest in the program to other teachers, so that the goals of the program could influence the entire school. Making 3s on all 11 Essentials was a stretch, but they wanted to improve.

ALL STUDENTS NEED MORE
OF A CHALLENGE

B y the time Jim Nelson succeeded Mary Catherine Swanson as executive director of AVID in 2006, his children were well launched in life. Like his wife and himself, all three Nelson kids had graduated from Permian High in Odessa, Texas, one of the nation's best-known schools because of its association with the book, film, and television series *Friday Night Lights*.

Permian was a good school with a diverse student body. It had managed not only to prepare many students for college but also to compile one of the best football records in the state of Texas. And yet, as Nelson, a successful Texas attorney and former state schools chief, learned more about the way AVID prepared students for college, he began to wonder if his children, and the vast majority of students in the United States, had missed something.

A POLITICAL EDUCATION

Nelson's youngest son graduated from Permian in 1999 and enrolled at Southwest Texas State University, now known as Texas State University. Like his father, he was a good golfer. He made the college team. After graduating, he launched a good career. He became an assistant golf professional at a country club in the Dallas area and married a bright and beautiful woman. But Nelson remembered how his son had struggled academically in college. Nelson was convinced that when his son left high school, "he was completely unready" for what university life would demand.

The more Nelson learned about AVID, the more he thought the program would be useful for nearly every family. Organizing time and work, taking notes, framing every lecture and reading assignment in terms of vital questions, learning how to conquer difficulties in mastering a skill or a concept—those were gifts AVID gave that far more students needed than ever received.

Nelson realized he could have used them himself. He fumbled opportunities when he was young. He graduated from Permian in 1968, a smart but shy student who was president of the National Honor Society. High school had been easy for Nelson. He got a golf and academic scholarship at Texas Christian University, but lost it due to poor grades. His father gave him a stern lecture. He transferred to the University of Texas at Arlington, where he matured. His grades improved. He managed to graduate from college in four years.

His father got him a job with an insurance adjustment firm, which he hated. He took the LSAT, did well, and enrolled at Texas Tech Law School in Lubbock, a choice motivated in part by having met an undergraduate there whom he would eventually marry. He got his degree and his law license, but went from job to job until he found a firm in Odessa that did trial work and had a partner named Perry Davis, who was willing to force Nelson out of his comfort zone.

If he had been an AVID student in high school, he told himself later, he would have developed presentation skills long before his late twenties. He finally learned what he needed to learn from Davis, who made it clear "I was either going to do it or they were going to get rid of me," Nelson said. "The first week I was there, he was trying a case representing Halliburton. We got to the end of it, and he said, 'I want you to do part of the closing statement.' I just about peed all over myself. But I did it."

Once Nelson had a good job and the confidence to do it, he looked for ways to contribute to his community. He and his wife, Karen, were interested in the schools. He had a talent for getting to know people and putting them at ease. He was elected to the Ector County School Board in 1984, and became the president of the Texas Association of School Boards. He worked closely with the board's governmental relations officer, Margaret LaFontaine, a gregarious and energetic staffer with wide-ranging contacts in Texas politics.

That relationship brought Nelson into the public eye. Margaret LaFontaine eventually became Margaret Spellings, a close aide to George W. Bush when he became Texas governor in 1994. She herself became a major force in US education policy as domestic policy adviser and then secretary of education when Bush became president. According to Nelson, she called him after Bush's election as governor and said, "Jim, we want to appoint you to something." She suggested a seat on the state workers' compensation board, but his firm had assigned him a workers' comp case that would be a conflict. So in 1996, he went on the state board for educator certification.

Nelson mastered the issues of finding and training the best teachers. He was so well known and admired in the higher reaches of Texas school administration that, in 1999, Bush asked him to be the state commissioner of education. "I was just scared to death, as scared as someone forty-nine years old could be, and kind of intimidated," Nelson recalled.

"Jim, tell me about your management experience," Bush said when they met to discuss the appointment. "This is a big job, an agency with eight hundred people."

"Governor," Nelson said, "truthfully I have one secretary."

Bush chuckled and said, "Well, that's a start."

Nelson had always been a master of self-deprecation. It charmed people. In this case, he knew he was out of his depth. He surrounded himself with experts and spent as much time as he could in schools. The more he saw, the more he wanted to involve himself directly in what was happening with kids. In 2002, he left government for an executive position at Voyager Expanded Learning Systems in Dallas. He took a leave from that to spend a year in Iraq as a senior adviser to the country's ministry of education. When he returned in 2004, he quit Voyager. He had something different in mind.

Passion and Commitment: An Introduction to AVID

People who have run state school systems almost never move into school district jobs, but that is what Nelson did in 2004. While eating breakfast one morning, he read in the *Dallas Morning News* that the superintendent in Richardson, a medium-sized district of thirty-eight thousand students north of Dallas, was retiring. Like many suburban districts around the country, it had changed from being mostly non-Hispanic white to being very racially and economically diverse. He got the job. There he encountered AVID for the first time.

"When I interviewed with the board, they told me we have this new program, and we really like it, and we want to see if it is going to work out," Nelson recalled. He was busy getting to know new people. He didn't do any more checking on AVID until the young district director, Eileen Friou, began to badger him. She wanted him to meet some teachers and kids. Finally, while attending a faculty meeting, he stopped by a school implementing AVID.

Friou knew that the best way to hook the new superintendent was to let him listen to a couple of students tell their stories. "One was an African American kid who had grown up in Dallas and one was a Hispanic young woman, and I was blown away," Nelson said. Their personal accounts of success through AVID were compelling. "I started paying attention to it, and it became one of the showcases of our district. Anytime we were trying to bring in state legislators or congressmen to get support for what we were doing, we would take them to an AVID classroom and have them sit down in the library with the teachers.

"In talking to the teachers, I saw a level of passion and commitment to these underserved kids that I had not seen in anything else in my experience," he recalled. "That's probably what excited me most." Friou became the Texas state AVID director, then went to work for AVID Center as director of the new AVID for Higher Education program.

Nelson met Swanson shortly after he became Richardson superintendent. "She was trying to pull together a group of superintendents as a cadre of advisers," he recalled. "It gave me an opportunity to meet her and kind of get a feel for what was happening. I was impressed.

"In 2006, she called me to tell me that the keynoter at the national conference that spring had some kind of crisis in his district—I think a teacher there had compared Bush to Hitler—and he couldn't leave town. She said, 'Can you come and fill in for him?'

"OK.

"And while you are here, I would like to talk about something else."

Swanson was retiring. She wanted him to take her job as executive director. "I really pushed back," Nelson said. "I loved the job I had and was committed to them for much more than just two years." But his wife and he began thinking about the chance to do something that was national, even international, in scope. "We thought of it as a five-year adventure," he said. "I thought AVID had the potential to become a big player in the college readiness world, becoming part of that culture that was developing around the country."

AVID was growing into an organization that had to deal for the first time with national and global policies and personalities. Swanson had always been, first and foremost, a teacher. She envisioned how to make classrooms work better for all students, particularly those in the over-looked and underserved middle range of the bell curve. She loved to write curriculum. She excelled at training teachers. The organization she cre-ated took thousands of students deeper into their lessons than they had ever been. It gave those students a vital comfort level when they arrived at college.

That focus would remain. Swanson would stay on the board. Nel-son was a disciple of her thinking and methods, but he had a taste for politics that she lacked. She could handle big egos based in Sacramento and Washington DC if she had to, but she didn't like it much. Nelson had been immersed in the politics of the nation's second-largest state. He had worked for Republican administrations but had many Democratic friends. As Swanson said, "Everyone loves Jim." He knew how policy was made in big states and in the federal government. Swanson thought he could steer AVID past any political and ideological shoals.

He also shared Swanson's financial conservatism, a blessing in a bad economy. "Our goal had been to save enough so that there was one year's budget available if a nightmare scenario occurred," Nelson said. His hiring of an experienced business executive, Mark Tanner, to handle finances brought new initiatives to trim costs.

The few complaints made about AVID usually involved how much it cost. Some educators argued that the program didn't do anything that schools could not do on their own. Swanson thought that critique was divorced from reality. What a school spent money on defined what it thought was important. Staffers were more motivated to work on projects that cost money than ones that didn't, because the money signified where action was, where good people could expect the most support and the most praise if they succeeded. A school that decided to do what AVID did without spending significant money on it would not make much progress. Tutoring and teacher training would still require funds even if the school did it on its own. Trying to do it on the cheap would communicate to staff that the effort wasn't important, and that would kill its chances.

SMALL STEPS FOR A BIG DIFFERENCE: TRACKING AND MEASURING SUCCESS

Nelson told the board in 2006 that he planned to stay on for five years. In 2013, well beyond that mark, he said that he planned to leave as soon as a successor was named. His legacy, he said, was not only AVID's growth at a time of fiscal restraint but also its movement toward a broader view of its responsibilities. "It has taken a while," Nelson said, "but we are moving to a schoolwide model. We tend to take small steps in order that we can make a big difference. We have developed some metrics that we will be rolling out in pilot schools.

"It is one thing to say you have AVID schoolwide, but you've got to be able to measure it some way to show that it really is effective in impact," Nelson said. "We are all about data. We have also taken the approach that if there are things that we see from our own data and from what our client is telling us that suggest we ourselves need to improve our methods, we are willing to do that."

One example was the gender gap, a problem not only for AVID but for nearly all programs trying to raise achievement for low-income students. Some African American mothers had complained that only 40 percent of AVID students nationwide were male. That percentage shrank to just 25 percent of African American AVID students. "So we brought together a group of experts to find out what we can do to address that," Nelson said. "And from that it grew into our African American male initiative, culturally relevant teaching to help teachers with strategies that will allow them to push these young men to a much higher level, to get them engaged and to be successful in AP and beyond. We have six pilot schools around the country that are focusing on these young men. We are willing to address what we see from our own data as problems."

Strengthening science and math instruction was also a priority. The Michael and Susan Dell Foundation asked AVID to find ways to coax more students into those subjects. That led to a pilot program of summer bridge classes preparing students for the hard work of science and math in the fall. Nelson pushed for more training for leaders, such as principals and superintendents, who often found breaking through the apathy of school districts toward average students just as troubling as AVID teachers did.

Nelson was in the job in part to handle the politics, but what he liked best about his assignment was that it was not very political. "We are not saying this is a Republican program or a Democratic program," he said. "We are just saying it is a program that works. I have taken both Democratic and Republican congressmen to AVID classrooms, from pretty hard right guys to more moderate ones, and they all came away saying they were impressed. They saw the passion of these teachers and the young people who come from families who don't even know what college is."

Just why AVID was so little known outside of education circles was a concern, Nelson said. "You don't hear people talking about us like they do Teach For America [the teacher recruitment program] or KIPP [the charter school network]. They're sexier for some reason. We work with just ordinary public schools."

The program had grown so much, he said, because "there is a hunger out there for a skill set to be able to figure out how to help these kids. So many students are coming to colleges not prepared to do that level of work, not even realizing what is going to be required of them, in terms of writing skills that are necessary, the ability to read critically, learning how to work together, learning how to ask questions. That is the kind of stuff that AVID starts doing as early as elementary school."

That was what Nelson found so startling when his own son struggled in college. "We talk all the time about this being a problem for kids in the academic middle, kids who typically are minority, kids whose parents don't have a college-going experience, but I argue it is not limited to them," Nelson said. "Here I have a law degree and my wife has a master's and two undergraduate degrees, and we didn't know what our kids were missing either."

Taking AVID to the Other Side of the World

Claire Brown began her career as an English teacher. She then became a teacher educator at Edith Cowan University in Western Australia. That evolved into a job as a university troubleshooter. She was a favorite of deans who had special projects. One day in fall 2008, the vice chancellor of Victoria University asked her to find a way to build more meaningful relationships between high schools and universities.

"Scan the world and find something," Brown was told. "There is no point in reinventing the wheel if something like that already exists."

On the Internet she found an article about AVID. It interested her. Students who might not otherwise go to college were being given support to make that happen. Brown had an American friend, Watson Scott Swail, who was president of the Education Policy Institute in Washington DC. He had visited Australia. She emailed him to ask if he knew anything about AVID. He replied that he not only knew about the organization but was on its postsecondary advisory board. "It's legit. It's good," he said. An AVID conference was scheduled for December in Texas. Brown's boss told her to go.

That was how it went for AVID's growth overseas, as well as in the United States. There was no plan. People discovered AVID, and in some cases, like Brown's, developed a serious interest.

Twenty-two percent of students at Victoria University were from low-income families. Its students had one of the lowest college completion rates. Australian educators debated the same issues American educators did. Could low-income children learn more if taught better, or did their family background doom them to failure? Could good teaching bring the poor into the middle class, or did they need good jobs to do that?

SUBVERTING BIASES AGAINST
AMERICAN INVENTIONS

There was another debate in Australia not heard so much in the United States. "Some people say don't raise the hopes of those students because many of them might want to get to a top university and get out of their socioeconomic status, but few will succeed," Brown said. "If you raise their hopes and then don't fulfill them, you do more damage than if you just leave them where they were in the first place. Leave them within those confines so they can redesign their own lives."

Brown took the long air trip to Grapevine, Texas, and checked into the Gaylord Hotel. "I came over with the classic Australian commitment to be skeptical of all things American," she said. "If it is American, it can't be good, which is a snobbery on our part."

That attitude did not last long at the conference, at least for her. "I was just gobsmacked," she said. First there was the artificial snow falling in the lobby, part of the Great Wolf Lodge water playground. Then there were her conversations with AVID teachers. "What blew me away was these people weren't just committed; they were absolutely passionate about what they were doing."

That struck a chord with Brown. She had been a star at her education school, the top graduate her year. She spent three years in urban schools and one year in a rural school looking for ways to raise the academic achievement of low-income students, many from Africa. At the Texas conference, she explored what the AVID teachers were doing that was different from traditional instruction. With her was the associate dean of teaching and learning in the school of education at her university, associate professor Bill Eckersley. He could back her up if she found something that might work in Australia.

She was not joking about the deeply engrained skepticism among her colleagues about American ideas. Australian educators saw themselves as practical people for whom progress was often slow and erratic. Any new method that involved speakers bringing audiences to their feet with thunderous applause was not to be trusted. You did not want to give the impression that the program you were selling had a cultlike aura. "They would often say about an idea, 'You've been drinking the Kool-Aid,'" Brown said.

That could be a problem with AVID, Brown realized. "This was unlike any conference I had ever attended," she recalled. "I just heard too many times before people say, 'I was jaded. I was ready to give up teaching. I didn't know how I was to get better. I was frustrated. And then I came to AVID. I can't wait to get back to my classroom tomorrow and try this out.'

"People who had been trying it out for a year or two said, 'This has changed my teaching. This has changed my life. I love my job again.'" She worried that she might seem too enraptured when she presented AVID to colleagues, but the associate dean told her to pursue it. She was not just going to write a report. She had bigger ideas. The Australian federal government wanted to support university and school initiatives that fostered deeper learning and provided more opportunities for students who did not usually have a chance to go to a university. By 2020, the government wanted 20 percent of the students enrolled at universities and 20 percent of the students earning bachelor's degrees to come from low socioeconomic backgrounds. By 2025, it wanted 40 percent of the population ages twenty-five to thirty-four to have undergraduate degrees.

The initiative was called the Higher Education Participation and Partnerships Program (HEPPP). Brown saw an opportunity for Victoria University's newly created Victoria Institute, where she was the associate director. Universities were to be given money based on their current enrollment of low-income students. Her university had 22 percent, higher than most Australian campuses. In addition, universities could then apply for competitive funding. The first grants would be announced in 2011. Brown thought AVID was exactly what the government was looking for. It was a proven way of raising the level of achievement of low-income students and making them much more likely to be admitted to college.

A SYSTEM OF RIGOR, NOT REMEDIATION

When Brown was in Texas, AVID executive Rob Gira told her that there was already a small AVID program at a school in Wodonga, northeast of Melbourne. It was a rural community. The school was for children of middle school age, most of them low income. Brown alerted her university's assistant vice chancellor for social inclusion, Katie Hughes, a sociologist who was interested in the project. They made the dusty five-hour drive to Wodonga.

"We were blown away," Brown recalled. "We found students who had had the usual low aspirations, and no aspirations in some cases. Now they wanted to go to university. They were focused. They said, 'I will go to university.' Their parents were saying, 'This program has transformed our lives.'" There were also people in the local education department who said the program was working and worthy of expansion in other parts of the country.

But there were still doubts back at her university. "People were saying, well, you can't just take this method and drop it into an Australian school," she said. "I was saying, no, no, it's far more complex than that. It's a system. It works simultaneously by equipping the students with academic, social, and emotional support by accelerating them around subjects of rigor rather than remediation. At the same time, it is working the metacognitive thinking and practices for both teachers and students that the teachers are using, and at the same time supporting the school leadership to go to whole-school improvement using these pedagogies."

She had to persuade the vice chancellor that it would work. He told her she could have thirty minutes. Granger Ward, the AVID executive who had grown up poor in New York City, had just arrived in Australia for a visit. He had told Brown he was planning a visit to Japan for some bird-watching. "Well, we have good birds in Australia," she said. "Come to Australia, and why don't you then do a couple of presentations on AVID?"

His presence at Brown's meeting with vice chancellor Peter Dawkins, plus the reams of data and firsthand observations from the Wodonga program, had the desired effect. The vice chancellor wrote AVID into his strategic plan. Bolstered by that positive development, Brown and Hughes submitted a grant proposal to the government. Not only would AVID raise the level of achievement for students thinking of going to college, they said, but it could elevate the level of teaching at the schools and participating universities.

They received a grant for $1.4 million, much more than they expected. They were one of only four individual university programs that were funded by the HEPPP money. Most of the grants went to large consortiums of universities in each state. "Our tiny little university put in its submission and got $1.4 million," Brown said. "We were shocked."

They consulted with researchers at the University of Bristol on a research design for determining the effect of the AVID program on Australian students. One aspect was to focus on seven dimensions of lifelong learning. Students would be surveyed at various times: before they were in the program, once they were in, and after they had left. They would use a research tool called the Effective Lifelong Learning Instrument (ELLI). Under the guidance of the director of the Victoria Institute, Professor Roger Slee, they realized that the complexity of AVID meant that an even broader range of mixed research methods would have to be employed to capture evidence of how AVID worked in Australia.

To enter university in Australia, students had to accumulate good grades in their final two years of school and achieve good scores on a set of final-year exams that were scaled to produce a ranking called the ATAR (pronounced "A-tar")—Australian Tertiary Admission Rank. Some subjects on the ATAR were perceived to be more difficult because fewer students took them—a process called scaling up. Chemistry and high-level math were in that category. Students chose which exams they would take from a broad array. They usually chose subjects on which they thought they would score well. "You are better off getting a subject score of 38 in a subject that isn't scaled up, like biology, than to take a scaled-up subject test like chemistry and get a 22," Brown said, "but students from disadvantaged areas often don't know how this system works."

The system was more complicated than the American SAT, ACT, AP, and IB testing systems. Many universities allowed applicants to submit portfolios of work rather than apply for entry by ATAR. Some universities had developed special relationships with certain schools that allowed them to specify subjects for which, if students did well in class, they would be admitted on the strength of those results alone.

SCALING AVID TO THE NEEDS OF AUSTRALIAN ACADEMICS

Brown met with a group of school principals to discuss how to direct the energies and processes of the AVID system to prepare students for the elastic Australian university admission system. The scaling-up process had been designed to eliminate the disparity between hard subjects like chemistry and softer subjects like art. The designers did not think it was fair to give students good in science an advantage over those whose talents were in other areas. They wanted a variety of students at each university. The question for Brown was, "How do we determine rigor? Which courses are we going to recommend for AVID kids to make sure they get the best ATAR they possibly can?"

Brown and Hughes saw that AVID could not only invigorate the teaching but also add more challenging courses to the schedules of some of the schools. Brown thought that the AVID emphasis on note-taking was key. "I have a son who is fifteen in the Academic Extension Program [advanced courses]," she said. "He can't take notes to save his life. As his mother, I am consumed with guilt. Why did I assume he would get note-taking instruction somewhere along the line?" As in US schools, note-taking instruction "is not something we do systematically," she said. "There are some schools that might do it, but traditionally it hasn't been something we all do consistently well."

AVID's binder system also filled a need, she thought. Brown's daughter was about to graduate from high school, but "her organizational skills are appalling," Brown said. "Papers are scattered everywhere. I am going to have a big bonfire. Paying attention to organizational skills is not something we have done well, especially at disadvantaged schools. Those high socioeconomic kids have a whole lot of other skills that get them through despite their lack of organization."

The original Wodonga program was in place. Brown and her colleagues arranged for AVID to be introduced to five more schools in Australia in January 2012. A high school named Victoria University Secondary College, attached to Brown's university, was one of them. There were three more schools in Wodonga and a school in New South Wales. Seven more were added in 2013. Nineteen more AVID sites were planned for 2014.

Brown, Hughes, other Victoria Institute colleagues, and some AVID teachers became staff developers and organized summer institutes. The big difference between AVID in Australia and AVID in the United States was that universities, not school districts, were setting up the program. This was advantageous for a program that relied so heavily on tutoring, as Brown's university had a ready supply of bright undergraduates with ambitions to be teachers and the energy to give strength to AVID. As part of the grant, Victoria University had set up a college class in AVID strategies, making the synergy that much better.

Amid the excitement, Brown and her colleagues encountered another wave of resistance, particularly from professors at the education school at Victoria University. They saw AVID as a rival for their students' loyalties. They were not experts on AVID; they taught other methods. One faculty member insisted that he had found a study by doctoral candidates that showed AVID to be no more effective than traditional high school programs in the United States. Brown investigated and found that no such research existed.

Even without evidence, AVID detractors continued to say that Brown and her colleagues were setting up schools for failure. They said "that the AVID people had gone to the conferences and bought the T-shirts," Brown recalled. "But AVID sent its best staff developers over for the Australian summer institutes. One hundred participants trekked to rural Wodonga for the first summer institute in 2011. And the US staff developers won them over."

The HEPPP grant for Brown's schools ran out in 2014. She anticipated that because a conservative government won in 2012, there would be no more federal funding for AVID. "One of the biggest challenges for us is that educational innovation takes time," Brown said. "Governments often want longitudinal data for a program's efficacy in an unrealistically short time frame. We need time to show whether AVID works in Australia or not. The first eighteen months of the AVID Australia project together with the evidence from the first AVID school in Wodonga is very promising, but we need the data and evidence over time."

New York Site Team's
Philadelphia Adventure

Robert Quinlan, AVID coordinator and administrator at Brooklyn High School of the Arts, kept a diary of his four days at the AVID Summer Institute in Philadelphia in late July and early August 2012. He had been promoted to assistant principal. His observations provided an unusually deep look at the personal interactions that were as vital a part of that AVID training exercise as the time spent with staff developers in hotel conference rooms.

Not for the Weary and Sluggish

Quinlan ran to the gym for a hard workout the Sunday before the institute. While doing dead lifts, he had this thought, which he wrote down in the diary: "Socratic Seminar is when you have an inner circle, a hot seat, an engaging topic." It was a typical moment for a teacher whose calling is always on his mind. He was about to go to his third summer institute, after previous sessions in Atlanta and San Diego. "AVID is not for the weary and the sluggish," he wrote.

The eight Brooklyn Arts staffers going to Philadelphia met in front of their school at 1 p.m. the next day, Monday. There would be two cars, four people in each. The three colleagues riding with Quinlan were Shavonne Milliner, Frank Proudfoot, and Lizette Soler.

Milliner was the driver, piloting her Ford Malibu. She was an AVID twelfth-grade English teacher with a love of Shakespeare. She had diverse musical tastes. The iPod mix she played on the car stereo ranged from the B-52s to Coldplay. She had been teaching for eight years and was in her third year at Brooklyn Arts. She headed the committee that oversaw student functions, such as the prom and graduation.

Sitting with Quinlan in the backseat was Proudfoot. He was a new AVID elective and AVID history teacher, but he was not new to Brooklyn Arts. He had been an AVID tutor there when he attended Hunter College. He also had a background in drama.

Soler rode shotgun. She was an AVID English teacher who had also begun as an AVID tutor while at Hunter. The tutoring experience, Quinlan noted in the diary, meant that Soler and Proudfoot "actually had a more solid framework of what AVID is all about as opposed to the veteran Milliner who would only be getting her feet wet for the first time this summer."

An indecipherable Google map got them lost, but eventually they reached the Embassy Suites in Philadelphia and checked in. They had sandwiches at Jimmy John's, then walked down Market Street to the Downtown Marriott/Philadelphia Convention Center, where the institute was being held. Jinan O'Connor, the AVID northeast states director, greeted them with hugs. The session would be just three days, a day shorter than usual under the new format that let participants do some of the learning online. They received lime-green AVID tote bags with the institute handbook, a Cornell notepad, a folder of reading materials, and, this being AVID, a one-inch binder.

Registration went quickly. Quinlan had time to go back and sign in for the four Brooklyn Arts teachers who had not yet arrived: AVID elective and AP World History teacher Kyle Wenz; AVID English and AP English Literature teacher Rebecca Levine; AVID elective and economics teacher Joshua Harris; and one of Quinlan's closest friends, AVID Global History and AP World History teacher Christopher McGugart. "Googs," as he was known, had been a fellow undergraduate with Quinlan at NYU. They had worked at the Smith & Wollensky Steakhouse together, shared the trauma of rooting for the New York Jets, and teamed up to improve Global History, leading to higher scores on the annual exam. McGugart was calm and cool, a contrast to Quinlan's hyper personality.

Wenz was a driven teacher. Quinlan had seen him calling parents from the school hallway when their children had come unprepared for tutorial day. In her first year at Brooklyn Arts, Levine had created the school's first literary magazine, titled *Ink*. Harris had guided several of Quinlan's former students successfully through the college application process. He enjoyed telling Quinlan every time a student said "Mr. Quinlan wouldn't do it that way."

Learning from Each Other

Quinlan got up at 5:30 a.m. to work out at the hotel gym. He met the team at the Embassy Suites ground floor for the free breakfast. They stopped at Starbucks for caffeine uploading at Milliner's insistence and convened their first site-team meeting in room 113A/B at the Marriott. There were many New York teams chattering, each at its own table. Each school introduced itself to the group. The morning topic was "Opening Doors to Opportunity."

Each team focused on key words and themes: the AVID College Readiness System, the 11 AVID Essentials in a Nutshell, particularly the 11th Essential, the AVID site team. The Brooklyn Arts group discussed rules for their meetings, ways of improving communication, and how to better use AVID data in instruction.

After forty minutes, the facilitators called the room to attention and introduced the concept of "Brain Breaks," a way of organizing teaching time. They called it "ten minutes of instruction and then two minutes of processing." Quinlan liked it. He had attended professional development sessions in New York that warned of loading kids with too much information at once.

They lunched at a local Mexican restaurant, then dispersed to their strand sessions. Quinlan found the room for the strand he had signed up for, Culturally Relevant Teaching. There were about eight participants at each of ten tables. An electronic SMART Board dominated the front of the room. The educators made name tags saying where they were from, how long they had taught, and the name of a teacher who had inspired them. They discussed how to create positive learning environments that were not blind to students' differences but also helped all reach the desired learning outcomes.

That night, the Brooklyn Arts team had a barbeque at Levine's brother's new house in New Jersey. The mosquitoes drove them inside, where they argued about technology in the classroom. Milliner "was confident in her nostalgic approach to literacy and staunch advocacy of reading a book, not a Kindle or iPad," Quinlan wrote. Wenz and Proudfoot "countered that devices had changed their lives for the better and believed that although physical books had their place, it was the iPads and Kindles that would win out in the long run." Brooklyn Arts had a multimillion-dollar tech grant. Quinlan struggled to summarize it in his diary. He said it advocated "personalized mastery learning with technology infused and utilized as a lever for increased student achievement within the realm of various learning environments, whether they be blended or online implementation of project-based learning." Lulled by stomachs full of hamburgers, hotdogs, iced tea, and beer, the team agreed to disagree.

Quinlan had heard of a change in the Tutorology strand. He had an itch to switch to it from the Culturally Relevant Teaching strand, as tutoring to him was the most powerful part of the program. He thought about it while he and McGugart drove the two cars full of sleepy teammates back to Philadelphia.

At the Embassy Suites breakfast the next morning, Quinlan was even more excited about switching to Tutorology. He interrogated Wenz and Harris about the new Tutorial Request Form. Brooklyn Arts would be receiving more tutors from Hunter College. Quinlan wanted to be ready for them. His strand switch was fine with the registration desk.

More Than a Program, an Attitude

On the third day, Quinlan's Tutorology strand broke into small groups. The participants simulated tutoring sessions, each with two students, plus a student presenting her point of confusion, an observer, and a tutor. They tried out the changes in the tutoring formula, which seemed to work.

Brooklyn Arts's relationship with Hunter College had transformed the school's tutoring system. Before Hunter came on the scene, tutorials were conducted mostly by Quinlan and other AVID teachers. When the Hunter tutors arrived, they not only deepened the process but also saw for themselves how much they liked being at Brooklyn Arts, and sought chances to be teachers there.

The Brooklyn Arts team meeting that afternoon was a formality. They had covered every conceivable topic on the night of the party in New Jersey. The facilitators approved their plan, signed their books, and wished them well on their trip back to New York.

That took longer than planned. Milliner's car wouldn't start. The dead battery problem was not solved until the next day. She and Quinlan got a day's extension on their cut-rate rooms at Embassy Suites.

In his diary, Quinlan praised the institute off-hours' salutary effect on team building, from the meals they spent together to their frustrating effort to revive Milliner's car. "Having enthusiastic members of your team with you is invigorating and makes the challenge ahead less daunting knowing that you have a solid squad working together," Quinlan wrote. "I believe that all teachers should at one point in their careers receive AVID training."

He remembered that in formal reports, even the most rabid AVID devotees would try not to be too partisan. They would praise not just AVID but something like "AVID or its equivalent." Quinlan shrugged that off. He did not think any other program approximated what AVID did.

By 2013, there were more Brooklyn Arts freshmen applying to be in the AVID program their sophomore year than the program had space for. The pressure was on for AVID to grow. "I always tell people that AVID is more than a program; it is an attitude," he wrote. He fed off the summer institute energy. It would be a long year. He would need those memories of him and his team, mixing teaching and technology and hamburgers.

"Precious Is Making a Big Mistake"

At Ray Kroc Middle School in an affluent neighborhood north of San Diego, Precious Jackson-Hubbard learned through AVID how to think and speak for herself. She was bused to the school each day from her south San Diego home. It was the same journey from the high-poverty south to the affluent north that Mary Catherine Swanson's first AVID students had taken fourteen years before.

Interviewed many years later after she had become an English teacher and assistant principal in the San Diego city school system, Jackson-Hubbard described the rigorous lessons and daily encouragement that had raised her academic skills in middle school. She had also learned life lessons in AVID that had given her confidence that she could go much further in life than her mother, who was on welfare.

Jackson-Hubbard became so sure of herself that she made a decision that shocked her counselor and teachers at Kroc. Like all middle school students in the busing program, she had to pick a high school. She had her choice of high-performing campuses north of San Diego, full of middle-class students taking advanced courses and going on to well-known colleges. She took the choice very seriously. She organized her own tour of prospective schools. She had her mother drop her off at each one so that she could interview the principal and some of the teachers. She wanted to see if the atmosphere was right.

Finding the Right Fit

That self-organized tour in 1994 was enough to raise eyebrows at the schools visited, and at Kroc. But it was the school she chose that caused a sensation. Instead of enrolling at one of the affluent suburban schools, she picked Lincoln High School near her mother's apartment in south San Diego. Most of its students were low-income minorities. Its AVID program consisted of just one class and one teacher for the few students with college ambitions it could find at that school.

When Jackson-Hubbard told her counselor at Kroc, the woman was devastated. "She called my mom," Jackson-Hubbard recalled. "She said 'Precious is making a big mistake. She cannot go to that school.'" Her mother instead embraced her daughter's choice. She was proud that this very bright and well-organized child had decided on Lincoln, her alma mater.

Jackson-Hubbard returned to Lincoln as a teacher after graduating from Howard University and getting her teaching credentials at San Diego State University. As a seasoned educator, she is more aware of the remarkable nature of her high school choice than she was when she was making it. She had found Kroc and its AVID program sometimes daunting and annoying, but she knew the hard work had been good for her. But she was uncomfortable being part of a little group of black and Hispanic students who were bused to the middle school each morning and never seemed to fit in with the culture of that neighborhood.

The bused-in kids were almost the only minorities on the campus. When some of them misbehaved, Jackson-Hubbard sensed that the image of the whole group was tainted. A teacher once asked her, "Why do your friends act like that?" She was offended that the adult assumed she was part of the same disruptive culture and should be able to explain it.

When she visited Lincoln on her tour, she found a "friendly, family-like environment," she said. "The teachers seemed to be having fun. The students seemed to be having fun. When I was introducing myself to people, there were warm smiles, and I didn't feel disconnected as I did at the other schools." The north San Diego high schools seemed to her "bigger, less friendly, very reserved, and very serious. I even felt that they looked at me funny. It didn't fit for me."

She wanted to prove that black students at a school full of other black students could make it. She felt good seeing students like her in Lincoln's advanced classes. The school was a medical magnet, designed to draw students who wanted to be doctors and nurses. Jackson-Hubbard had that dream until her freshman physiology class worked on cadavers at University of California, San Diego School of Medicine. She was grossed out. They put her in another room to work on a less frightening skeleton. She knew then that medicine was not for her.

She asked Janet Singleton, the AVID teacher who would become her guide and inspiration, if that meant she had to leave Lincoln. "No," Singleton said. "Let's talk about other things you like to do." Singleton was African American and had attended a historically black college, Norfolk State in Virginia. At first Jackson-Hubbard was intimidated by Singleton. She had a reputation as a rebel teacher. Sometimes she broke the rules. Three of the boys in Lincoln's AVID class were active gang members, but Singleton supported their right to be there and pursue their college dreams. "I grew very fond of her level of energy," Jackson-Hubbard said. "I respected the fact that she respected everyone despite what their flaws were." The chat about not wanting to be a doctor was the first personal conversation she had had with Singleton. There would be many more.

Running with It: Keeping Organized and Going After the Journey

Jackson-Hubbard made an immediate impression at Lincoln. Staffers joked about the girl who came to interview them before deciding to attend. Her people skills were remarkable. She was elected freshman class president, sophomore class vice president, junior class president, and student body president. She was also a cheerleader. Her orderly approach to her work, learned at AVID, helped her excel. "I was the one who would go down to the school board meeting or go to this town hall meeting or serve on this committee," she said. "I believed in students from our community getting access to the same opportunities that those other kids did."

She took the required science courses in the summer so she would have more time for the humanities courses she preferred in the regular school year. She took two AP courses, US History and English Literature. On each of those final exams she got a 2 on the 5-point scale. That was below passing, but 2s on AP exams were above average for inner-city schools. That experience with college-level work helped when she went to Howard. Her SAT score was 1180 for verbal and math, also well above average for a school in her neighborhood. Her class grades were mostly A's.

While compiling a strong academic record, she had to deal with tumult at home. When she was in eighth grade, her mother had been jailed on a drug charge. At one point it was so bad that she moved into the home of her paternal grandparents.

As a top student and leader at Lincoln, Jackson-Hubbard had opportunities to visit college campuses on the East Coast. Howard made a deep impression on her. She chose it over USC because the Los Angeles university did not have room for her until spring. She wanted to leave home and start college right away.

She had enough scholarship money to pay her freshman bills. Each successive year, she had grades good enough to qualify for financial aid, although her mother had to borrow money near the end. She majored in English and planned to go to law school, but her LSAT score was disappointing. She began to think about teaching. She got into the education program at San Diego State at the last minute. She taught English at a middle school for a year and then transferred to Lincoln, where she taught English and was the senior AVID teacher.

In 2013, she became vice principal of a middle school in San Diego. She still thought about law school, but her strongest urge was to start her own charter school. The organizational skills taught by AVID had become part of her self-image. In college, she said, "I did make sure I stayed organized, and I surrounded myself with organized people, and I encouraged them to be organized."

She remained close to AVID, sometimes speaking at summer institutes. Her rejection of the high schools her middle school advisers suggested remained a remarkable moment in AVID history. When Swanson was asked in 2013 what she would have said if anyone had asked her what to tell the willful Jackson-Hubbard at age twelve, she called the question "a tough one." Swanson said, "Lincoln has traditionally had the lowest scores in the San Diego Unified School District. Teachers tried to avoid being sent there." But she recalled that much money had been spent to upgrade the school's facilities, and class sizes were small. "It caters to inner-city black students, and their football teams are legendary," Swanson said.

"If I had been her adviser," Swanson said, "I would have questioned her regarding her personal goals, the colleges she might have been thinking of attending, what their entry requirements were, whether she could meet those requirements at Lincoln."

To Jackson-Hubbard's mind, Swanson did advise her, as the spirit of the AVID founder was in much of what she had learned about life choices in her middle school classes. "I was just doing what my AVID teacher and my English teacher were telling me. They told me, 'Precious, go after your journey. Show people how smart you are. Show people how capable you are.'

"And I just kind of took it and ran with it," she said.

Escaping Death, Making AVID Cost-Effective

Late on the night of December 4, 1999, business executive Mark Tanner, who would bring the latest business practices to AVID, was driving back to his Salt Lake City home after visiting his daughter at Brigham Young University in Provo. Tanner was a star executive. He had had major jobs with United Technologies, PepsiCo, and the planning for the 2002 Winter Olympics. He was a top executive at Mrs. Field's when he stopped on I-15 that night because he had run out of gas. A defective gas gauge had given him that unpleasant surprise.

It got much worse. He was in the fast lane, unable to get off the highway. His wife was in the front seat. His two sons, ten and twelve, were in the back. He turned on his hazard blinkers. He got out and went to open his trunk to see if he had flares. A second later he was flying through the air.

A car behind him had slowed so as not to hit him, but the driver of a second car coming fast right behind the first car did not see the problem until it was too late. That nineteen-year-old driver was going about eighty-five miles per hour. She swerved to the left, hitting the car slowing down and then slamming into Tanner as he reached into his trunk. He landed forty feet away on his head. A woman in one of the cars backed up by the accident ran to the scene; she said she worked in a hospital. The woman thought Tanner was dead. He could hear her, but could not move.

From the Edge of Death to Engineering Efficiencies

After a long recovery, Tanner moved to California, switched to working as a management consultant, and put his energy into helping schools. He was elected to the Carlsbad school board in northern San Diego County. He heard that AVID needed a chief operating officer and a chief financial officer. He had only a vague notion of what AVID did, but it sounded interesting. When Jim Nelson offered him the chief financial officer job, Tanner said he would only take the chief operating officer job, but would be happy to handle the finances at the same time.

Nelson said fine. No one at AVID had ever had Tanner's experience in big business. He was a public school graduate and committed to public education. At South Pasadena (California) High School, he had been quarterback of the freshman football team, star of the school play, and student body president. But money was always short because although his father was a psychologist, it was difficult to support thirteen children. Tanner worked at a hardware store in high school. He had three jobs while attending Stanford and two while at graduate school at UCLA. He believed that all students could be successful if they worked at it. He believed in AVID's future and looked for ways to make the program more effective without costing more.

When he arrived in 2008, AVID still had a small and collegial central office. He liked the collaborative style, but that ability to work together also meant that it was not always clear who was supposed to do what. The management team discussed issues until they reached consensus. Tanner began to emphasize what he called role clarity—making sure each person's job was well defined. He thought that would lead to more powerful outcomes.

AVID Center started with just four employees in 1994. In 2004, it had thirty-five people on the payroll. That number had risen to fifty-seven by the time Tanner arrived. By 2012, the staff had doubled to 140. The organization could no longer make all decisions by consensus. Tanner's instincts for corporate success meshed well with a growing realization that AVID had to become more efficient and effective to serve all of its schools at the highest level. "We want to make AVID more accessible, affordable, higher quality, and consistent for all of our clients," Tanner said.

Tanner encouraged reducing the summer institute from the five-day system that was used in 2008 to the three-day institute that had become the standard by 2013. There had to be more instruction, but that could be done with online preinstitute introductions called launches. New online postinstitute material called boosts helped teachers follow up on what they had learned. Tanner made sure that the participant fee for the summer institute was the same price in 2012 as it had been in 2008.

The teacher training methods were also reorganized. Over the years, with so many institutes and so many trainers, AVID had developed seven different guides for Socratic Seminars and a similar number of primers for Cornell notes. A team reviewed the different versions and came up with the best approach for each AVID practice and strategy. Putting the work online and on discs solved another problem. AVID teachers would often remember a great session they had had on, for instance, higher-order thinking, but could not find the right workbook. Now it was a few clicks away.

Tanner looked closely at the data. The number of schools in the program was growing at about 17 percent per year. Of the 250,000 students in AVID, 62 percent had family incomes low enough to qualify for federal lunch subsidies. Eighty-five percent of their parents had not gone to college. Fifty-five percent of the students were Hispanic; 25 percent, African American. Ninety-one percent of seniors with at least three years in AVID completed all requirements for a four-year state college or university in their state by the time they graduated.

The numbers seemed to fit the organization's long-term goals. It had little competition. Other programs providing college preparation services were relatively small and local, and usually were after school, not part of the daily schedule.

BRINGING A LONG-TERM PERSPECTIVE TO THE SHORTSIGHTED

One of the greatest obstacles to AVID's growth, Tanner thought, was the shortsightedness of some districts. They knew they needed to give average students better instruction and college preparation, but thought they could do it on their own. "They say, 'There is nothing special about what you are doing. We can do it ourselves.' Of course we have data showing schools do better if they have AVID," he said. He agreed with Swanson's key insight: schools and teachers only devoted themselves effectively to programs they considered important, and the only programs they considered important were the ones they were spending serious money on.

Tanner agreed with the AVID board's decision to move toward making AVID districtwide, not just schoolwide. Tanner was also in tune with the board's interest in getting more programs into large urban districts. "We have not figured out AVID for larger districts," Tanner said. "We are in the Los Angeles Unified School District. We are in a few classrooms in New York City. But if you look at a typical NBA or NFL team, and take the cities those teams are in, you are going to search for a long time to find AVID in those places in a meaningful way.

"It may mean a different approach," he said. "Larger districts are very bureaucratic. You need a champion with influence inside the district for AVID to work. . . . People are going to have to believe in it because there is so much turnover in such districts you can lose influence pretty quickly. . . . Even if you get an enlightened superintendent, you know that he or she is going to be leaving in two or three years."

Tanner had watched AVID grow slowly in his own district, Carlsbad. He was on the school board for eight years and then decided he was too busy to continue. His wife ran, won the election, and soon became school board chair. Fifty-five percent of the students in that district had parents who did not go to college. Tanner said AVID would help a great deal, but it was difficult to convince educators in a system that was mostly middle class.

"I think there is a perception that AVID is just for smart brown kids," Tanner said. "I don't think there is a perception that all of our kids can benefit from this." After eight years of effort, Carlsbad managed to require that all students take the courses required for admission to the state university system before graduation. "That was a huge fight in the school board," Tanner said. "But we can do this."

Tanner's talent for persistence was obvious. He brought himself back from the edge of death. Making AVID better did not seem so tough from that perspective.

RESEARCH RESULTS
Slow Groups Make You Dumb

The most impressive AVID data, at least to the teachers and school administrators I interviewed around the country, were the high percentages of AVID students who passed college preparation courses and enrolled in four-year colleges, compared to state and national averages.

The portion of AVID seniors completing course requirements for four-year colleges was 93 percent in California, 93 percent in Texas, 89 percent in Florida, 92 percent in Maryland, and 89 percent in Washington State for the 2013–2014 school year, according to AVID. This compared to a 36 percent rate for all high school seniors nationally, as reported by the Manhattan Institute for Policy Research in 2003. For minority groups, the difference was even greater. Ninety-two percent of blacks and 92 percent of Hispanics in AVID completed four-year college requirements as seniors in the 2013–2014 school year, whereas national figures reported in 2003 by the Manhattan Institute said the rate was 25 percent for blacks and 22 percent for Hispanics.

In the 2013–2014 school year, 88 percent of AVID seniors applied to four-year colleges, and 78 percent of AVID seniors were accepted at such colleges, considerably higher than the national average. Comparing AVID and College Board figures for the class of 2014, 65 percent of AVID seniors took at least one AP test in high school compared to 33 percent for all seniors. Among blacks, the figures were 57 percent for AVID and 21 percent nationally. For Hispanics, the difference in AP test taking was 68 percent for AVID and 33 percent for all Hispanic seniors.

Data from the National Student Clearinghouse Research Center show that the college-going habits persist. In fall 2011, 86 percent of black AVID graduates and 90 percent of Hispanic AVID graduates reenrolled after completing their first year of college. In fall 2012, 86 percent of black AVID graduates and 89 percent of Hispanic AVID graduates reenrolled after completing a second year.

Many programs attempt to raise achievement for low-income and minority students, but none involve as many high school students as AVID. No other program places such emphasis on advanced courses, tutoring to create college-level study habits, working on college application skills, and training of teachers to help average students. A 2012 paper in the *National Teacher Education Journal* by doctoral candidate Patrick T. Peabody Jr., an AVID middle school coordinator, cited studies showing AVID students outperforming similar non-AVID students, as well as a Texas study of the effect of AVID training on teachers. "AVID Institutes place teachers in highly structured, intense sessions where they learn strategies and gain tools to help their students succeed," he said. "The AVID site team grew leaders, and many members stepped out and took on tasks they may normally not have."

Research Findings beyond the Numbers

There is a catch to judging education programs by research results. A program's leaders may invest much time and money in collecting data, as AVID did, but find that critics discount positive results as tainted because the organization being studied did the research, or at least paid for it. Major independent studies of educational approaches are rare because they cost so much, particularly if the program is found in many schools. A study of forty-three middle schools in the KIPP charter network by Mathematic Policy Research took five years and cost $4 million. It was the only study of its size ever done of a charter school network and had very positive results, but it was still criticized. There will eventually be a major independent study of AVID, I suspect, but for the time being, the smaller studies that do exist are almost all positive. Most of the data about AVID were collected by AVID. The program requires schools to keep track of how their students are doing.

Dennis Johnston, AVID's senior director and chief research officer, said, "There are consistent findings around the positive metacognitive development of AVID kids, student attendance, and discipline impacts that the research community might be less likely to embrace as a 'significant research finding' due to the lack of a randomly assigned control group, but nonetheless, due to their consistency, can be attributed to AVID and should be shared."

Lea Hubbard, a sociologist focusing on education at the University of San Diego, said her research on African American girls in AVID illuminated a feature of the program that the usual measures overlook. The students in her study "relied on each other to keep them out of trouble and motivated academically. . . . Often at home, in their neighborhoods, students were distracted from academic pursuits, and that's putting it mildly."

I found one independent study of AVID to be unusually deep and descriptive. It was done twenty years ago, but its conclusions buttress more recent reports and reflect what I have found in interviews. From October 1991 to June 1993, four researchers from the University of California, San Diego (UCSD) studied 248 students at eight high schools with AVID programs in the San Diego city school district—Bay Meadows, Churchill, Golden Gate, Keeneland, Monrovia, Nassau, Pimlico, and Saratoga. The team was led by sociologist Hugh "Bud" Mehan. The AVID research was the core of their 1996 book, *Constructing School Success: The Consequences of Untracking Low-Achieving Students.*

Mehan and his fellow researchers, Irene Villanueva, Lea Hubbard, and Angela Lintz, emphasized that Hispanic and black AVID students were more likely to go to four-year colleges than San Diego students and American students of those ethnicities in general. The four-year-college-going rate for black students with three years in AVID was 55 percent, compared to 38 percent for San Diego black students and 33 percent for US black students. For Hispanic students, the portions going to four-year colleges were 43 percent for AVID, 25 percent for San Diego, and 29 percent for the United States. At that early date, they found some good signs of persistence. Eighty-nine percent of the AVID students they surveyed were still in college after two years.

The researchers reported several cases of AVID teachers becoming confidants of students troubled by family tragedies, abusive relatives, and teachers who did not explain lessons very well. The UCSD team was concerned that AVID teachers might burn out from so many extra responsibilities. "Will the program be able to replace them with other committed teachers?" they wrote. "The AVID untracking plan tries to spread the responsibility for students' academic success to school site teams and wider segments of the faculty. It will be necessary to institutionalize these practices in order for the momentum of the program to be sustained." AVID's strong growth and still positive results in the last twenty years suggest that has happened.

The UCSD report was particularly useful in giving a flavor of the resistance to AVID from some educators in early years, a phenomenon less evident two decades later. A counselor who was part of the AVID site team at Pimlico had an impression similar to that of many new to AVID. "She wanted to limit the AVID experience to one course, which would be taken only once, probably in the freshman year, instead of a course that is taken every semester for 3 years," the researchers said. "She believes that offering AVID for 3 years is not necessary because students can be taught study skills in one semester." She did not think of AVID as an instructional innovation or a supportive structure that average students would need throughout high school to succeed.

The researchers found a graphic arts teacher in San Diego who attacked AVID publicly several times, with support from some parents and teachers, on an issue that does not appear to have gained much support since. The researchers said,

> [He] characterized AVID in terms of reverse discrimination, asserting that AVID is an unfair preferential program. He claims that AVID gives advantage to people who don't really deserve it. Minority students who have not done well, but have been designated as having potential, are given opportunities that are denied to whites. He feels there are "lots of students who could benefit" but they are not classified as acceptable under the AVID guidelines. Furthermore, [he] asserts the students AVID chooses are not really getting good grades and wonders, therefore, why these underachieving, mostly minority students should be rewarded with a special program while other deserving kids don't get the same benefits.

The researchers quoted him saying, "They are creaming the best students" who might choose his vocational course instead. He said he had "the leftovers," which he did not think was fair.

Parallel Ladders:
Combating Bias and Competition with Community

The researchers noted resistance to AVID students from counselors and teachers who were not in the program:

> Several African American males reported tales of systematic discrimination at the hands of a particular counselor. This counselor repeatedly tells African American males that they "won't make it to a big time college." One student reported asking for information about a 4-year college and being told, "What for? It's just a waste of your time and mine. You won't make it anyway." The counselor then gave him only information about 2-year colleges and vocational schools . . . When one student tried to add chemistry to his schedule, the same counselor said, "You don't need that for what you are going to do after graduation. Only college-bound kids need academics."

Those students stopped seeing the counselor and relied on their AVID teacher to supervise their college applications. They advised new AVID students to do the same.

Just identifying a student as part of AVID seemed to trigger this bias, the researchers said. "It appears as though some teachers think that AVID students are only in advanced classes because they are AVID students. One AVID student commented that her Advanced English teacher told her on her first day that she wouldn't make it in her class. Her AVID teacher intervened on her behalf the next day, telling the English teacher that the student 'would make it because [she] was getting extra help from AVID.' The student finished the semester with a grade of B," the book said.

The UCSD researchers reported that many AVID students said the program felt like a family that helped each other and fought together against outside opposition. "Several Saratoga students told us that they did not know anyone in AVID when they joined but, after a few years, almost all of their friends were from AVID. These friendships developed because they were together in classes throughout the day and worked together in study groups," the researchers said. "Coordinators encouraged these friendships by minimizing competition. The AVID coordinator at Monrovia High School, for example, told her students that they should think of themselves 'on parallel ladders with each other. There should be not competition between students, but rather an opportunity to share notes and to help one another.'"

The UCSD assessment was not completely admiring. It found that tutoring often strayed from forcing students to derive the central concepts of their lessons. More often than not, the tutors just helped with homework, giving answers far more often than Swanson and other AVID leaders wanted. But the program had achieved enough success to convince the researchers that it was an effective way to loosen the grip of tracking. Isolating minorities and low-income students in remedial classes is still common in US schools, but it was even more prevalent in the 1990s. The UCSD team thought that was wrong.

"The sorting practices of the school constitute the very identities of the students they touch," their book concluded. *"It is not that dumb kids are placed in slow groups or low tracks; it is that kids are made dumb by being placed into slow groups or low tracks.* [italics in the original] And as we have seen in this study, students can be made smart by being placed in challenging courses when they have a system of social scaffolding supporting them." That summed up the reigning philosophy of AVID in both the 1990s and the 2010s.

SURPRISE LEADER CREATES
GIANT AVID DISTRICT

In 2005, the Hillsborough County (Florida) public school system, eighth-largest in the country, needed a new superintendent. The incumbent at district headquarters in Tampa had retired. As usually happens in such large and important districts, the school board announced that it was launching a national search for a replacement.

Then something unexpected happened. One of the district's assistant superintendents, a woman named MaryEllen Elia, applied for the position and got it. Unlike many superintendents of big districts, Elia had never been a superintendent anywhere before. Also unlike superintendents in most big districts, she had spent sixteen years as a classroom teacher. She had not even been a principal. She had come to Hillsborough from Buffalo, New York, only a decade before because her husband had a job opportunity he couldn't turn down. She became a reading specialist for the district, a role likely to get little notice. When one of her colleagues suggested she apply for an opening as supervisor of reading for grades 6 through 12, she said, "Listen, there is no way that this New Yorker is going to get hired into an administrative position in Florida."

But she was wrong. She got the job. And even though most of Elia's administrative work in the years before she applied to be superintendent was devoted to the drudgery of building new facilities, the school board, despite the nationwide search, hired her.

Their new superintendent was someone who had never attended a single public school in the course of her Catholic upbringing. She was famous at school headquarters for saying exactly what she thought whenever asked a question. But the board members seemed fond of her precisely because of her candor. It was also important that Elia had gotten to know all of them and seemed—in contrast to many superintendents—eager to listen to them before she made decisions.

When she took a big risk and pushed the district to give low-income students daunting challenges like AVID, AP, and IB, the board stuck with her. Before long, Hillsborough had more schools with AVID programs than any other district in the country.

AVID AS AN ENABLING PROCESS

As a high school social studies teacher in Buffalo, Elia had become interested in what she saw as a decline in student reading skills. She took graduate work in the subject. When she got to Florida, she took a job coaching high school teachers, whatever their subject, on how to improve student reading. When she became superintendent, she applied for a large grant from the College Board for the EXCELerator program. Overseeing the expansion of EXCELerator was Eric J. Smith, the much-traveled leader of the movement to make high school more rigorous for low-income students. He had been a very early adopter of AVID when he headed the school system in Newport News, Virginia. "There were four high schools in our original grant proposal, and one of the components of the model was AVID," Elia said. "So I put AVID in those four high schools, and we worked really hard."

She got the grant. Elia had never met Mary Catherine Swanson before AVID became part of the Hillsborough County program. But they had both taught in high schools. They thought alike about the need to reverse the decline in reading skills and make secondary education more challenging than it was.

Elia loved the way AVID was designed. "The background I had in reading was aligned with AVID," she said. "AVID is an enabling process. It helps kids be learners. It gives them the skills they need to be able to figure out how to organize themselves, how to think how to put things in the context of an academic subject, or their lives. It helps kids become better organized, both physically better organized and mentally better organized.

"All those years, I had been trying to teach teachers to be better teachers by getting kids organized and putting the information they were giving to students into contexts they would be able to identify. All of that fit with what the AVID program was," Elia said.

Inquiry-based tutoring made sense to her. She had taken a social studies education course at the University of Buffalo from Barry Byer, author of a book on learning through inquiry. "Kids have to be able to test their knowledge base and talk about things they are learning with other people," Elia said. "It is like a kid sitting in front of a TV. They don't really learn much from it. They have to explain it to other people, and have to answer their questions about it. Then they start to put it in context.

"So we used the idea of the EXCELerator model and did AVID districtwide," she said in 2013. "We have forty-six middle schools and twenty-seven high schools. Every middle school has an AVID program, and every high school has an AVID program."

That led her to push for more support from AVID Central. She was sending her staff to Orlando for the Summer Institute, but didn't see why she couldn't have the training in Tampa and save money. "I have more people going to training in AVID that most states do," she said. AVID did what she asked.

THE CHALLENGES OF EXPANSION

Elia was careful about how the district picked AVID teachers. School principals usually selected the AVID teams for their buildings. Elia vetoed that "because you might not get what you want," she said. "I had a committee of teachers and principals, those who were really on the cutting edge of challenging kids and curriculum, to vet the teachers."

Both Elia and AVID took heat for the sudden and rapid expansion of the numbers of low-income students with noncollege parents taking AP and IB. When she taught in New York, Elia had encountered critics of increasing rigor for average students "who thought the only kids who should be challenged are the ones who could get a 5 on an AP test even if they were fast asleep," she said. She heard similar criticism in Florida. People said AP and IB were too much for AVID kids.

"I had lots of pushback," she said. "The editorial board of the *St. Petersburg Times* [now the *Tampa Bay Times*] took me to task for it." As typically happens, average AP scores dropped when so many students were added to the courses. "The guidance counselors had said to us, 'Well, those kids just don't seem to have the infrastructure in their families to support this,'" Elia recalled.

She was not sympathetic to that view. "We went crazy. We really pulled out all the stops to get this thing in place. And I had battles with the teachers. They were concerned, not just with AVID but with challenging students with higher course work. They were emailing my board, and I was trying to work with the board to understand this. You have to understand that some of these AP teachers are revered. So if they say something, people listen."

She stuck with her plan. She persuaded her board to believe in teachers eager to move low-income students to the next level. "We start in the ninth grade with AP Human Geography," she said. Then the number of AP courses increases in the tenth grade, and the eleventh, and "all that time they are getting AVID support."

The College Board had complained about giving high school freshmen a course designed for eleventh and twelfth graders, but that doesn't impress Elia. Granted, she said, the College Board was right if it was talking about "most places where you don't have support for such kids in middle school. It is a negative to put a kid in that class then. But I have been providing that support in middle schools and high schools with AVID, so using the same logic with me doesn't make sense."

———————

AVID began to focus on spreading its methods to entire middle and high schools, including students who did not take AVID elective courses. "That's our goal too," Elia said in 2013. "Our teachers are accepting AVID. They are seeing it as a positive thing. They are seeing a difference in the kids who are in AVID." But to grow, she said, AVID has "to catch schools at just the right time." When reformers tried to bring AVID in a big way into the largest non-California city ever to embrace the program, the timing was off.

Up and Down in Chicago

The ambitious effort to turn Chicago into America's largest AVID district began in 2002 when a group of high school students, accompanied by a few teachers, parents, and community activists, appeared at a school board meeting to complain about their terrible schools. Trashing Chicago public education was nothing new. In 1987, Bill Bennett, the US secretary of education, said the city had the worst schools in the country. What was unusual was seeing Chicago students raise the issue. Normally they just tried to get through the day. They and their parents assumed the schools were bad and would continue to be bad.

The members of the Southwest Youth Collaborative who addressed the board that night thought differently. They were bright teenagers, mostly minorities from low-income families, who argued that much could be done if the board did its job. The schools they were attending seemed to them to be run as if they were temporary holding cells for kids on their way to prison. Their teachers weren't even making a pretense of preparing them for college.

Usually school boards let angry testimony flare, then thanked the speakers and quickly adjourned. That fall in Chicago was different. The school system was going through a leadership change. Chief executive officer Paul Vallas had quit to run for governor. Arne Duncan, an experienced Chicago educator and friend of future US president Barack Obama, succeeded him. A board member suggested that in this time of transition, new ideas were welcome. The students were told to do some research, come back, and tell the board what specifically they wanted done.

Student-Led Push for AVID in Chicago

The students set to work, led by community activist Jeremy Lahoud. They found encouraging data about AVID. They told the board that was what they wanted. A new member of Duncan's administrative team,

Ron Raglin, talked to Lahoud. Then forty-two, Raglin had known Duncan since Raglin was a student in the after-school program for African American students run by Duncan's mother, Sue. Raglin went to college and eventually became an AVID teacher in California. His firsthand experience with the program was influential in the formation of AVID Chicago. Many Chicago educators had also seen the *60 Minutes II* report broadcast a few months before.

Duncan made Greg Darnieder, an educator and foundation head, head of a school district division for preparing students for higher education. Duncan asked Darnieder what he needed. "It will take $4 million, unrestricted, and authorization to create a research unit of at least four people that would be separate from the district's research team," Darnieder told Duncan. He did not want to lose his data-crunchers, vital to making the reform work, to other assignments.

"Go for it," Duncan said.

The AVID Chicago group started with eight high schools, including Gage Park in the southwest, where some of the Southwest Youth Collaborative members had been students. Alfredo Ortiz, formerly head of the high school division under Vallas, became Gage Park's new principal. He and his top assistant principal, Kathy Notter, called in Gage Park social studies teacher Jonathan Keith, who had a reputation for motivating students. The Academic Decathlon team he advised had done well in competition with much wealthier campuses. They thought he would make a good AVID coordinator.

Keith had grown up in Chicago. He had bounced from one college to another, mostly night schools while he worked construction, until he settled down to get a degree in history and political science with a minor in education at the University of Illinois in Champagne-Urbana. Keith had been told that everyone had to reapply for their jobs as the school moved to AVID. "If you are interested in being a part of AVID, then you can keep your job," Ortiz said.

"Where do I sign up?" Keith said.

He flew to Austin with a massive Chicago delegation for the summer institute. He thought it would be a nice vacation at the Radisson Hotel. Instead he had the usual near-religious AVID conversion experience. "It was so riveting," he recalled. "It was by far the best professional learning experience in education I had ever witnessed, and I had been to them all, from IB to AP to the College Board to Touchstone." He loved meeting the other teachers. "These were educators who had all been through the same ringer I had been through, and they had found someplace where they had a voice," Keith said. "It was very cultish. I am not the first person to say that. We fell in love."

That devotion, at least at Gage Park High School, was soon tested. Ortiz decided to ignore AVID Essential 2, voluntary participation by students and teachers. He enrolled every student in the program. Raglin said he thought this was a worthy experiment, even if it departed from AVID principles: "Alfredo thought this was good stuff, and he said 'I want to set this thing up wall to wall.'"

Keith's view of what happened at his school was mixed. His AVID elective class of ninth graders worked well. The tutorials were particularly useful, he thought. It took time for inquiry-based learning to click, but eventually the questioning helped his students go deeper into their subjects than they had before. Compliance with Cornell notes, however, was less successful. By his estimate, only half of his students took them. Even worse, the school's faculty and student body were not ready for the advanced classes that AVID required. "We started creating honors courses to meet the certification rules," Keith said, "but they weren't real."

Requiring everyone to take AVID was a sore point among students. "They just saw this as a very generic thing that they were being subjected to, so a lot of the really great kids were being rebellious," Keith said. "This was something they were being forced into. Those exact same kids, if we had recruited them properly and explained what we were doing, they would have been our star AVID students."

Still, Keith thought his school was better with its warped version of AVID than it had been with no AVID at all. AVID in Chicago looked like an improvement to many teachers, parents, and students. It got favorable press attention. AVID district director Chandra Taylor-Smith worked hard to keep the quality high as the program expanded. When Mayor Richard Daley announced that he wanted AVID in every school, the pressure increased to make AVID even bigger. Darnieder had sent out videos of the *60 Minutes II* report and got an eager response. Principals who liked the program convinced other principals to sign up. "It is the only program that I have ever been involved with that sold itself on a peer basis, principal to principal," Darnieder said. "Once we got it established, the phone was ringing off the hook. We literally at any time had thirty to forty schools on the waiting list."

KEEPING CLOSE TO AVID'S CORE

But when a new principal came to Gage Park, Keith persuaded her to switch to the standard AVID model and stop putting everyone in the program. Gage Park had 1,850 students. Keith and the new principal recruited only students who wanted to participate and who fit the AVID kid-in-the-middle profile. That was about 250 students, or eight sections.

"It really started to bloom," Keith said. "It was what the kids wanted." The faculty finally had the capacity to create challenging honors and AP classes. "In a couple of years we had twelve sections of AVID and thirteen sections of AP," Keith said. Individual students began to shine. One girl on her own organized a group of Gage Park AVID students who joined Keith for a conference in the suburbs after he called to tell her that an award-winning AVID school that had promised to provide students had not followed through.

Keith eventually transferred to a middle school that was starting AVID. He watched with disappointment as support for the program dis-integrated in Chicago after Duncan was named US education secretary in late 2008 and left for Washington.

Just why that happened is a matter of dispute. Raglin became the district's AVID coordinator at about that time. My interviews convince me that there was little he could have done to stop the decline. Duncan's successors had their own plans that did not include AVID. Darnieder, who went to Washington with Duncan, acknowledged when asked in 2013 that the program declined after they left, and that the absence of Duncan was a factor.

When I asked then AVID executive vice president Granger Ward about this in 2013, however, he said that the change of administrator was not the only problem. "While new leadership changed some directions," he said, "the district director's inability to implement AVID with fidelity was a significant and contributing factor." Ward said, "When the summer institute was in Chicago, Ron's lack of planning and organization reduced the potential numbers of Chicago Public Schools (CPS) teachers scheduled to attend from almost five hundred to slightly more than one hundred. That significantly impacted implementation. Ron created a CPS certification process for AVID schools in addition to the AVID Center certification, which created additional challenges for schools. Ron's belief was that 'his' certification criteria were better and more rigorous than ours."

Ward said that AVID Center officials "met with him and others within CPS to assist them in getting back on track continually." But, he said, "I believe the efforts failed as a result of the combined shift by new leadership and Ron's counterproductive efforts."

Raglin, interviewed in late 2013, vehemently disagreed. He said he had to change the certification rules because of pressure from his Chicago bosses. He said that AVID was only one of many initiatives supported by Duncan that were "systematically destroyed" under Duncan's successors as Chicago schools CEO. He said the number of Chicago teachers attending the summer institute declined sharply because Chicago officials diverted money to other projects and because AVID Center insisted on moving the main training site from Chicago to Indianapolis for those teachers. Raglin acknowledged that he and Ward took different approaches to keeping AVID strong in Chicago, but in the end nothing worked.

Jean-Claude Brizard, who was appointed schools CEO by new mayor Rahm Emanuel after two short-term occupants of the job, said AVID Chicago was "already in spiraling decline" when he arrived, due to a shift in priorities by school leaders immediately after Duncan's departure. "Unfortunately these things happen when leadership and priorities change," Brizard said.

Darnieder said that despite the decline of AVID in the city, the attention it had focused on data collection had changed the culture at CPS headquarters and helped future programs of every kind. The city schools began to develop statistics on completion of financial aid forms, college enrollment, and college persistency. The one attempt to use AVID data to judge the effectiveness of the program in Chicago did not get far, however. University of Chicago researchers found little difference between achievement levels attained by ninth graders after a year in AVID and similar students in the Chicago system in years just before AVID arrived. The short-term nature of the study left many unanswered questions.

Keith left Chicago in 2013 when the YMCA recruited him to start a public charter school in Detroit, the YMCA Detroit Leadership Academy. He began with just a ninth grade, all students enrolled in AVID. He said he had no intention of repeating the AVID-for-all mistake at Gage Park, but had no opportunity in his first year to figure out which students qualified for the program before they arrived. "The freshman AVID curriculum is really life skills and tutoring, and that is good for everyone," he said. His ninth-grade class would have no more than a hundred students, so his teachers could handle it until they sorted out who would qualify for AVID in higher grades.

SOME SETBACKS AND SUCCESSES

Raglin left Chicago in 2012 after his position of AVID coordinator for the district was eliminated. In a farewell memo to AVID educators, he said that the district leaders had decided to "devolve resources." That meant schools henceforth decided what programs they wanted and had to find their own funding for them. In that memo, Raglin shared the data he had accumulated, a summary of what AVID had accomplished before it had shrunk to just a few schools.

During the ten years the program was active in Chicago, nearly all of the city's high schools had adopted AVID. The total was more than 250 campuses, including some middle grades and a few elementary schools. More than two thousand Chicago educators had had AVID training. More than seven hundred college students had become AVID tutors. There were more than one hundred AVID partnerships with colleges to improve access for Chicago students.

About fifty thousand students had taken AVID classes. More than 90 percent of students who completed at least three years of AVID had passed all the courses needed for admission to a four-year state college in Illinois. More than 90 percent of that same group had completed the required federal forms for college financial aid. Seventy-two percent of the AVID completers had graduated from high school. Forty-three percent of AVID students had taken at least two AP courses. More than 65 percent of the students who had completed at least three years of AVID had enrolled in college.

Raglin said he wished the AVID organization in San Diego had fought harder for the program at the end. "They could have tried to get an audience with the CEO or the mayor and said, 'Here's your data,'" he said. But he also said that he had not lost faith in what AVID did. He took a job in Elgin, one of the Chicago suburban school districts, as chief of equity and social justice. Fifty-five percent of Elgin students were from low-income homes. Every school in the district had an AVID program.

Noting that AVID's national board had discussed becoming more involved in large urban districts, Raglin said he hoped they would be tougher than they were in Chicago. Change would never go smoothly in such places, he said, so when obstacles appeared, it was best to push against them, and have faith that children's achievement would improve with perseverance. "You've got to know how to navigate and negotiate that terrain," he said.

FROM 7-ELEVEN TO AVID

The press release announcing Michelle Mullen's appointment as an AVID executive vice president in February 2013 described an accomplished educator. She had a master's, bachelor's, and teaching credential from the University of San Diego and an administrative credential from California State University San Marcos. She was a National Board Certified teacher, and had been director of the Single Subject Credential program at Cal State San Marcos, as well as the leader of AVID's English Learner College Readiness program.

What the announcement did not say was that among the team of five executives who ran AVID, Mullen, fifty, may have had the most troubled childhood. At age sixteen, after frequent misbehavior, including missing school, she arranged to become a legally emancipated minor when her mother told her to go live with her father and she refused. If AVID had existed then, she would have been a likely recruit for the program and perhaps wasted less time the next few years. She moved in with her boyfriend, had a short-lived marriage, and didn't quite know what to do until age twenty-four, when she decided to go to a four-year college and become a teacher.

The announcement also did not say that she was the first top AVID executive since Swanson to have taught an AVID class. The announcement made no effort, because such matters were not appropriate for press releases, to illuminate the missionary zeal Mullen had for the program, and how in that potent mix of conscience and determination she was very much like thousands of teachers teaching Cornell notes, time management, inquiry-based learning, and college preparation across the country.

GET OUT OF THE WAY: REMOVING ROADBLOCKS TO SUCCESS

Mullen had spent her career trying to persuade traditional educators that many students who had skipped school and had bad grades could do well in challenging courses and succeed in college if taught the best ways to learn and to organize their lives. The struggle to instill those lessons was frustrating for such teachers, making AVID something of a godsend. The program's growing size and influence had given them more opportunities to persuade recalcitrant educators to reconsider their views and, if that didn't work, to enroll promising students into AP and other demanding courses even in the face of opposition.

"It is going to drive us to keep the dialogue going in this country around who gets to have access to success and worth and all that," Mullen said of AVID after her 2013 appointment. "I think AVID is becoming high-profile enough . . . that it's going to be harder for us to go back to old ways of doing things that would keep kids down . . . I do feel that it provides me and others who think like this an avenue or platform to be seen, be heard, and basically tell other people to shut up and get out of the way."

She laughed nervously after saying that at the end of a long interview, but her words were similar to what AVID teachers were saying across the country. College Board research showed that half of students who showed likelihood of success in AP never got to take those college-level courses and tests. Schools often failed to recognize the potential of students whose ambitions had been stunted by their impoverished upbringing or misfortune. Some American teenagers were so distracted by what was happening to them when they were not in school that they did not see until later how much better they could have done in school if they had been better supervised and taught.

That was Mullen's story. Her father had been in the Coast Guard and then worked in insurance. Her mother was a secretary. Neither had gone to college. When they divorced, Mullen's mother had difficulty making a living while raising four high-spirited girls. She finally gave up and told all of them to go live with their father. Mullen was not on good terms with the man, and wanted to leave high school altogether. But she had a counselor named Harvey Royer at Vista High School, the school where Rob Gira would later be principal, who persuaded her to stick it out until she got a diploma. Royer was also the one who explained to her that she could petition a court to let her live on her own if she could not stand being with either of her parents.

She got involved in a student organization that sponsored competitions in retail merchandizing. She had been accepted at the Fashion Institute of Design and Merchandizing in Los Angeles when she got pregnant and decided instead to marry the father, just two years older than she was, and move to a rural part of San Bernardino County after graduating from high school. She miscarried and decided she no longer wanted to be with a man "who was really interested in doing some work and then going to parties every night." The next several years were filled by a series of jobs, including managing Fotomat kiosks, working as an account manager for a title company, managing a 7-Eleven store and then ending up at the parent company, Southland Corp., as a training manager for new franchisees of 7-Eleven stores. She took general education and business courses at a community college, but began to think that her negative reaction to her business law class meant that private enterprise wasn't the right choice for her.

Her work at Southland reawakened her old love of teaching. She had enjoyed instructing her younger sisters when she was in school. "But I was sick of teaching people how to make money," she said. "I really wasn't contributing to a better world, in my mind." She transferred to the University of San Diego, which had scholarship money for students like Mullen coming to college late. She earned a degree in English, followed by her teaching credential, then got a job at Granite Hills High School in El Cajon in San Diego County.

The school was heavily tracked, which appalled her. A student was assigned to the remedial track at the bottom, the applied arts track somewhat higher, the college prep track above that, or the honors track at the top. She was a new English teacher, so she was given students in the bottom two tracks. When she was a student, she said, "I could have been easily dumped in those classes because of how much I was gone from school, and there were a zillion other reasons why people would think I wasn't serious about school."

She created community public service opportunities for her students. They wrote articles on community activities and worked with a group that supported foster children. This did not sit well with some other teachers. "They thought that I was trying to show them up, that I would take kids like that and do those things when the kids they had that were in honors weren't even doing those things," she said. The school administration questioned her about the possibility that the school might be liable if anything went wrong when she took her students off-campus. "It was all about putting up blockades rather than finding out about the ways you can maneuver safely and make things happen," she said.

WARMING UP TO AVID

The next semester she transferred to San Dieguito High School, on the coast north of the city of San Diego, where she had friends she had made in graduate school and at a summer workshop on teaching writing. It was an affluent suburban school. Only 35 percent of the students were low income, but it had a substantial minority of Hispanic students. Many of them had been enrolled in an AVID program that had just started.

Her friends at San Dieguito knew she would like that approach. Indeed, when she was still a student teacher, she had spent one semester at Clairemont High, three years after Swanson had left. She had worked some days for Don Thorpe, Swanson's successor. Her first impression of AVID was not entirely favorable. "There were a lot of people in the room," she recalled. "There were tutors and kids and the teacher, and I thought, what am I supposed to be doing? It felt chaotic to me. My attitude changed, but I always felt it was a little bit chaotic, and that was a function of the way Don managed the class. He was pretty laid back."

She also remembered that the AVID classroom was "the place where I had the most authentic kid conversations." Those teenagers had a sense of what was possible. They revealed their dreams and listened when she talked about college and how they could get where they wanted to go. This was a big change from the other school she had worked at as a student teacher, Kearney High. That school was full of the children of Southeast Asian immigrants. "I was in a class where the first thing the teachers did was give every kid an American name," she said. "The rationale for that was that their names were too hard to pronounce." There were few attempts, she said, to give newly arrived students a sense of the strength of their culture and themselves. "I worked primarily with kids who were second language learners and I walked out of that school feeling really disappointed and dissatisfied with what we were doing for kids," she said.

So becoming an AVID coordinator just a year into her career as a full-time teacher felt good to Mullen. San Dieguito High School had just one AVID class, with students from every grade of the tenth- through twelfth-grade school. "I loved it," she recalled. "I felt like I was really purpose driven. I knew why I was in public education. I knew what my calling was. I thought I was living it out in my English classes, but AVID was a place where I could get all the facets of a kid and wrap them in a web from all directions, which I couldn't do in English class. I embraced it wholeheartedly."

From the beginning, she had to fight to get the teachers of advanced classes to take her kids, as the AVID rules required. As a new teacher, she lacked the power to steamroller teachers who didn't think low-income students could handle AP. To get the advanced-course teachers to comply, she said, it often took "lots of persuasion." Within her English department, where she had friends, the advanced-class teachers "would take any of the kids I asked them to. They said, 'Bring them in. We'll figure it out.' There was one teacher in English who really didn't want them. So we ignored her and gave her no kids.

"As we got into the math and science world, we had more skeptics and fewer teachers who were willing to consider their own pedagogy and to consider how that correlates to kids' success," she recalled. "There was more lockstep, people saying 'This is sequential, this is how we do math, first you do this and then you do this. Your kids have not shown enough proficiency yet to be here.'" She pointed out that her students had the benefit of college students tutoring them twice a week. As more AVID students demonstrated their ability to handle math and science courses, the resistance lessened.

Still, she lost kids. The attrition was greatest between eleventh and twelfth grades. "In the early days there was misunderstanding about why kids should do AVID," she said. The students' attitude was "what's in it for me? It wasn't clear to them," she said. "They didn't have enough hooks to hang their beliefs on. They thought it was for at-risk kids, kids who were not sufficiently intelligent and needed to work extra hard.

"The best way to counter that argument was developing a real core group of kids who saw it all the way through and could speak to their own transformation. That was the key for the adults on the campus as well as the kids," she said.

In 1996, San Dieguito High transformed itself as the district added a high school. The school board moved to make sure that San Dieguito would not become a ghetto school because it was located in the part of the district with the most low-income families. It became a school of choice, renamed the San Dieguito Academy. Any student in the district could attend. The lure was a block schedule that had much more room for student electives. "That allowed us to offer these amazing music and art and foreign language and tech courses," she said.

By the time she left in 2002, San Dieguito had four AVID elective classes and many more students in advanced classes. From the mid-1990s, as both a consultant and a distinguished teacher in residence, she helped the new Cal State San Marcos campus start a teacher education program that supported AVID. "All the teacher education students who came to get their single-subject credential spent time in partner high schools or middle schools working in an AVID program where they would tutor or do student teaching," she said.

She had met Swanson at her first summer institute in 1991, just before she took over the AVID program at San Dieguito. "I thought she was tough talking, bigger than life, this big presence," Mullen recalled. "She took up space in the room, no nonsense, driven." But Mullen was on the fence about whether Swanson was as much a force for good as she was told. "I trust people easily, but I don't see them as credible very easily," she said. "I have to get to know people to know how credible they are. I reserved judgment." Swanson sounded good, but would she deliver?

Gradually, as Mullen attended regular monthly meetings with Swanson and other AVID coordinators, she was won over. She was impressed that Swanson was able to get experts from UC San Diego and San Diego State to explain the connections between what colleges were doing and what AVID was doing. "Lots of data would come to us," she said. "That helped cement for me who she was and what this work was."

AVID Excel: Closing Gaps for ESL Students

In 2006, while Mullen was working at Cal State San Marcos, she got a call from Swanson asking if she would work for AVID as a consultant to run a grant from the James Irvine Foundation. The idea was to look at a few low-income Los Angeles County high schools and find out what might be done to help low-achieving English language learners.

"What we learned was that we had lots of second-language kids who got into AVID elective courses and whose needs were partially met but not fully met," Mullen said. "Many of those kids would end up in the remedial courses when they hit college, or they wouldn't follow the college application process all the way through. They needed more explicit instruction around language that wasn't happening in the AVID elective course because the teacher and students were immersed in all the other stuff."

Mullen used the learning from the three-year Irvine grant to develop a new middle school program that came to be called AVID Excel. It was for students who had completed sixth grade at only the intermediate level of English proficiency, even though they had been in American schools for four years or more, and were poised to become long-term English language learners. "Their trajectory didn't look good for completing course requirements for college and having the opportunity to go to college," she said.

"The AVID Excel program we call a cousin to the traditional AVID elective because students learn some of the same stuff they would in the middle school AVID elective, but there is a particular focus on academic English language, reading and writing," she said. These English language learners enrolled in the AVID Excel course in seventh and eighth grade rather than the traditional AVID elective, and committed to a two-week summer course during two summers.

By 2013, there were AVID Excel programs in sixteen schools in California, Florida, and Washington State. "The goal is for the English language learners to come out of eighth grade and land in a traditional ninth-grade AVID elective and not be tracked in any way," she said. "We want them to be as prepped and ready to go as soon as possible from a linguistic standpoint, so they can hold their own in a traditional AVID elective and be in advanced courses in high school."

For more than twenty years, American educators had noticed this gap between students who grew up in English-speaking homes and those who did not, but hadn't found a reliable way to close it. Mullen acknowledged that it was a difficult task, but she thought AVID's skill in supporting the whole student—his academics, his habits, his dreams, his way of learning—would give the new approach more chance of success.

In 2011, Mullen became director of curriculum initiatives for AVID. She had married a biologist and had two daughters, some years working just part-time as a consultant. She thought her daughters were old enough, with one of them at the San Dieguito Academy, that she could take a full-time position. When she was promoted to be AVID executive vice president for curriculum and learning in 2013, it felt natural to her. "I was in my element," she said. "We are known as a high-caliber professional learning organization, but what does that mean, and how do we codify that and brand that, and how do we ensure that we hold up our end of whatever we say we are doing, and what is the integrity of that?" she said. It doesn't feel to her like an organization, but "a grassroots activist movement, and I think as a movement builds, you have more and more real people who sink their teeth into this work and believe in it and live it," she said.

"It keeps front and center on the table the issue of the haves and the have-nots, and keeps on the table the awareness that our own constraints driven by hierarchical thinking and power and all the other things that drive our biases, that every day we can bust those. Every day there is a kid who proves that wrong."

Spreading AVID to Elementary School and College

Eileen Friou and Shannon McAndrews both began their teaching careers earlier than they expected. They had savvy and energy so obvious that they were hired with emergency credentials and given full-time classroom assignments before they finished teacher training. That was a good sign. The same had happened to teaching legends like Jaime Escalante. The best talent often blossoms early.

Because of their personal qualities, Friou and McAndrews eventually got challenging jobs at AVID. They began directing efforts to take the program beyond its secondary school beginnings, in Friou's case into colleges and in McAndrews's case into elementary schools. By 2013, when this book was completed, those initiatives were still too new to be well measured. But the first results were promising, and seemed to reinforce AVID successes in middle and high schools.

Friou's father had been a U-2 pilot, with missions over Cuba. Her mother was a teacher. She graduated from Southwest High School in Fort Worth, Texas, and attended several colleges on the way to her degree and teaching credential because her parents, preferring she do something more lucrative like accounting, resisted her yearning for a classroom.

She spent eleven years in the Richardson school district as an instructional specialist for elementary schools. She was called back there in 2003 to become district director of a program she had never heard of, AVID. The next year, when former Texas state education commissioner Jim Nelson was named superintendent in Richardson, Friou became part of AVID legend by allegedly harassing the future AVID executive director into visiting an AVID classroom and promising he would expand the program.

Interviewed years later, Friou conceded that "I am very persistent" and was at the time concerned that the new superintendent would cancel a program he had not initiated himself, as superintendents often did.

But, she said, she was only one of many AVID advocates in Richardson who coaxed Nelson into a classroom, where the AVID students quickly won him over.

AVID FOR HIGHER EDUCATION

Friou became AVID director for the state of Texas in 2007. Colleges were not a priority for her until 2010, when the Texas Coordinating Higher Education Board asked if AVID could assist in its campaign to close the gap between whites and minorities in college success. Nelson and AVID executive vice president Rob Gira were interested. Friou was enthralled. "I am really good at starting something from scratch," she said.

Only about half of American undergraduates who started college then ever got degrees. The record was worse for students who enrolled in two-year community colleges. A study completed by the College Board Advisory and Policy Center in 2012 said that only 34 percent of students in community colleges had attained either a degree or certificate six years after enrolling.

By 2013, Friou had AVID for Higher Education programs on forty-one campuses in fourteen states. The campuses included Los Medanos College in California, Augsburg College in Minnesota, Skagit Valley College in Washington, Wiley College in Texas, Mount Hood College in Oregon, and Tougaloo College in Mississippi. Sixty percent were four-year colleges, and 40 percent were two-year, but the number of AVID college students in four- and two-year schools was about equal.

Many colleges for years had required freshmen to take one-term courses on how to study. "Those courses tend to rely heavily upon theory and often do not offer students the opportunity for practical application," Friou said. Her staff trained college instructors to use AVID techniques. "In AVID, students are taught and practice taking Cornell notes, being self-advocates, reading and thinking critically, and organizing and managing their learning," she said.

College classes didn't meet often enough to have time for tutoring, so the AVID tutors worked in AVID centers, usually a classroom on campus. They not only did inquiry-based tutoring in the centers but also helped students set up study groups in which they tutored each other using AVID techniques. At one college, an external evaluator found the AVID tutoring method so popular that the college's administrators, seeing the results, "started doing all of their training of all of their tutors in all of their tutoring centers in our Socratic tutoring methods," Friou said. There were also manpower savings. Colleges were accustomed to having tutors work with just one student at a time. When one college complained that it had a shortage of tutors for its popular but difficult anatomy and physiology courses, "we helped them realize that one tutor could work with five or six students at a time with AVID, and you were getting those students to work collaboratively so they could also study without a tutor at the AVID center," she said.

The freshman-year AVID courses are often called AVID seminars. "Around the AVID seminar there are informal seminars, which keep the students bonded as a group and keep them coming back to the center so we can be giving them emotional and academic support," Friou said. "Second-year students mentor the first-year students."

Friou said that the new AVID programs sometimes encountered the same resistance from college faculty as AVID coordinators did from high school teachers leading advanced courses. Some were troubled that someone else was telling their students how to study for their course. But once the nature of the program was explained to them, Friou said, their objections faded. "Faculty truly wanted students to be passionate about their disciplines," she said. "The professors realized that we were not going to talk to students about course content at all. We were going to talk to them about delivering the work that the professors wanted. Helping students come to their classes more prepared and better able to make meaningful conversation and be passionate about their areas—that meant a lot of buy-in."

In some colleges, AVID began what it called the Teacher Preparation Initiative, preparing future teachers in AVID methods long before they were hired by a school. AVID schools were eager to hire such teachers, and often already knew them well because those teacher candidates were a prime source of tutors at their schools.

McAndrews built similar connections between AVID's core secondary school program and the AVID elementary school program she developed. By 2013, there were 658 schools with AVID Elementary programs in twenty-five states and Australia.

AVID for Elementary School

McAndrews grew up in Fallbrook, north of San Diego. She got her bachelor's degree in elementary education at San Diego State University, and her master's in curriculum and instruction as well as three teaching credentials at the University of San Diego. She eventually entered a doctoral program at Pepperdine University. When she first heard about AVID in 2002, she was teaching a special class for twenty-eight fifth and sixth graders who had failed to pass a set of exams, called Multiple Measures, that the state then used to assess children. The school was James Dukes Elementary in the Ramona district of San Diego County.

When she went to the district office in search of expert guidance in helping such a group, she was handed a notice from the county education office saying that AVID, an organization with which she was unfamiliar, was offering a summer course for fifth- and sixth-grade teachers. When McAndrews later became director of the AVID Elementary program, she tried to pin down its early experiments with children that age, but did not get far. There were scattered grants around the country to try AVID in elementary schools. The project that worked most closely with AVID Center was in the Cherry Creek school district near Boulder, Colorado. Some of its teachers were the staff developers at the 2002 Summer Institute that introduced McAndrews to AVID ways.

When she first heard about the program, she was not sure that it would work in elementary schools. "We had every child at all developmental levels in our classes. Students did not select or apply to be in our classes. We had all ability levels of students all day, every day," she recalled. AVID had built its reputation on helping kids in the middle who showed promise. The Cherry Creek staff developers agreed with her that the American elementary school model did not allow that. But AVID offered teaching strategies, particularly an emphasis on note-taking, organization, and critical thinking, that McAndrews thought might assist all students regardless of their developmental level.

At the end of the weeklong institute, she recalled, "I was very excited. I felt like with my curriculum and instruction background I could take what they had given and scaffold, adjust, and refine the strategies to make it work within my classroom." She stayed in touch with Gira and Mark Wolfe, director of curriculum at the AVID Center office. They showed up to watch her teach and ultimately put her in charge of the national AVID Elementary initiative.

At Dukes Elementary that first year, McAndrews experimented with something that the Cherry Creek staff developers had not recommended but that she thought would help engage her students. "They were typical kids that had already disconnected from school," she said. "They had a fear, an apprehension about school." Unlike most elementary school teachers well versed in the thinking and jargon behind their classroom practices, she told the students exactly what she was doing and used some of the professional language associated with those practices. She explained the AVID foundations of instruction: writing, inquiry, collaboration, organization, and reading to learn (WICOR). When students did critical thinking work, "I was open with them on why I was doing the things I was doing and the research behind it, something we never shared with kids before." Instead of being bored, they responded to the secret language of teachers and did better than they had before.

In AVID Elementary classrooms, teachers and their students do not have tutors coming to teach them to ask questions. But the teachers eventually introduce Arthur L. Costa's three levels of questions. If a visitor in class asks an AVID fifth grader a level one question, the child will likely say, "I can answer level two and three questions, too, if you like," McAndrews said. "They may not always have an adult understanding of what Costa was talking about, but they definitely have a practical and life experience of what that looks like."

Instead of tutoring groups, they start with study buddies or study groups when they are doing their work. She recalled one AVID Elementary school where third-, fourth-, and fifth-grade students were working in the computer lab on a monthlong project focusing on a hero of their choice. Several students were editing and reviewing their peers' work. Eventually AVID Elementary students move up to focus groups more like a secondary school tutorial but without a tutor present. They aren't required to keep binders, but each must have a backpack and some kind of notebook inside. Note-taking is introduced gradually. In the beginning, the teacher models three-column notes. They are shown in posters hung on the classroom wall. "We ask the elementary teachers to pick one subject area that they are most comfortable teaching, and that is the subject area the students take notes from," McAndrews said.

AVID often is found in just the two highest grades in the elementary school, although some have it in all grades. "We require if they are going to do only one grade level, then it be the exit grade level," she said. That would be fifth or sixth grade at most elementary schools.

About 60 percent of the AVID Elementary schools are in districts with well-established AVID programs in the secondary schools. About 10 percent are in districts where there is no secondary school AVID program. McAndrews said it was sometimes more difficult to persuade the districts that have AVID secondary that the elementary program would work for them. "Their mindset is [focused on] what they need in high school, and when we introduce AVID Elementary it is a difficult concept," she said.

The reactions to AVID Elementary from teachers are surprising to people who don't spend much time in classrooms. There are aspects of the school day that are important to teachers but that nobody else thinks about. McAndrews said the number-one thing she heard about from teachers was the difference AVID made in the time it takes to switch from one topic to another, what teachers call transition. "It can take an unskilled teacher twenty-five minutes to transition kids from math to language arts if the teacher doesn't know what she is doing. It takes an AVID Elementary–trained teacher less than two minutes to transition students at any given moment," McAndrews said. Because the AVID school day is so structured, and children are used to having their materials in hand and their time organized, "students are on task, on time in transition, and that happens very quickly," McAndrews said.

One teacher she visited raved about AVID's focus on calendars' making it less likely that students and their parents will be unprepared for changes in the routine. "It is such a simple thing of putting the schedule here and having the kids be responsible for their schedule," the teacher said. "I am no longer getting calls about what time is lunch, when is assembly, when do we have recess. I came home and told my husband that I have not had that what-time-is-recess question for three weeks straight."

That was not, however, the argument McAndrews and other AVID Elementary officials used when talking to superintendents and principals. She said, "Our biggest pitch is, what we are trying to do with elementary school is leveling the playing field for kids and giving them tools before the doors start closing or, worse, students are trapped under low expectations."

THE GROWTH MINDSET: A COMMITMENT TO LEARNING ABOVE ALL ELSE

Both in Friou's college-level AVID and McAndrews's elementary-level AVID, the idea was to create in students an attitude about learning that will enrich the rest of their lives. The research of Stanford psychologist Carol Dweck has had a great influence on the program. In her book *Mindset: The New Psychology of Success*, Dweck describes what teachers like those in AVID are after: "In the growth mindset, people believe that their talents and abilities can be developed through passion, education and persistence," Dweck wrote. "For them, it's not about looking smart or grooming their image. It's about a commitment to learning—taking informed risks and learning from the results, surrounding yourself with people who will challenge you to grow, looking frankly at your deficiencies and seeking to remedy them."

That is difficult to do. The college and elementary parts of the AVID program have gone only a short way and have few results yet to show for them. But as with all AVID programs, the educators involved have seen how such attitudes have changed their lives, and have no doubt of the benefits for their students if they stand firm against tendencies to lose heart, become distracted, and put responsibilities off until tomorrow, whether a student is eight, twelve, or twenty.

A Veteran Superintendent Becomes AVID Leader

By 2013, few school district superintendents in the country had as much experience starting and running AVID programs as Sandy Husk. She had installed Cornell notes, binder checks, and inquiry-based tutoring in districts in Colorado, Tennessee, and Oregon. She repeatedly told AVID leaders in San Diego that they ought to communicate better with superintendents, because people in jobs like hers were the key to the program's growth. Apparently the AVID board listened. In August of 2013, it made Husk chief executive officer of AVID, replacing Jim Nelson, who was retiring.

Husk was an interesting choice. The first executive director had been Swanson, the program's founder and a very experienced classroom teacher. The second was Nelson, an attorney who had been the Texas state commissioner of education, a close friend of US Education Secretary Margaret Spellings, and a gifted political operator.

Husk had much less teaching experience than Swanson. She lacked Nelson's White House ties. But she knew a lot about being a district superintendent, having performed that role for eighteen years, since she was thirty-nine years old. Swanson had never been a district superintendent. Nelson had been one for only two years. It appeared that the AVID board wanted a leader who knew what district leaders wanted and needed, as they were the people who invited AVID in and occasionally, as has had happened in Chicago, forced AVID out. Husk knew the intricacies of the district budgets where money for AVID had to be found. She had much practice selecting and motivating school principals, whose attitudes and priorities would make or break outside initiatives like AVID. She could also quickly read how politically secure district superintendents were. Did their school board support them, or were they on their way out?

COMMON SENSE

Husk's father was a civil engineer who did mostly airport construction. Her mother was a secretary and housewife. She lived in Florida, West Virginia, and New York until her family landed in the Atlanta suburb of DeKalb County, where she attended high school. She joined the drill team at Sequoia High School to make friends. She became a good student, accelerated in French and math, taking some local college courses her senior year. She had known she wanted to be a teacher since she was nine.

Husk always had part-time jobs in high school and at the University of Georgia, where she majored in elementary education. She completed college in three years, graduating in 1977. Her first job was teaching sixth grade in Jonesboro, Georgia, while living at home and working a night job so she could save every penny for graduate school. She moved to Boulder, Colorado, and substitute-taught while she studied for her master's degree. For several years, she worked as both a teacher and a counselor in Colorado schools. Then she began a career at the central office of the St. Vrain school district near Boulder. She did curriculum work in health and wellness and became a staff development coordinator. She worked as principal of a bilingual center school called Columbine Elementary, then transferred to the Westminster district near Denver, where she was executive director for curriculum and instruction. She earned her PhD in administration, curriculum, and supervision at the University of Colorado Denver.

Her first superintendency began in 1995 in the same area, the Mapleton Adams County district on the northern edge of Denver. It was a small district with six thousand students, a good place to experiment with a program called AVID, which she had discovered along with a friend, Karen Lewis, who worked in another Adams County district. Both of them were inspired by Jonathan Freeman's AVID book, *Wall of Fame*. Husk hired Lewis to be a high school principal in Mapleton. Bringing in AVID was one of the first things on their agenda.

"It occurred to me that it was really common sense," she recalled when interviewed in 2012. "This is what it took to get kids to believe in their futures. . . . I loved the part where Mary Catherine taught them to respectfully, politely confront their teachers about what they needed in their classrooms. Instead of her trying to convince the teachers, she taught the kids to respectfully request that instruction be changed. The teachers who were really dedicated to the profession but had not had successes with lower-income minority children needed to take a risk. Once they did, you couldn't get them to stop.

"I had a whole background in professional development," Husk said. "My dissertation was related to that topic. I knew enough about how to change adult behaviors. Early innovators will take a risk because they are not fearful. Other teachers will not take a risk because they believe what they are doing is working, and they don't want to let go of it. They need to see that the new behavior is actually getting new results in kids. You can get some teachers to take a risk just by saying, 'Hey, here's a new idea.' Those are teachers like Mary Catherine. But for others you needed some kind of evidence. Once they saw kids' behaviors changing, even if they weren't kids in their own room, they were comfortable taking a risk."

Husk said that Lewis "was a major part of my experience of success because she has a real drive, and she knew what it took to get a staff to change." Lewis was running Mapleton High School. It was in a former agrarian community that had become a bedroom suburb. There were many small, older brick homes and apartment complexes full of blue-collar families, many of them Hispanic. The previous principal had left a staff with low morale and a parent community worried about safety. Lewis, fluent in Spanish, began to rally people behind the school and the plans she and Husk had to energize the instruction.

They carefully analyzed what was being taught and how much was being learned. They showed teachers the data on AVID results. They sent staffers to a summer institute in San Diego and started AVID elective classes in the ninth and tenth grades at Mapleton High. "What I think is the power of AVID is once you do that, the result will grow out of the AVID classrooms because the teachers will see that when kids are encouraged and given rigorous expectations, through the way they are taught to debate or the Cornell note-taking or the Socratic method of dialogue, other teachers will start copying it," Husk said.

"The transformation of the high school itself was amazing," Husk said. The leadership was strong. Students and their parents had new hope. They created a summer academy so that new ninth graders enrolling in AVID would be better prepared for the increased rigor. Husk and Lewis didn't fix everything, but saw that the improvements were changing attitudes. "There was a mentor program we did. The older senior high kids were mentoring and helping introduce the younger students to the school, so a feeling of camaraderie and safety was created, instead of the usual pecking order," Husk said. AVID was added to the middle school that fed into Mapleton High.

BEYOND ORDERLINESS

In 2001, Husk accepted the superintendent's position in Clarksville, Tennessee, part of Montgomery County. The district had twenty-seven thousand students, about 35 percent of them minorities, mostly African American. Many of the families were military. Fort Campbell sat in the middle of the county. About 45 percent of the students were low income.

The district's test performance was above the state average, but when Husk looked deeper she found that the scores of low-income and black students were low, and few were going to college. District leaders had been more focused on orderliness. "When I would go to a school, they would show me how clean their halls were and that the backpack straps weren't hanging out of the lockers," she recalled. "They didn't seem to be real motivated to show me the classrooms. And if they did, it was again about orderliness. The kids weren't fighting and were well behaved. They wanted to talk about instruction, but they didn't have a framework to do it."

She reorganized the central office, pulling in some of the best principals to supervise other principals. She upgraded teacher training and aligned instruction with the state exams. She brought in AVID, telling staffers that it was a way to improve achievement for low-income students. A good supply of foundation money let her send enough teachers and administrators to summer institutes to start AVID programs in all six high schools at once.

In 2006, she became superintendent of the Salem-Keizer district, with forty thousand students, in the state capital of Oregon. It had many children of state officials, but it also had the highest proportion of low-income students Husk had ever supervised. Salem was in a rich valley full of agricultural workers. Sixty percent of the students were poor enough to qualify for federal lunch subsidies. Forty-five percent were minorities, mostly Hispanic. Who were once migrant workers now lived in her district. Its low-income percentage was higher than even the state's largest urban district, Portland. About 25 percent of students lived in homes where English was not the first language, also the highest for any Oregon district.

Husk saw immediately that the district had not addressed its demographic situation with as much urgency as she thought was necessary. "We had a lot of hard-working people who wanted to do good things but were doing that in spite of the district, not with the district," she said. She knew by then that when she came into a new system, she had to understand the perspective of the people there as to what was working and what was not working. She asked many questions, listened carefully, and put together a strategic plan.

For instance, "They wanted central office to perform a service," Husk said. "If they ordered books, they wanted the books delivered. If they ordered a sub, they wanted a sub to show up, and that was not always happening." Once she dealt with the basics, she asked them what they would like for an intervention strategy, a way to improve instruction for low-income and minority students who were not being encouraged to go to college. She would show principals and leading teachers the programs that she had confidence in, including AVID. Its track record caught their eye, and the program was on its way.

The Salem-Keizer school board applauded the results. Invitations for AVID students to address evening board meetings were not uncommon, but one night the warm atmosphere got an extra jolt. A student had given a moving presentation, but had to leave for a wrestling match. His father was there to give him a ride. The student's dad could not resist interrupting the next item of board business. "You've changed this family's life," he said loudly, "not just this kid's life."

Husk had ideas to make the program even better. She was pleased to see that the people at AVID Center responded to what she said. In 2012, she had a complaint similar to that of MaryEllen Elia, the superintendent in Hillsborough County, Florida: AVID Summer Institutes and other trainings were too far away. "You could get basic training offered locally and we could avoid travel costs," she said. "Then we could expand a lot more locally."

When Husk had problems with AVID, she called or emailed her old friend Karen Lewis, the woman who helped her start the program in Mapleton, Colorado. Lewis had since become the western division director for AVID, based in Denver. When AVID announced that it was looking for a replacement for Jim Nelson, Husk told Lewis that she was going to give it a try.

She passed the initial screening by AVID's executive search firm, then took two trips to San Diego for extensive discussions with the top AVID staff and the AVID board. The board members in 2013 were chairman Melendy Lovett, a senior vice president at Texas Instruments Inc.; vice chairman Monte Moses, National Superintendent of the Year in 2005; secretary and treasurer Clarence Fields, a member of the first AVID class and an award-winning Xerox sales executive; AVID founder Mary Catherine Swanson; Dave Gordon, Sacramento County school superintendent; Todd Gutschow, a software innovator retired from Fair Isaac & Co.; Gene I. Maeroff, author, former *New York Times* reporter, and member of the school board in Edison, New Jersey; Carol E. Malloy, retired mathematics education professor at the University of North Carolina at Chapel Hill; Lionel "Skip" Meno, former Texas state education commissioner and former San Diego State University education college dean; Aracella Vila, former vice president of pharmaceutical company Schering-Plough; and Stephen Weber, former president of San Diego State University.

The board had many questions. "They wanted to know what was my vision around education and how do we move students into higher levels of course work, especially college, and how that aligns with their existing strategic imperatives," Husk recalled in 2013 after her appointment was announced. They asked about her leadership style and personal strengths. She said she told them, "I think I am really good at building a team, and I think I have the ability to focus on the assets of an organization while creating an appropriate passion or tension toward improving and driving the mission forward. I think I establish a culture where people feel comfortable taking a risk but also really keep their eye on the data and the matrix of what it is we are accomplishing and how do we continually get better."

She and her husband moved to San Diego, keeping a vacation home in Oregon. She started work January 1, 2014.

McKay Wins One
in Madison, Indiana

At Madison High School in southern Indiana, Kande McKay continued to fight to involve more students in her program and keep them until graduation. She was an illustrative example of an AVID coordinator three decades after the program had begun. She had had some successes, but every year she wondered if she and her teachers could maintain the energy they had had in the past. They could not coast. Coasting would be disastrous.

She started with the parents. In January every year, the school district had a meeting at the high school for the parents of eighth graders who would be ninth graders in the fall. McKay handed out applications. "AVID is a program that will prepare your students for college," she told them. "We are looking for students in the middle who want to go to college. By that we mean B and C students who know they can do better, who just need that extra oomph. We are looking for students who would be the first in their families to go to college."

NOT A REMEDIAL PROGRAM: A WILLING-TO-WORK PROGRAM

In 2013, her thirteenth year running the program, McKay worked at improving what she was telling the parents and the students. In the early years, many people in Madison saw AVID as a remedial program. The part of McKay's pitch that stuck was that it was for kids whose parents had not gone to college. That usually meant students whose parents had lower incomes, which Americans traditionally translated as kids not doing so well in school. In most schools, AVID students would mostly be Hispanic or black, which added to the remedial impression because minorities were more likely to be assigned to such classes. But there were few minorities at

Madison High. It still took McKay a while to quash the view that AVID courses were less challenging than regular or college prep courses.

She didn't want to say that AVID didn't take kids with learning disabilities who had individualized education programs (IEPs). AVID did take them. "But we fought the idea that all kids with IEPs go to AVID," she said. "I said it is not that either. We take kids with IEPs if they want to go to college and will do the work."

She met with the eighth-grade teachers to compile a list of likely recruits. "I need kids who can do honors-level work and want to go to college," she told them. "They don't necessarily have to be in honors right now, but have the willingness to work hard that would get them there." The eighth-grade teachers were happy to list students they thought fit the profile. McKay would then send each child a letter: "Congratulations! You have been recommended for AVID, the Advancement Via Individual Determination program." She wanted them to consider this an honor, a recognition that they had the makings of a successful college student.

McKay emphasized that although the program was for kids from noncollege families, its students were going to be placed in the most, not the least, challenging courses. What was new about AVID, she said, was that they would have support to succeed in those courses, particularly the tutoring that college-educated parents could afford but that these parents could not. McKay found she could change some minds about AVID by having her students speak to community groups. "They talked to churches, they talked to organizations, they talked to Kiwanis," she said. "That really helped." There was no way to dismiss as remedial the young people giving such polished talks and answering questions with such aplomb.

The first question McKay asked AVID applicants was, "What do you think AVID is?" In the early years, students weren't sure. They usually said something like, "My teacher said I needed to do this." It was not until McKay's third year that she first heard from an applicant, "Well, I know it's for smart kids." After that student left, McKay did a happy dance.

Progress was always slower than she hoped for. The first year of AVID at Madison, before she became the coordinator, twenty-five students enrolled, but only six stuck with the program through senior year. Her first year as coordinator she enrolled twenty-five, of which nine students, a slight improvement, were still in AVID when they graduated. Her second cohort had fifteen of its original twenty-five freshmen graduate as AVID students. Her third year, she enrolled thirty students, creating two AVID elective classes of fifteen each. Of the twenty-five original AVID students in the class of 2013, twenty-two stayed in the program, the first time McKay had gotten more than twenty to graduation. Madison in 2013 had 142 AVID students: two classes of freshmen with twenty-five in each class; two classes of sophomores, one with twenty-two students and one with twenty-three; one class of twenty-five juniors; and one class of twenty-two seniors.

Like that of most AVID programs, the Madison teachers' goal was to get the students into AP courses and make sure they succeeded in them. In the early years, the only AP classes the school could provide were in English Language and Calculus AB. The AP English Language teacher had no problem teaching students from noncollege families. The AP Calculus teacher was less certain, given the program's reputation for being remedial. "What are all these AVID students doing in my class?" he asked McKay.

"Because they can do the work," she said. "If they are not, let me know."

That calculus teacher never said another word of complaint about AVID to her. "I worked with him," she recalled, "and there were a couple of times when some students weren't pulling their weight, and we would get the tutors in there and help them work. Then the next year he came to me and asked, 'Who are my AVID kids?'"

She gave him the names. "They work harder than anybody else," he said.

"Absolutely," she said. "If they fall off, you let me know."

Growing Up with AVID: Changing Hearts and Minds

The school eventually added AP courses in statistics, art history, US history, government, and chemistry. McKay put AVID students in those courses. She insisted that they take the three-hour AP exams at the end. Non-AVID students were not required to take the AP exams, but McKay sensed that the growing AVID influence might lead to a toughening of rules for students not in AVID.

One of McKay's priorities was to persuade the district to fund an AVID program in the middle school. She has been pushing for that since 2004. "It always comes down to my district not having enough money," she said. To get started, the middle school would need to send eight teachers to a summer institute. That would cost about $600 per person, plus $200 each for travel expenses. There would be a $3,000 license fee and probably $4,000 a year for tutors. The total for that first year would be about $14,000.

The middle school teachers were eager to do it. They had applied for grants several times, but had not been awarded any. McKay had hope because her district's new superintendent, Ginger Studebaker-Bolinger, appeared to like AVID. There was a summer institute in Indianapolis in 2012, which the superintendent attended. One of McKay's students was a speaker. "Where do we need to go with this?" Studebaker-Bolinger asked McKay.

"We need the middle school," McKay said.

McKay said the superintendent shared her view of a disturbing disconnect between the middle and high schools. "The culture of our middle school is we don't assign homework because they won't do it. And then those kids come to the high school and implode because the high school has become very rigorous," McKay said. The middle school's culture was so laid back that her son Ethen, a good student, only brought home one book a night for homework. McKay's solution was to treat him like an AVID student. "He is naturally smart. He was in our gifted program. But he doesn't like to work a whole lot. So he has a binder and a three-hole punch, and we have binder checks at home," she said. "He kind of rolls his eyes at me, but he does it because if he doesn't, he can't play with his Xbox."

McKay and Ethen's father divorced when Ethen was five. Her ex-husband was a great father, she said. He was coping with the effects of his stroke, and remained in Madison. After the divorce, she reconnected with her high school sweetheart, an accountant in town. They married and had a baby, Colin, who in 2013 was six years old.

"I feel that AVID and I have grown up together," she said. "I am telling people who are just getting started it is so much easier to implement AVID with fidelity now than it used to be, and that is the key. Once I knew what I was doing, it took off. . . . More people want to be AVID teachers now at my school. They know it's hard work, but they see the relationship we have with our kids. When I get up on honors day and I am crying because my kids have gotten hundreds of thousands of dollars in scholarships, that says something."

THERE IS ALWAYS MORE TO DO

Among the many former students she kept track of was Jill Storm. "She was in that first freshman class that I had," McKay said. "She came from nothing practically. She lived in one of our trailer parks and had an older brother. Nobody was at home, so she could do pretty much anything she wanted, and she did. But we stuck with her. We made her do school, Jill Wiley and I. We told ourselves when we got that girl educated we were going to get a drink, since we deserved it."

The student "was the most creative thing. She loved music. We would talk about Ani DiFranco and all sorts of other artists forever. She was a musician, and I developed a really close relationship with her, as Jill Wiley did." Wiley got the girl into St. Mary-of-the-Woods College. McKay said, "We were looking for St. Mary-of-the-Woods. It was the perfect place for her. . . . She graduated from St. Mary-of-the-Woods, and she is a music and art therapist now. So she is amazing," McKay said. The true excitement, McKay discovered, was in finding ways to get to the hearts of teenagers and convince them how much better they could be, and how much more they could do, if they listened in class, learned how to ask questions, and tried harder than they had tried before.

In 2013, McKay was promoted to digital curriculum integration specialist for the district. She would focus on teacher training in curriculum and integrating technology. "I can infuse AVID strategies in the training I do with our teachers," she said. She continued to be district coordinator for AVID. She was not going to give that up. She still had much she needed to do.

In April, one of her biggest prayers was answered. McKay and Studebaker-Bolinger persuaded the school board to authorize the funds to start an AVID program in the middle school.

McKay cried in the boardroom when the decision was made. That was her way, but only for a minute. She was amazed at how much had changed. Now she had a chance to put everything she had done on a firmer foundation, and show even more kids how far they could go.

CONCLUSION

Toward the end of my work on this book, I asked the readers of my weekly column in the *Washington Post* what they knew of AVID. If the program was familiar to them, did they like it or not? Why? I confessed in the column that I had had trouble finding people who had complaints. Journalists like me are not comfortable writing about any endeavor until we have talked to its critics. I told readers that if AVID had not impressed them, they should email me or post a comment on the web version of the column, washingtonpost.com/class-struggle. There were then ninety-three Washington-area schools participating in AVID and more on the way, so I hoped for a good sample of opinion.

FEEDBACK ON AVID

A flood of responses poured in from parents, teachers, and students, although it was clear most of the student input was not voluntary. Their AVID teachers had seen this as an ideal opportunity for them to practice an important form of writing. They would have to share their thoughts with a stranger who wanted facts, not their feelings.

Almost all of the emails, comments, and letters were positive. I paid close attention to the few that were not, particularly one revealing the confusion created by AVID's rapid growth and its indefinite rules for who qualifies and who doesn't. Anne Arundel County (Maryland) parent Julie Hummer told me that when she first encountered AVID, she could not understand why a program meant for average students accepted even one of her twin sons. Both Eric and Ben were top students, she said. But Meade Middle School's AVID program enrolled Eric. That puzzled her even more because the twin who was rejected, Ben, had some learning disabilities that would seem to put him closer to the middle of his class. She said that she and other parents got little information before applying. To her, the AVID admissions system at her school was confusing and contradictory,

251

particularly troubling because she liked what the program did and wanted
both sons in it.

"I am certain that a great many candidates were disqualified simply
because they did not express enough enthusiasm for a program they knew
little about," she said. When the interviewer asked Ben if he wanted to be
in AVID, Hummer told me, "He said he wanted to be in the band and play
the tuba." He thought wrongly that being in AVID would preclude that.
There were so many applicants that any students indicating they did not
want in were rejected automatically, Hummer was told by school officials.

Hummer said she could see why the program is popular. She saw
that students were taught to organize their schoolwork and lives in ways
parents loved, but found hard to instill in their children. Several emails
and letters to me from AVID students said that at first they thought the
program required too much work, such as the Cornell notes, but after
they enrolled, they realized that those skills made school easier, not harder.
Jordan Taylor, a tenth grader at Fairfax High School in Fairfax County,
Virginia, said he thought an elective course in marketing would be more
fun, but had since been convinced that AVID "is the best class in my
schedule." Heidy Palencia, also a tenth grader at Fairfax High, said she
signed up because friends already in AVID told her "it's like being in one
big family that helps each other with school work."

"When my son's grades start declining, the support that is given is
exceptional," said Mary Ann Sabo, an AVID parent at Central Middle
School in Anne Arundel. That district had the largest AVID program in
the Washington DC area, with classes in all thirty-one middle and high
schools. The key to that support was the tutoring. Many parents and teachers praised the depth of the inquiry-based sessions. Mikhailina Karina, an
AVID tutor in Fairfax County, said, "I always have to explain to people
that I am not actually tutoring anyone, but facilitating learning."

Asked about AVID's admission problems at Meade Middle School,
AVID eastern divisional director Robert Logan said that in the rapidly
growing program "the selection process is not pure science." Hummer
made several calls and persuaded the school to put Ben in the program
along with Eric. Logan said both boys are within the average range for
their school. It was hard for parents, and me, to understand that. AVID
is going to need better explanations of how its admission system works.

Ever a Work in Progress

I have been writing about schools for more than thirty years. I have seen innumerable programs, most of which frustrate the teachers who are asked to adopt them and then are discarded for something new and equally aggravating. A legendary teacher in the Washington area, Patrick Welsh of T.C. Williams in Alexandria, Virginia, wrote of this phenomenon in a 2013 *Washington Post* piece: "In the four decades between when I started teaching English at T.C. in 1970 and my retirement this year, I saw countless reforms come and go; some even returned years later disguised in new education lingo. Some that were touted as 'best practices' couldn't work. . . . Others were nothing but common-sense bromides hyped as revolutionary epiphanies. All of them failed to do what I believe to be key to teaching: to make students care about what they're studying and understand how it's relevant to their lives."

Like all good reforms, AVID is a work in progress. Unlike the reforms that so irritated Welsh, AVID encourages good teachers to point out weaknesses in the program so that its schools can be improved. Mary Catherine Swanson revised her methods several times while creating AVID. The people who currently run the organization have the same attitude of modesty and flexibility.

There is much discussion among education policymakers about turning schools around. Can that be done? Or should we close failing schools and start afresh? The AVID experience does not settle the argument, but it reveals some key parts of any successful resuscitation. If you give a failing school a dose of well-organized classes in behavior, time management, study skills, and college preparation, if you bring in tutors trained to show students how to ask good questions rather than just memorize answers, you have the beginnings of a change that can become more deeply rooted and last longer than the usual turnaround and start-up projects.

One of the greatest strengths of AVID when compared to current educational fashions is that it trusts teachers, once trained, to make good decisions. It does not insist that schools force their staff to reapply for their jobs before anything can be done. For that and many reasons, thousands of teachers have embraced the program. It fits their own experience of what will take their teaching to a new level and what won't.

Wouldn't we be better off if we asked teachers what they preferred before barging in with the latest brilliant innovation? One of the most effective whole-school reforms, Success For All, achieved that record in part because, unlike any other program I know, it did not go into a school until at least 75 percent of staffers approved the program in a secret ballot. The best schools I know are run by teams, a principal and teachers united by a shared view of what must be done, and a willingness to change their minds based on results.

AVID is the largest program I have ever encountered that inspires so much devotion from teachers. In a country failing to prepare most students for college, its methods seem to work. When they don't, the organization tries very hard to find the solution. As Julie Hummer in Anne Arundel County noted, it has its problems, but so does every other initiative to improve our schools. When good teachers tell me something is working for them and their students, and the data confirm that view, I say good, keep it up, and let the rest of us know how we can help.

About the Author

Jay **Mathews** is an award-winning education columnist. He writes regularly for the *Washington Post* and is the author of nine books, including *Work Hard. Be Nice: How Two Inspired Teachers Created the Most Promising Schools in America* (Algonquin Books, 2009) and *Harvard Schmarvard: Getting Beyond the Ivy League to the College That Is Best for You* (Three Rivers Press, 2003). Mathews is the creator of the annual Challenge Index rankings of high schools, now published on washingtonpost.com, which has drawn as many as twenty-one million page views a year. He has won numerous awards for education writing, including the Upton Sinclair Award as "a beacon of light in the realm of education" and the Eugene Meyer Award for distinguished service to the *Washington Post*.

ACKNOWLEDGMENTS

I thank all the teachers, students, administrators, and staffers at AVID who assisted my exploration of their complex and vibrant organization. I learned much from them, but also had complete independence to judge what they were doing in whatever way I thought the facts indicated. I am particularly indebted to AVID executives Rob Gira and Liz Morse and AVID founder Mary Catherine Swanson for giving me the opportunity to write the book and responding to my many questions and requests so quickly and professionally.

All of the names and people in this book are real. Every person mentioned whom I could locate has been given relevant portions of the manuscript to check for errors, but any mistakes remain my responsibility. Conversations and events that I did not hear or see have been reported as the participants remembered them, with emphasis on those elements found in more than one account.

Marjorie McAneny, senior acquisitions editor at Jossey-Bass, was my principal guide getting the book ready for publication. Lesley Iura, vice president and publisher, led the team for *Question Everything* and remains the person at Jossey-Bass I have known longest and best.

Others at Jossey-Bass who have my gratitude are Max Coleman, senior editorial assistant; Tracy Gallagher, assistant editor; Robin Lloyd, senior production editor; Michele Jones, copyeditor; Robyn Gretzinger, senior publicist; and Jennifer Wenzel, associate marketing manager.

My editors at the *Washington Post*, particularly education editor Josh White, local editor Mike Semel, managing editor Kevin Merida, and executive editor Marty Baron, have been, as usual, understanding and supportive. I also owe much to the kindness and educational expertise of former Washington Post Co. board chairman Don Graham.

My wife, Linda, like me a lifelong journalist, helped with some of the reporting for this book, including an extended visit to Foothill High School in Bakersfield, California. My mother, Frances Mathews, and my brother, Jim Mathews, are both educators and continue to help me see the reality of their profession. My children, Joe, Peter, and Katie; daughter-in-law, Anna; son-in-law, Matt Struhar; and grandsons, Ben, Tom, and Sam have kindly tolerated my tendency to talk too much about what I am writing. I will be exploring AVID for the rest of my life, so anyone who has anything to share with me on that subject should contact me at jay.mathews@washpost.com.

INDEX